CONTENTS

ABBREVIATIONS

BL	British Library
CFMA	Classiques Français du Moyen Âge
EETS	Early English Text Society (e.s. extra series, o.s. original series, s.s. supplementary series)
ELH	*English Literary History*
MLN	*Modern Language Notes*
N & Q	*Notes and Queries* (n.s. new series)
OED	*Oxford English Dictionary*
PMLA	*Publications of the Modern Language Association of America*
STS	Scottish Text Society
TLS	*Times Literary Supplement*

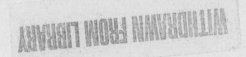

ESSAYS ON
MEDIEVAL
LITERATURE

J.A. Burrow

CLARENDON PRESS · OXFORD
1984

Oxford University Press, Walton Street, Oxford OX2 6DP

London Glasgow New York Toronto
Delhi Bombay Calcutta Madras Karachi
Kuala Lumpur Singapore Hong Kong Tokyo
Nairobi Dar es Salaam Cape Town
Melbourne Auckland

and associated companies in
Beirut Berlin Ibadan Mexico City Nicosia

Oxford is a trade mark of Oxford University Press

Published in the United States
by Oxford University Press, New York

British Library Cataloguing in Publication Data
Burrow, J. A.
Essays on medieval literature
1. English literature — Middle English,
1100–1500 — History and criticism
I. Title
820'.9'001   PR281
ISBN 0-19-811187-8

Library of Congress Cataloging in Publication Data
Burrow, J. A. (John Anthony)
Essays on medieval literature.
Includes bibliographical references and index.
1. English literature—Middle English, 1100–1500—
History and criticism—Addresses, essays, lectures.
2. Scottish literature—To 1700—History and criticism—
Addresses, essays, lectures.   3. Chaucer, Geoffrey, d.
1400—Criticism and interpretation—Addresses, essays,
lectures.   I. Title.
PR260.B8 1984   820'.9'001   83-19498
ISBN 0-19-811187-8

Typeset by Hope Services, Abingdon,
and printed in Great Britain by
Hazell Watson & Viney Ltd.,
Aylesbury, Bucks.

PREFACE

The essays in this volume are chiefly concerned with English and Scottish writings of the fourteenth and fifteenth centuries. Those on Chaucer's *Knight's Tale*, Langland's second vision, *Sir Gawain and the Green Knight*, and Henryson's *Preaching of the Swallow* belong together as attempts to clarify the meaning of particular poems from this period by explaining concepts or institutions which are more or less unfamiliar nowadays: the scheme of the three ages in Chaucer, the sequence sermon-confession–pilgrimage–pardon in Langland, honour and shame in *Sir Gawain*, and the virtue of prudence in Henryson. Of the two other essays on Canterbury Tales, that on the *Merchant's Tale* represents a kind of 'new criticism' of Chaucer which has become common since the time of its publication (1957), whereas the second, on *Sir Thopas*, indicates one way forward for Chaucer criticism now, through the detailed study of his poetic language. The essays on *The Cloud of Unknowing* and on the audience of *Piers Plowman* are both primarily concerned with questions of style. The latter has been revised and brought up to date with a post-script. The remaining four pieces range more widely, in pursuit of the following topics: the importance of context, the medieval poet's presentation of himself, the 'nature ideal' in thinking about the ages of man, and the integrity of the literal level in allegories.

Four of the essays have not appeared in print elsewhere: 'The Title "Sir"', 'Honour and Shame in *Sir Gawain and the Green Knight*', 'Allegory: The Literal Level', and the J. A. W. Bennett memorial lecture delivered at the University of Perugia, 'Chaucer's *Knight's Tale* and the Three Ages of Man'. The rest are reprinted with only slight alterations (except in the case of 'The Audience of *Piers Plowman*') from the publications in which they first appeared. For their generous permission to reprint I would like to thank the editors of *Anglia*, *Chaucer Review*, *Essays in Criticism*, *Notes and Queries*, *Review of English Studies*, and *Studies in the Age of Chaucer*. Where appropriate, details of earlier

publication of each essay are recorded in an asterisked foot-
note on its first page.

Bristol   J.A.B.

1. POEMS WITHOUT CONTEXTS:
THE RAWLINSON LYRICS*

I

By comparison with their modern colleagues, medievalists generally know rather little about the contexts of the works they study. Even a relatively well-documented work such as Chaucer's *Troilus* suffers in this way by comparison with, say, Milton's *Paradise Lost*—not to speak of Eliot's *Four Quartets*; and we know far less, of course, about most medieval English poets than we do about Chaucer. Many of the surviving works, in any case, are anonymous; and we often do not know exactly when they were written, or with what purpose, or for what audience. These are the poems which I have called, in my title, 'poems without contexts'.

There is, I should confess straight away, an element of dramatic exaggeration in this title. Of course no medieval English poems come down to modern times entirely 'without context'. The very fact that we identify them as medieval and English means that we can consider them in the context of England and the Middle Ages. Those are very broad categories of time and space, certainly—England and the Middle Ages; but they do provide a rudimentary context for interpretation and understanding. They are enough to encourage some kinds of reading and to rule out others. So these poems are 'without context' only in a relative sense—relative to modern English literature. Absolute contextlessness would be a different matter. A text absolutely without context would need, I suppose, to be written in a language no one understood. It would also have to be found in a place which offered no clue to its provenance—under the seat, perhaps, of an international air liner at the end of a busy week. Obviously nothing in Old or Middle English lies at all near such an almost unimaginable degree zero.

Yet, if one conceives a scale running from that zero to an almost equally unimaginable maximum, one can safely say

* First published in *Essays in Criticism* 29 (1979), 6–32. A text of the lyrics under discussion will be found at the end of this essay.

that most medieval poems do lie significantly lower on it than most modern ones. So it seems appropriate for a medievalist to approach the problem of context, as I shall, from the negative side. I have picked on a group of texts about which very little is known: the poems of Bodleian Library Manuscript Rawlinson D. 913. The question I want to consider is this: how far does our ignorance of the context of these poems impair our ability to understand them? I shall go through some of the processes of interpretation, rather slowly, for the sake of demonstration; and I shall invite you to observe what kinds of conclusion can and cannot be safely drawn in a case such as this, where there is almost no external evidence to guide us. The demonstration will have a certain theoretical interest, I hope. Also, some of the poems are very beautiful.

II

My 'poems without a context' survive only on a single strip of parchment about 4 inches wide and 11 inches long. This strip forms part of Manuscript Rawlinson D. 913 in the Bodleian Library. However, that manuscript provides no relevant context for the strip, because it is a collection of separate fragments bound together by the Bodleian Library at least a century after it received Rawlinson's collection in 1756. Nor is anything known about the history of the strip before Rawlinson had it in his possession. What, indeed, is it? One scholar speculated that it may have been a small roll; but Malcolm Parkes things it was most probably cut from a larger leaf. The palaeographers agree on only one fact: the handwriting belongs to the first half of the fourteenth century, perhaps somewhere near 1325.

The contents of this unique strip are in places difficult to decipher. Clearly there are a number of distinct items, probably twelve, generally separated by spaces. Most of them are English; but there is some French. All the items are written as prose; but most of them are clearly poems. Some may be fragments. In places the writer has abbreviated his text by missing out repeats. The whole document has a casual and fugitive appearance; and it succeeded in eluding scholars (apart from the Bodley cataloguers) until as late as 1907. In that year, the German scholar W. Heuser printed its contents for the first time in the learned journal *Anglia*, under the title 'Fragments from some unknown minstrel-songs [*Spielmanns-liedern*] of the fourteenth century'. Despite this rather obscure and tardy début, some of the Rawlinson poems found their way into anthologies such as Sisam's *Fourteenth Century Verse and Prose* (1921), and two in particular soon acquired a certain celebrity. Item 7, 'Icham of Irlande', as we shall see, was adapted by Yeats to form the refrain of one of his 'Words for Music Perhaps', published in *The Winding Stair* in 1933. In 1950, Edith Sitwell described Item 8, 'Maiden in the mor lay', as a 'miracle of poetry'.

I shall return later to these two mysterious and haunting poems. Let me look first at the other pieces on the strip.[1]

Three of the pieces are the merest scraps: Items 2, 3, and 4. I can make little of them. No. 3, 'Ichave a mantel ymaket of cloth', sounds like a line of verse. It is hard to imagine any prose context in which someone might have occasion to write down such a message: 'I have a mantle made of cloth'. The information content is low (many people had mantles, and most mantles were made of cloth), and that suggests the language of poetry, where redundancy has always had a special licence. Perhaps the line is the beginning of a song, jotted down as a reminder or cue by whoever compiled the collection. The same may be true of No. 2, 'The godemon on his weye', which means something like 'The master of the house on his journey'. No. 4 appears to be a rough rhyming couplet. It may be translated as follows: 'I never saw such a man as Jordan was; he went to Gogeshale without money'. 'Gogeshale' is perhaps Coggeshall in Essex, where there was an annual fair. A man who goes to a fair without money is either a rogue or a fool; so perhaps these lines introduced some comic or picaresque narrative. One scholar has deduced from the reference to Coggeshall that all the Rawlinson pieces come from Eastern England, and even that they were written down at the Cistercian monastery of Coggeshall;

---

[1] The texts appended to this essay are normalized in spelling and presented (as far as possible) in coherent and continuous form. Major expansions are indicated by square brackets. Minor conjectures and emendations are left unmarked.

but it will be obvious that both conclusions are purely speculative.[2]

Among the other items can be distinguished three short poems quite clearly concerned, in their different ways, with sexual love. These are Items 1, 10, and 11. The simplest of them is No. 11, 'Al gold Jonet is thin her'. This poem exhibits a highly repetitive style characteristic, as we shall see, of several of the Rawlinson poems. Its kernel is formed by two simple sentences: 'Al gold Jonet is thin her' and 'Save Jankin thin onlye dere, lemman dere'. From these thirteen words the whole poem is generated. The slight semantic gap between the two kernel sentences produces a faint effect of teasing economy, as if the poem consisted of two simple yet suggestively related brush-strokes. But any reader who knows how men address beautiful women in Western literature can easily supply the missing connection: 'Your hair is all gold [and because of your beauty I love you so much that I shall die unless] you save me.' There can be no argument here about the basic message.

Yet even this very simple poem suffers somewhat, I believe, from our ignorance of its context. How sophisticated is its simplicity? That is the difficult question. A poem in which a lover pleads with a golden-haired mistress to save his life might claim to be a lyric of courtly love; but 'lemman' is not a courtly word in Middle English, and the names Jankin and Janet carry homely associations. Suppose, however, that a document turned up which proved beyond doubt that 'Al gold Jonet is thin her' was the work of Geoffrey Chaucer. We would then unhesitatingly read it as a version of the pastoral, in Chaucer's 'small-town' manner, and perhaps compare it with the love-song of Absolon in the *Miller's Tale*. We would learn to appreciate the almost Chinese delicacy with which the two kernel sentences are set in relation one to another; and we would perhaps begin to see subtlety, too, in the varied repetitions of the second sentence. Does the omission of 'thin' in the fourth line serve as a faint check to the lady's

---

[2] R. L. Greene (ed.), *The Lyrics of the Red Book of Ossory*, Medium Aevum Monographs, n.s. v (Oxford, 1974), pp. ix-x. I am indebted to Norman Davis for a new reading of this item in the Rawlinson MS.

complacency? Is the phrase 'thin onlye dere' in the last line
to be read as a claim or as a reminder?

I hope these observations do not strike you as too cynical.
I do not mean to suggest that we see subtleties in texts only
when we know them to be the work of persons of good education or breeding. On the other hand, it is simply naïve to
suppose that such considerations do not affect our judgement
in these matters. Working on 'poems without contexts' makes
you realize that. Whether we like it or not, interpretation
does rely quite heavily upon promptings from outside the
text itself.

The second poem I want to consider is Item 1, 'Of everykune tree'. Like Item 11, this poem consists of two simple
kernel sentences: 'Of everykune tree the hawethorn bloweth
swotest', and 'My lemman she shal be the fairest of every
kinne'. In this case, the two sentences generate by repetition
two parallel stanzas, rhyming a a b a / a a c a. The two un-
rhymed lines are linked together by the presence in them of
two parallel superlatives: 'sweetest' . . . 'fairest'. The semantic
gap between the two constituent sentences is considerably
wider here than in the Janet poem. The first sentence states
that the hawthorn bears a blossom sweeter than that of any
other tree. The second expresses, apparently, a young lover's
determination that his mistress will be a very beautiful
woman. It is a curious fact, surely, that most readers should
have no difficulty in making sense of this gross *non sequitur*.
They unhesitatingly assume that the unexpected relationship
between the tree and the lady is of a familiar metaphorical or
symbolical kind. Furthermore, most readers would probably
agree that the tree is a symbol of the woman, rather than
vice versa. The main reason for this decision is presumably
the fact that poems about women are more common, in
Western literature at least, than poems about trees. Western
writers use nature-imagery to describe women much more
often than they use woman-imagery to describe nature.
Perhaps, too, the fact that the woman occupies the latter part
of the poem helps to establish her primacy. If one tries the
experiment of reading the stanzas in reverse order, the poem
creates, I think, a rather more equivocal effect.

In this case, then, a very general context indeed—little short of the whole Western literary tradition—seems sufficient to establish an agreed interpretation. The poem may appear enigmatic; but only a reader from Mars, or perhaps China, would misunderstand it. However, interpretations which appeal to such very general contexts are always rather vulnerable. It is an axiom of interpretation that a specific or narrow context always carries more weight than a broader one. So in cases such as the present one, a critic who suggests an interpretation which implies a more specific context will always have a certain theoretical advantage. An example of such an interpretation is provided by John Speirs. This is what Speirs says about 'Of everykune tree':

This song, to judge from the repeated lines, was a song for several voices and the singers were dancers round a hawthorn tree (or its human impersonator, wreathed in hawthorn, perhaps in a May dance). The song may have belonged with the worship or wooing of the hawthorn tree or its spirit or its human impersonator—the fairest of earth creatures. Even if we regard the 'lemmon' of the last four lines as not identical with the hawthorn tree of the first four, it would still be hard to escape the impression that this more human type of wooing-song had evolved from the earlier type and that it still shares the quality of the earlier type.[3]

Now, if the poem could indeed be shown to belong to the specific ritual context described by Speirs, then one would certainly be justified in ignoring more general considerations and reading it as a poem about a hawthorn bush. Those who continue to believe that the poem is a mere 'human type of wooing-song' will object that there is no other evidence that Englishmen worshipped, let alone wooed, bushes in the days of Edward II; but then any specific context they may themselves propose, in answer to Speirs, will itself be hypothetical. We may all know which side we would be on in such a dispute—I certainly do—but how would one *settle* it?

Item 10, 'Alnight by the rose', is even shorter than the two poems we have just discussed. It is also superficially more enigmatic, since it makes no mention of a 'lemman'. Yet nearly all readers agree that it is concerned with love, or at least with sex. They read it, that is, as an allegory. But how,

[3] J. Speirs, *Medieval English Poetry: The Non-Chaucerian Tradition* (London, 1957), pp. 61-2.

it may be asked, can they know that it is an allegory? The answer turns out to be rather obvious. Medieval theorists say that texts betray their allegorical character when they do not make sense on the literal level; and this rule fits the present case. One can imagine circumstances in which a person who was afraid to steal a whole rose-bush might steal a single flower; but why should anyone spend a whole night lying by a rose-bush? No competent reader, of course, spends any time on such problems. The unlikely hypothesis that this is a poem about rose-stealing barely enters his head. He looks instantly for an allegorical interpretation, and finds one without difficulty. The rose (unlike the hawthorn tree) is a commonplace symbol of the beloved in Western literature; and the image of maidenhood as a flower survives in the English verb 'deflower'. A lover, we see, is claiming to have spent the night secretly with a woman whom he dared not carry off. The poem therefore turns out to be more witty, and perhaps more cynical, than the Janet poem or the hawthorn poem. It opens in the same ecstatically repetitive vein; but the style of the third and fourth lines is different. They are linked together, not by simple parallelism, but by paradoxical antithesis. There is chiasmus in 'the rose stele' and 'bar the flour away'; and the last line rhymes with line two to produce a compact quatrain: a b c b.

The element of wit in this poem seems to arise from the presence in it, by implication, of a third person. Nos. 1 and 11 concern only the lover and his lemman; but here there is someone else—a husband, or a father, or a duenna—who forbids the lover to steal the rose. The lover has outwitted this adversary; and his glee finds expression in sprightly word-play. The dramatic character of this poem, as one might call it, links it to two other pieces in the collection: Item 5, 'Ami tenez vous joyous', and Item 9, 'Wer ther outher in this toun'. Both these poems, like 'Alnight by the rose', involve an adversary as well as the two lovers themselves; but they are both more explicitly dramatic. Let me look first at No. 5.

'Ami tenez vous joyous' presents fewer problems than any other piece on the Rawlinson strip. Like the English poems we have been looking at, this French poem is highly repetitive; but it is repetitive in a different fashion. In 'Al gold Jonet is thin her', as we have it in Rawlinson, the repetitions and near-repetitions obey no formal principle, and therefore create a somewhat mysterious incantatory effect. In the French poem, by contrast, all the lines are repeated exactly, and in a regular way, to make up a 'chanson à danser'. This was the French equivalent of the medieval English carol. As usual in this type of poem, the burden or refrain is given first. It consists of a repeated couplet. There follow three regular stanzas, also in the form of repeated couplets. Each stanza is followed by the burden couplet (which should perhaps again be repeated). Thus the poem conforms exactly to the pattern of the carol. It also represents, equally clearly, the type of French lyric known as the 'chanson de mal mariée' or 'song of an unhappily married woman'. The wife addresses her absent lover ('ami'). He must keep his spirits up, she says, because her husband will die. Her husband is *lui gelous*, 'the jealous one'. She asks her lover for a 'loving look' (*douz regars*) when he returns. He must think of her in his sufferings and keep himself *gai*. She is, and always will be, his love: 'Vostre amie sui et serrai'.

The 'chanson de mal mariée' was a favourite genre of the medieval French *trouvère*; but it is not often found on this side of the Channel before the fifteenth century. The presence of this particular piece on the Rawlinson strip is therefore somewhat surprising. It seems to belong to a world more polite than that of the other pieces. Its basic triangular situation—a woman, a *gelous*, and an absent lover—is one which appears in many courtly French lyrics, as well as in the *Roman de la Rose*. The ideal of joy and gaiety is also courtly. So is the prizing of a 'douz regars'. Even the ruthless frankness of 'Si murra lui gelous' may be read as aristocratic: well-bred ladies do not stoop to euphemism. However, we should note that the poem is a 'chanson *à danser*'. This would mean that it was primarily intended, like the medieval English carol, for festive performance. A soloist would sing the stanzas, while the rest of the dancers joined in with the burden. Of such dance-songs Peter Dronke observes that 'their melodic and poetic simplicity made them intrinsically suitable for dancing and festivities irrespective of class'.[4]

4 P. Dronke, *The Medieval Lyric* (London, 1968), p. 189.

'Ami tenez vous joyous' is certainly simple. The very high degree of repetition suggests that it was indeed sung, and perhaps danced to. If so, this would provide a link with at least some of the other items on the Rawlinson strip. We have already seen a good deal of repetition in the English poems; and at least one critic, as we have noticed, has suggested that 'Of everykune tree' is a dance-song of some sort.

Let me leave this question for a moment and turn to the other 'dramatic' love-poem, No. 9, 'Wer ther outher in this toun'. This is in every way more difficult than the French poem. The text is illegible in some places and obscure in others. The metrical form is irregular. I have divided it into four quatrains, apparently rhyming a b c b; but that leaves two lines over, which may be all that remains of a fifth quatrain. The dramatic situation is also obscure. The French poem belongs to a specific lyric type; and the situation which it portrays is completely determined by the conventions of that type. By contrast, the situation in the English poem is—or appears to be—much more singular. As it stands, indeed, the poem calls to mind one of those puzzling dramatic monologues by Browning. Sometimes Browning sets the reader to deduce a situation so peculiar that he is teased into thinking that he must have got it wrong. But a medieval poet, one supposes, would hardly do that. So we are left imagining that this poem is fragmentary, or else that it belongs to a lost type —neither very satisfactory solutions to an intractable problem.

The first quatrain may be translated as follows: 'If there were any ale or wine in this place, I would buy it for my mistress'. That could be the opening of a poem, certainly— indeed, a strikingly vigorous opening. But the situation is already somewhat misty, by comparison with the bright, sharp light of the French poem. One should not, I suppose, be surprised to find a lover trying to buy a drink for his lady. But the mention of ale perhaps suggests that this lover is less than a complete gentleman. One may recall the parish clerk Absolon, in Chaucer's *Miller's Tale*, who sends 'pyment, meeth and spiced ale' to the carpenter's wife. But what kind of *toun* is this, where ale and wine may not be available? Or does *toun*, as some have thought, mean 'tun, cask'? In that case, the setting is presumably a tavern. We read on, already puzzled, only to find that the mistress has apparently suffered some kind of violent assault. Lines 5 and 6 seem to mean: 'It was a very miserable thing for anyone to be so bold as to make my beloved all bloody'. In the following quatrain, the lover vows vengeance: 'Even though he were the son of the King of Normandy, yet I would be avenged for my mistress'. The poem has by now taken us into a very strange world indeed. A lover is apparently trying to find drink for a woman who has been assaulted by another man. The next quatrain opens with an echo of line 5: 'It was a very miserable thing for me then, miserable for me then. That is how it is for a man who loses what he loves'. The change to the past tense here coincides with a sudden change of tone. In the previous quatrain, the assault was a present subject for vengeance; but here it has dwindled into a past subject for reflection. The tone is resigned and gloomily philosophical, rather in the manner of Anglo-Saxon elegies such as the *Wanderer*. The same tone prevails in the last quatrain, or so it would seem. You will get some idea of the diffculty of reading the manuscript at this point from the fact that Kenneth and Celia Sisam, in their *Oxford Book of Medieval English Verse*, start this stanza with the line 'No lore I ne lerde' ('I have not been educated'). My own text is based, after much hesitation and long staring at the parchment, on Dronke's transcription: 'That is what she taught me, and I can say no more; but to Christ I commend her who was my mistress'.[5] On this reading, the text ends with an aposiopesis. The mistress is now a thing of the past—dead, perhaps, or carried off by the brutal adversary—and the speaker 'can no more'. It does not sound as if there were any more stanzas to come.

So we are left with a very enigmatic poem of tragic love. To make matters worse, I should mention that there is no space in the manuscript separating what I have distinguished as No. 9 from the equally enigmatic No. 8, 'Maiden in the mor lay'. The one runs straight on from the other—unlike all the other pieces, which are separated by spaces. There is also one curious verbal link between the two poems (if such they be). Compare lines 11 and 12 of No. 9, 'Well wo was me tho, / Wo was me tho', with lines 8 and 9 of No. 8, 'Well was

[5] P. Dronke, 'The Rawlinson Lyrics', *N & Q* n.s. 8 (1961), 245–6.

hire mete, / What was hire mete?' Certainly it is hard to read
the two poems as one, and the editors are probably right to
separate them; but a lingering doubt remains. The problem
would be easier if one could see in the lines beginning 'Wer
ther outher in this toun' a poem of some recognizable type.
R. H. Robbins entitles the piece 'A Toast to His Lost Mistress'
and suggests that it might be a drinking song. Basil Cottle sees
the poem as deliberately 'choked and incoherent', supposing
it to represent the monologue of a deserted drunk.[6] The
latter conjecture seems to me distinctly better than the
former; but both rest on slender evidence. Both Robbins and
Cottle read line 16 as 'Ne—no more in can!', i.e. 'nothing left
in the mug!' That certainly would suggest either a drinking
song or a drinker's monologue. But Dronke's reading, though
it involves a small emendation, is more likely; and if one
adopts it, as I have done, the poem is left with only a single
reference to drink, at the opening.

However, there is another place in the Rawlinson collection which certainly does concern drinking. This is the
extraordinary item No. 12. This appears at the bottom of the
verso side of the strip, and it is hard to make out, especially
in its opening lines. My reconstruction, which is very hypothetical, displays two closely parallel stanzas (lines 1-5 and
lines 10-14) but leaves six lines formally unaccounted for. It
is clear, however, that the poem represents, in part at least,
the words of a drinker to his companions. The repetitive
manner so characteristic of the Rawlinson poems here creates
an effect of tipsy and slightly incoherent excitement. This
kind of mimesis is definitely not a feature of drinking songs.
Hence R. H. Robbins concludes that the poem 'is not a song
to be sung on festive occasions . . . but a very clever literary
production describing how a man feels and reacts when
drunk'.[7] But this conclusion takes insufficient account, I
think, of the latter part of the poem, beginning 'Stondeth alle
stille'. This hardly makes sense as part of a purely literary
production. Robbins says that the poet 'is trying to represent
the emotions of a drunken man, who wants everything to

    [6] R. H. Robbins (ed.), *Secular Lyrics of the XIVth and XVth Centuries* (Ox-
ford, 1952), pp. 7 and 230-1; A. B. Cottle, *The Triumph of English 1350-1400*
(London, 1969), p. 297.   [7] *Secular Lyrics*, pp. 230-1.

stand still; then, when he trips, is able to relax his body'.[8] But surely the three imperatives *stondeth*, *trippe*, and *let gon* must all have the same reference. To me they sound most like instructions to dancers, built into the text of a dance song. A modern analogy is the Hokey-Cokey, where the dancers sing 'You put your right leg in, You put your right leg out', and so on. I suspect, therefore, that the whole poem may be the text, not of a drinking song, but of a dance song. Perhaps the dance itself involved some imitation of drunken behaviour. Possibly the dancers stood and stamped during the heavy, repetitive parts of the song: 'Tabart is ydronken', 'Stondeth alle stille'. At other times they may have skipped and 'let their bodies go'—dancing in a ring, perhaps, round a leader who impersonated the drunken Tabart.

This is, of course, speculation; but I hope you will agree that it is not idle speculation. To argue whether this poem is a literary piece of dramatic monologue or a fragment of dance song is to argue about the very meaning of the poem. One cannot avoid such conjectures, however resolutely one sets one's face against mere scholarly speculation. Those who insist on sticking to the 'words on the page' simply drive the business of conjecture underground. For one cannot interpret or evaluate a text without identifying what *kind* of text it is. In some cases that identification is so easily made that we do not notice ourselves making it; but there is no difference in principle between these easy cases and difficult ones like 'Tabart is ydronken'.

These considerations apply with particular force, I think, to the two best-known Rawlinson poems, 'Icham of Irlande' and 'Maiden in the mor lay'; but before discussing these, let me deal briefly with the one other remaining piece, No. 6, 'Ore alom, alom'. Like the other French poem, this one appears to be a 'chanson à danser'; but in this case the refrain or burden is followed by only one stanza, so perhaps the poem is fragmentary. On the other hand, the fundamentally dance-like character of the carol is more evident here. The repeated 'alom, alom, alom' appears to correspond, like 'Trippe a littel with thy fot' in No. 12, to what dancers actually did as they sang. In his standard work, *The Early*

[8] *Secular Lyrics*, p. 265.

English Carols, R. L. Greene describes the typical performance of a carol as follows: the leader would 'sing the stanzas of the song to which the carole was being danced. During the time of such singing the ring moved to the left. At the close of the stanza the entire company of dancers would respond with the refrain or burden of the song, dancing in place the while. Then, as the circle revolved again, the leader would sing the following stanza . . .'.[9] It is easy, in this case, to imagine the dancers stamping as they chorus 'Ore alom, alom, alom', expressing an impatience which gives way to relief as the leader sings 'Ore est temps d'alier a diner' and the ring revolves.

The content of this poem presents no difficulties. It is plainly a song of 'pastime and good company', such as might be sung and danced just before dinner on some festive occasion. We may notice here the curious fact that neither of the French pieces in Rawlinson presents any problems of interpretation. They are both equally lucid and orderly—quite without the turbid passages and occasional glimpses of deep water which we find in the English poems. The contrast is not uncharacteristic of the literary cultures of English and French in the Middle Ages.

This contrast appears most strikingly when we turn from No. 6 to No. 7, 'Icham of Irlande'. Like No. 6, this famous piece appears to be a carol, or a fragment of one. There is a three-line burden, followed by a single stanza, the last line of which (as often in carols) serves as a transition back to the burden—which is presumably to be repeated. The invitation to 'come ant daunce with me' leaves little doubt that this carol really was meant to be danced. If the dance followed the pattern described by Greene, the stanza would have been sung by a soloist, the burden by the rest of the company; but the poem makes no dramatic use of this distinction of persons. The Irish speaker in the burden seems to be the same as the (presumably female) speaker in the stanza who invites a gentleman to dance with her in Ireland. Since this speaker would inevitably be identified with the soloist (herself presumably female), we must imagine that the other dancers are, as it were, echoing her words in their burden. Perhaps the

[9] R. L. Greene, *The Early English Carols* (2nd edn., Oxford, 1977), pp. xlv-xlvi.

dance took the form of a Ladies' Excuse Me, with the soloist singling out whichever man stopped opposite her, when the ring of carollers had finished dancing round as she sang her stanza. In that case, she may have repeated the same stanza at each invitation. Otherwise, the text must be fragmentary.

However, such a reconstruction of the dance, even if it were generally agreed, would not in this case lead to a complete interpretation. In Nos. 6 and 12, the dancers impersonate revellers and drunks, respectively. In No. 5, the soloist impersonates a 'mal mariée'. Those are familiar human types, with no mystery about them. But who or what, in the present poem, does the soloist impersonate? Who is this Irish woman (if she is a woman) who prays the men to come and dance with her in Ireland?

One answer to this difficult question has been given by John Speirs: 'Ireland, the Isle of Saints because earlier it had been the Isle of the Gods, is here sacred still perhaps in a pagan as well as a Christian sense. The dancer from across the sea—from a sacred or magical *other* country—is still perhaps essentially a faery or otherworld visitant. . . . Essentially, or symbolically, the dancer will steal away or abduct her partner.'[10] Now Speirs may be right in suggesting that we have here, as perhaps in the case of the Holy Grail, a fragment out of pagan antiquity. If so, however, the original pagan form and meaning are beyond the range of conjecture. In any case, such conjecture would be relevant to the interpretation of the fourteenth-century poem only in so far as that poem itself has ancient or pagan meanings. On this crucial point, Speirs is somewhat evasive: 'sacred *still perhaps in a pagan sense . . . still perhaps essentially a faery*'.

I would prefer to approach the problem from a different angle altogether, and speculate rather on what the poem meant to the dancers. It may have been enough for them to identify 'Ireland', in the make-believe geography of the dance floor, with the area occupied by the soloist at the centre of the ring of carollers. The symbolism of dance would then quite naturally explain why this area represented a 'holy land' ('Weave a circle round him thrice'). It would also,

[10] *Medieval English Poetry*, p. 60.

perhaps, justify to the dancers the strange pleading insistence of the woman's cry:

> Gode sire, pray ich thee
> For of sainte charite
> Come ant daunce with me
> In Irlande.

These are, of course, themselves conjectures; but they may at least suggest the peculiar nature of the problem presented by 'Icham of Irlande'. In the case of the other ten pieces I have so far discussed, problems seem to stem from our ignorance of the original, fourteenth-century context. If only we could talk to the scribe or his friends, we may imagine, we would find out what we want to know—about the man who went to Coggeshall without money, for instance, or about the blood-stained mistress. But the scribe may not have understood any better than we do who the Irish dancer 'really was'. He would, perhaps, have understood the poem only in so far as it referred to the actions and symbolic geography of the dance. How many people nowadays could explain the unseasonable nuts in 'Here we go gathering nuts in May'?

I cannot leave this poem without referring briefly to Yeats. Yeats runs burden and stanza together, alters the wording slightly, substitutes a line of his own for line 4, and so produces a five-line burden for his own carol:

> 'I am of Ireland,
> And the Holy Land of Ireland,
> And time runs on,' cried she.
> 'Come out of charity,
> Come dance with me in Ireland.'

In his two stanzas, Yeats portrays 'one solitary man' who hears this call, but refuses it. As Ellmann says, he 'finds many pretexts for preferring comfortable expedience to the discomforts of idealism'; but at the end the woman is still singing 'as if indifferent to his prudential explanations'.[11] In

---

[11] R. Ellmann, *The Identity of Yeats* (London, 1954), pp. 280-1.

the context of Yeats's poem, the mystery of the Irish woman is partly dissipated. Her words are to be understood, as Ellmann says, as 'the cry of all idealism and heroism'—but also, surely, as the cry of Ireland. Yeats has reset the Middle English poem in the world of contemporary politics. Yet even so, the poem retains something of what Speirs rightly calls its 'trance-like or rapt' quality.

It is time to turn, however, to the last of the Rawlinson 'Words for Music Perhaps': No. 8, 'Maiden in the mor lay'. Once the much-abbreviated text of the manuscript is expanded by necessary repeats, this proves to be the longest piece in the collection; but its four seven-line stanzas are so repetitious that the prose sense can be summed up in a single sentence: A maiden spent seven nights and a day in the wilds, eating primroses and violets, drinking cold spring-water, and sheltering in a chamber of red roses and lilies. The utterance is very simple, but also very strange; and it has attracted much more attention from interpreters than any other piece in the collection. Let me summarize briefly some of their conclusions.

A number of critics interpret the poem in terms of Christian tradition. Some have seen the maiden as an ascetic or penitent (perhaps Mary Magdalene?) who has given up the comforts of civilization for the sake of her soul.[12] Others interpret her allegorically. Thus D. W. Robertson, in an essay on 'Historical Criticism' published in 1951, identified her as the Virgin Mary. Robertson suggested, among other things, that the roses allegorically represent martyrdom or charity, and that the lilies represent purity. The spring-water is God's grace. The maiden is the Virgin, awaiting the coming of Christ (the 'day' of line 7) in the 'wilderness of the world under the old law' (the 'moor').[13]

Several scholars have questioned this interpretation, among them E. T. Donaldson. Donaldson admits that medieval readers may have 'thought of the Virgin' as they read the poem; but he maintains that it makes sense without allegorical interpretation. He compares the maiden to Wordsworth's

[12] E. M. W. Tillyard, *TLS*, 11 May 1951, p. 293; J. Harris, *Journal of Medieval and Renaissance Studies* 1 (1971), 59–87.

[13] D. W. Robertson, 'Historical Criticism', *English Institute Essays 1950*, ed. A. S. Downer (New York, 1951), p. 27.

Lucy: 'In each case the poetic *donnée* is the highly primitive one which exposes an innocent woman to the vast, potentially hostile, presumably impersonal forces of nature; and the Middle English lyric suggests the mystery by which these forces are, at times, transmuted into something more humane, even benevolent, by their guardianship of the innocent maiden.'[14] Others have looked for a more definite secular interpretation, and have found it in the counter-cultures of folk-belief. The maiden, they suggest, may be 'undergoing some rite of initiation or purification', or else she is under a spell. Or she may be a fairy creature. Thus Dronke, taking a hint from Speirs, presents an elaborate reading of the poem as a dance song celebrating a water-sprite who dwells by a spring on the moors.[15]

Anyone who reads these discussions of 'Maiden in the mor lay' will be left with a strong sense of how hard it is to establish any interpretation of such an enigmatic poem in the absence of an agreed context. We seem to be trapped in what is known as the 'hermeneutic circle'. E. D. Hirsch explains the idea of this circle as follows: 'The whole can be understood only through its parts, but the parts can be understood only through the whole.'[16] So, in this case, it seems that we cannot determine the meaning of parts such as the rose or spring without first knowing what kind of piece the poem is. On the other hand, we cannot determine what kind of piece the poem is without first knowing what at least some of its parts signify.

One possible way of escaping from this circle suggests itself at once. Can we not take the other Rawlinson pieces as themselves providing the necessary context within which to consider this particularly difficult case? For the Rawlinson collection is itself, we might argue, a 'whole' some of whose parts *can* be known. It contains, as we have seen, five poems concerned in various ways with love between the sexes: Nos. 1, 5, 9, 10, and 11. We have also identified No. 6 as a festive

---

[14] E. T. Donaldson, 'Patristic Exegesis in the Criticism of Medieval Literature— The Opposition', in *Critical Approaches to Medieval Literature*, ed. D. Bethurum (New York, 1960), p. 23.

[15] *The Medieval Lyric*, pp. 195–6.

[16] E. D. Hirsch, *Validity in Interpretation* (New Haven, Conn., 1967), p. 76. See also discussion in Hirsch's later book, *The Aims of Interpretation* (Chicago, 1976).

song, and No. 12 as a poem about drunkenness. Three of the pieces, we may add, are in the form of the 'chanson à danser' or carol and may themselves be dance songs: Nos. 5, 6, and 7. No. 12 appears to be another dance song. Nos. 1, 10, and 11 are also 'words for music perhaps'. The general character of the collection, therefore, seems to be secular, even popular, with a predominance of song-like or danceable pieces mostly concerned with food or drink or love.

It does not follow from this, however, that all the Rawlinson pieces must be secular or worldly. The matter might be settled if we knew who wrote the strip and why; but we do not. Some scholars have supposed that the scribe was a minstrel noting down items from his repertoire. But this is no more than a bare hypothesis; and in any case, a minstrel might well have a song of the Virgin among his miscellaneous party-pieces. It is certainly true to say that 'Maiden in the mor lay' *sounds* as if it were the same sort of poem as the other Rawlinson pieces. Its highly repetitive, song-like manner, for example, resembles that of Nos. 1, 10, 11, and 12. But similarity of manner does not exclude difference of meaning. I would conclude, therefore, that consideration of the Rawlinson collection as a whole does not offer a sure way out of the hermeneutic circle, though it does lend some circumstantial support to secular interpretations of 'Maiden in the mor lay'. So far as this argument is concerned, Robertson is more likely to be wrong than right; but one can say no more than that.

However, since 1951, when Robertson published his interpretation, two fresh pieces of evidence have most unexpectedly come to light. These are the only two known medieval references to the Rawlinson poems; and both of them, as it happens, concern 'Maiden in the mor lay'. The first, published by R. L. Greene in 1952 in *Speculum* (xxvii. 504–6), occurs in an Irish manuscript known as the Red Book of Ossory. The last pages of this volume contain the text of sixty Latin poems, written in fourteenth-century hands. On the first page of this section of the manuscript is the following note:

Be advised, reader, that the Bishop of Ossory has made these songs for the vicars of the cathedral church, for the priests, and for his clerks, to be sung on important holidays and at celebrations, in order that their throats and mouths, consecrated to God, may not be polluted by songs that are lewd, secular, and associated with revelry. Furthermore, since they are trained singers, let them provide themselves with suitable tunes according to what the texts require.

The bishop in question was an English Franciscan Friar, Richard de Ledrede, Bishop of Ossory from 1317 till 1360. Now, a number of his Latin lyrics have prefixed to them scraps of English or French verse. These scraps evidently indicate the 'suitable tunes' to which the pious Latin was designed to be sung. One of the Latin poems, a song of the Nativity, has at its head the words: 'Mayde y[n] the moore [l] ay'. Evidently Ledrede intended his Ossory clergy to sing this particular piece to the tune of our Rawlinson poem.

The second new piece of evidence was published more recently, by Professor Wenzel in the 1974 issue of *Speculum* (xlix. 69-74). It was discovered by Wenzel in a Latin sermon collection written down about 1360 in a manuscript in Worcester Cathedral Library. The preacher is lamenting the moral deterioration of man. In the Golden Age, he says, citing the familiar authorities of Ovid and Boethius, men lived in joy and innocence. They ate only the foods that nature provided. And what, he asks, did they drink? His answer is unexpected. I quote: 'And what was their drink? The answer appears in a certain song [*in quodam cantico*], namely a *karole* that is called "the mayde be wode lay". Note in margin: "the cold water of the well spryng".'

These two remarkable allusions throw some light, I think, on the Rawlinson poem. First, they confirm the suspicion that 'Maiden in the mor lay' is a song or 'canticum'—evidently a popular one, for its tune was known even in far-off Kilkenny. Second, we note that the Worcester preacher calls the poem a *karole*, which probably suggests that he regarded it as a song for dancing. Third, and most important, we find clues to the meaning of the poem. The Worcester allusion may seem to prompt an interpretation quite different from any that has previously been proposed. Is 'Maiden in the mor lay' a lyric about the Golden Age? I do not think we can draw that conclusion. The Worcester preacher seems to be making no more than a graceful literary allusion, prompted by his own rhetorical question, 'And what was their drink?' The question reminds him of the song, and the song provides a felicitously appropriate answer.

More significant, I think, is the Ossory allusion. The Bishop, it will be recalled, intended his pious Latin pieces to replace 'songs that are lewd, secular, and associated with revelry'. It has been argued that the accompanying scraps of English and French do no more than suggest suitable tunes. They do not necessarily, on this argument, indicate the particular lewd songs which the Bishop intended to supplant. If that is so, then of course 'Maiden in the mor lay' might still be a Marian lyric. But this rather strained argument gains no support from the other vernacular Ossory scraps. There are eight of these, and all of them seem to indicate popular secular songs, mostly love-songs.[17] The longest scrap, for instance, represents the opening of a rare English 'chanson de mal mariée'. Another reads simply: 'Have god day, my lemmon'. In short, 'Maiden in the mor lay' keeps much the same sort of company in the Red Book of Ossory as it does in the Rawlinson Manuscript. We are surely safe in assuming that Bishop Ledrede did indeed regard it as one of those 'cantilenae teatrales, turpes et seculares' which he so much deplored. He may have been wrong, of course; but then so may Professor Robertson. And who is more likely to be wrong: a fourteenth-century bishop or a twentieth-century professor?

I conclude, then, that the Ossory allusion offers us a possible way of escape from the hermeneutic circle in the case of 'Maiden in the mor lay'. It discourages, if it does not absolutely rule out, interpretations which see the maiden as Mary Magdalene or the Virgin Mary. On the other hand, it does not help us to select the right secular interpretation; and I doubt whether we shall ever be quite sure of that, unless yet another allusion turns up, perhaps. One suspects, as in the case of 'Icham of Irlande', that the singers of the *karole* may themselves not have known the significance of their mysterious damsel who lay in the moor—or, in the Worcester variant, 'by wood'. Originally, perhaps, she *was* a water-sprite; but for the carollers she may well have been, as she is for us, a creature of mystery.

---

[17] Greene, *The Lyrics of the Red Book*, Nos. 8 (also 19 and 28), 17, 18, 22 (also 34), 24, 30, 40, 41.

III

This discussion of the twelve Rawlinson pieces has ended on an inconclusive note; but I do not apologize for that. My purpose, it will be recalled, was to display what kinds of difficulties arise in the interpretation of 'poems without contexts'. I therefore do not have to claim to have solved all problems presented by these poems. Indeed, I have suggested that some of them hardly *can* be solved, in the absence of further external evidence.

In his masterly book entitled *Validity in Interpretation*, E. D. Hirsch refers to the famous experiments reported by I. A. Richards in his *Practical Criticism*. The Cambridge undergraduates were presented with the text of certain poems, without title or attribution, and failed rather dismally to understand them. Richards thought, no doubt correctly, that this failure reflected on their education; but Hirsch thinks it has a more general significance as well. All interpretation, Hirsch argues, depends upon an ability to guess what *type of meaning* is being expressed; and our ability to guess this correctly is much impaired when we have no external evidence to guide us. Our sense of what to look for in a text, in other words, depends more than we may like to admit upon being given an external context. Texts do not have 'semantic autonomy'. Indeed, one and the same text may support two radically different interpretations, if we have occasion to read it in more than one context and hence look for and see different things. The story by Borges entitled 'The Man Who Wrote *Don Quixote*' is based on this curious fact.

I said earlier that Item No. 11, 'Al gold Jonet is thin her', would read differently if we were to discover that Chaucer wrote it. We would take it, then, as an exercise in a sophisticated pastoral manner. In fact, however, the general character of the Rawlinson collection, so far as that can be determined, does not support such an interpretation. The poems seem generally to belong rather to some world of popular song and dance than to the courtly literary world of Chaucer. But such a conclusion, even if it were universally accepted, would by no means end the matter. A phrase such as 'a world of popular song and dance' is easily spoken; but what kinds of guess about meaning does it encourage, and what kinds does it exclude? What, indeed, does 'popular' mean in this context? We may recall that at least one of the Rawlinson poems was 'popular' with vicars, priests, and clerks in the diocese of Ossory. What does *that* imply?

The truth is that our knowledge of the social and human context of the Rawlinson pieces is too uncertain and indefinite to help us much with their interpretation. It is enough to rule out the more abstruse, patristic readings of 'Maiden in the mor lay', no doubt; but that is almost all.

So how *do* we decide what 'type of meanings' to look for in these poems? The full answer to this question is no doubt very complicated; but one point emerges clearly. We rely heavily upon our ability to identify positively from internal evidence the literary genre to which each poem belongs. Thus, No. 5 presented no difficulty, because it recognizably belonged to a well-known medieval genre: the 'chanson de mal mariée'. This genre is so specific in its conventions that it determines, not just the situation of the unhappily married woman, but also even the choice of individual words to express it. *Lui gelous*, in this kind of text, can only mean 'the husband'. So once the genre of this particular piece had been identified, everything else became clear. The work of interpretation was performed at a stroke.

Not all genres, of course, are as specific as the 'chanson de mal mariée'. One does not arrive at a complete interpretation of 'Icham of Irlande' simply by identifying it as a dance song. That identification helps in so far as it enables one to subsume the poem's meanings into a reconstructed dance. But the reconstruction leaves a residue of obscurity: Who, after all, *was* the Irish dancer? In the case of 'Maiden in the mor lay', identification of the poem as a dance song or *karole* is less helpful. The meanings of this poem cannot easily be subsumed into the dance genre. Yet even here the interpreter enjoys some advantage, in being able to tell at least what type of poem he is dealing with. One way of feeling that advantage is to compare 'Maiden in the mor lay' with No. 9, 'Wer ther outher in this toun'. I called the latter a 'dramatic monologue'; but that convenient phrase will not have concealed the fact that I was unable to make any coherent sense of the piece. I did not really know what kind of poem it was.

In conclusion, let me sum up this general point as simply as I can. In interpreting any text, we need to be able to guess what kinds of meaning to look for in it. These guesses are usually guided, to some considerable extent, by our knowledge of the 'external context'—the title of the text, who wrote it, when, for what occasion, for what audience, etc. But we can do without such knowledge under certain circumstances. The text must clearly declare itself as belonging to a known genre or type; and that genre must be such as to determine certain specific types of meaning. Otherwise, in the absence of external evidence, we are in most cases condemned to conjecture and controversy. Another way of saying the same thing is to describe genre as an internal substitute for context.

APPENDIX

THE POEMS OF BODLEIAN MS RAWLINSON D. 913

1.
> Of everykune tree,
> Of everykune tree,
> The hawethorn bloweth swotest,
> Of everykune tree.
>
> My lemman she shal be,
> My lemman she shal be,
> The fairest of every kinne
> My lemman she shal be.

2.
> The godemon on his weye.

3.
> Ichave a mantel ymaket of cloth.

4.
> Ne sey never such a man as Jordan was; wente
> he to Gogeshale panyles.

5.
    Ami tenez vous joyous,
    Si murra lui gelous.
    Ami tenez vous joyous,
    Si murra lui gelous.

Ami, quant vous turneiez,
Un douz regars moi donez.
Ami, quant vous turneiez,
Un douz regars moi donez.
    Ami tenez vous joyous,
    Si murra lui gelous.

Ami, quant vous soufrerez,
De vostre amie pencerez.
[Ami, quant vous soufrerez,
De vostre amie pencerez.]
    Ami tenez vous joyous,
    Si murra lui gelous.

Ami, si vous tenez gai,
Vostre amie sui et serrai.
[Ami, si vous tenez gai,
Vostre amie sui et serrai.]
    Ami tenez vous joyous,
    Si murra lui gelous.

6.
    Ore alom, alom, alom,
    Bele companie avom.
    Ore alom, alom, alom,
    Bele companie avom.

Ore est temps d'alier a diner,
Ore est temps d'alier a diner.
    Ore alom, alom, alom
    Bele companie avom.

7.
    Icham of Irlande
    Ant of the holy lande
    Of Irlande.

    Gode sire, pray ich thee
    For of sainte charite
    Come ant daunce with me
    In Irlande.

8.
Maiden in the mor lay,
In the mor lay,
Sevenight fulle [ant a —]
Sevenight fulle [ant a —]
Maiden in the mor lay,
In the mor lay,
Sevenightes fulle ant a day.

Well was hire mete,
What was hire mete?
The primerole ant the —
The primerole ant the —
Well was hire mete,
What was hire mete?
The primerole ant the violet.

Well [was hire dring,]
What was hire dring?
[The chelde water of the —
The chelde water of the —
Well was hire dring,
What was hire dring?]
The chelde water of the welle spring.

Well was hire bour,
What was hire bour?
[The rede rose an te —
The rede rose an te —
Well was hire bour,
What was hire bour?]
The rede rose an te lilie flour.

9.
Wer ther outher in this toun
Ale or wyn,
Ich hit wolde bugge
To lemman myn.

Well wo was so hardy
Forte make my lef al blody.

Though he were the kinges sone
Of Normaundy,
Yet icholde awreke be
For lemman myn.

Well wo was me tho,
Wo was me tho;
The man that leseth that he loveth
Him is al so.

So she me lerde —
Ne no more I ne can,
But Crist ich hire biteche
That was my lemman.

10.   Alnight by the rose, rose,
Alnight by the rose I lay.
Darst ich nought the rose stele,
Ant yet I bar the flour away.

11.   Al gold Jonet is thin her,
Al gold Jonet is thin her.
Save thin Jankin, lemman dere,
Save Jankin, lemman dere.
Save thin onlye dere.

12.   [Tabart is] ydronken,
Dronken, dronken,
Ydronken is Tabart,
Ydronken is Tabart,
[Ydronken] atte wine.

Hay [   ] Malkin,
Suster, Walter, Peter!
Ye dronke al depe
Ant ichulle eke.

Stondeth alle stille,
Stille, stille,
Stille stondeth alle,
Stille [stondeth alle,]
Stille as any ston.

Trippe a littel with thy fot
Ant let thy body gon.

2. CHAUCER'S *KNIGHT'S TALE* AND THE THREE AGES OF MAN

Two discussions of the *Knight's Tale*, one by Richard Neuse, the other by Douglas Brooks and Alastair Fowler, have drawn attention to age as a variable factor to be taken into account when considering the main actors, human and divine, in Chaucer's poem.[1] In the present essay I attempt to take this idea further by analysing the characters in the Tale, men and women, gods and goddesses, specifically as representatives of the *three* ages of man: youth, maturity, and old age.

Medieval writers inherited from classical and patristic times several different schemes of the ages. From the twelfth century onwards, two dominant schemes are those invoked by Brooks and Fowler: seven ages, and four. The former, which is familiar from Shakespeare's *As You Like It*, has an astrological character, for it rests on a parallelism between the ages and the seven planets. The latter is a scientific scheme, linked by multiple parallelisms with other natural tetrads, notably the four elements, the four humours, and the four seasons of the year.[2] Dante's discussion of the four ages of man in his *Convivio* was certainly known to Chaucer; and the structure of the *Knight's Tale*, with its evident parallels between the god-planets and the human characters, calls astrological seven-age schemes to mind. However, the age-structure of the Tale's population, as Neuse clearly saw, asks to be analysed in terms not of seven or four,

---

[1] R. Neuse, 'The Knight: The First Mover in Chaucer's Human Comedy', *University of Toronto Quarterly* 31 (1962), 299–315, reprinted in J. A. Burrow (ed.), *Geoffrey Chaucer: A Critical Anthology* (2nd edn., Harmondsworth, 1982), pp. 242–63, cited from the latter; D. Brooks and A. Fowler, 'The Meaning of Chaucer's *Knight's Tale*', *Medium Aevum* 39 (1970), 123–46; also, more briefly, P. Tristram, *Figures of Life and Death in Medieval English Literature* (London, 1976), pp. 88–91.

[2] On age-schemes in antiquity and the Renaissance, see the works cited below, Essay 11, n. 14. On seven-age schemes, see Boll, 'Die Lebensalter', pp. 112–37. On four-age schemes, see Boll, pp. 101–6, and R. Klibansky, E. Panofsky, and F. Saxl, *Saturn and Melancholy* (London, 1964), pp. 292–7. For Dante's version of the latter, see *Il Convivio*, ed. G. Busnelli and G. Vandelli (Florence, 1964), IV. xxiii–xxviii.

but three ages. Neuse sets out Chaucer's 'image of different generations' in tabular form.[3]

Saturn			Egeus		
Jupiter			Theseus		
Mars	Venus	Diana	Arcite	Palamon	Emily

Schemes of the three ages have a tradition less distinct than those of four or seven ages, because they rest not upon some learned analogy but upon the easily observable three-generation structure of any human community, a structure exhibited also in the community of the gods in the *Knight's Tale*: Saturn the grandfather ('aiel', 2477), his son Jupiter, and his granddaughter Venus ('doughter to Jove', 2222). Yet the history of three-age schemes in the Middle Ages shows that even they did acquire certain more specific associations. Two texts, one of which at least Chaucer probably knew, will illustrate this: the *Parlement of the Thre Ages* and the *De Regimine Principum* of Giles of Rome.

The *Parlement of the Thre Ages* belongs to a homiletic and moralizing tradition, which associates the three ages especially with the thought of death.[4] In this fourteenth-century alliterative poem, the poet reports a debate between three personifications: Youthe, Medill Elde, and Elde. It is Elde, naturally enough, who preaches the vanity of things and the inevitability of death to pleasure-loving Youthe and worldly Medill Elde, just as it is old Egeus who states these truths most unequivocally in the *Knight's Tale*. But the homiletic tradition also stresses the fact that death can take people unexpectedly in any one of the three ages. The *locus classicus* for this idea in the West was St. Gregory the Great's interpretation of that parable of Christ's which concerns the servants who wait for their returning Lord to knock without

---

[3] Neuse, p. 248, and cf. p. 259. For a discussion of three-age schemes in two fourteenth-century French poems, *Echecs d'Amour* and *Chevalier Errant*, see P.-Y. Badel, *Le Roman de la Rose au XIVe siècle* (Geneva, 1980), pp. 288, 326–30.

[4] Ed. M. Y. Offord, EETS o.s. 246 (1959). See B. Rowland, 'The Three Ages of *The Parlement of the Thre Ages*', *Chaucer Review* 9 (1975), 342–52; and T. Turville-Petre, 'The Ages of Man in *The Parlement of the Thre Ages*', *Medium Aevum* 46 (1977), 66–76, especially pp. 67–9 on associations between three-age schemes and death.

knowing in which of the three *vigiliae*, or watches of the
night, to expect him (Luke 12: 36-8). Gregory interpreted
the knocking at the door as the summons of death (compare
Parlement of the Thre Ages, 292, 654) and the three *vigiliae*
as the three ages of man. This interpretation was followed by
many medieval preachers, and by Langland in *Piers Plowman*,
as I have shown elsewhere.[5] The suddenness of premature
death is, of course, a shocking reality in the *Knight's Tale*,
where Arcite is carried off at a moment of triumph in the
first of his three ages. As Theseus observes (employing, however, the even simpler binary division of life):

> Of man and womman seen we wel also
> That nedes, in oon of thise termes two,
> This is to seyn, in youthe or elles age,
> He moot be deed, the kyng as shal the page.

(I. 3027-30)

Nearer to Chaucer's poem, generally speaking, is the conception of the three ages which he could have found in the
De Regimine Principum. Giles of Rome's discussion of the
ages here (I. iv. 1-4) in fact derives largely from Aristotle's
Rhetoric (II. 12-14); but the latter was relatively little
known, whereas the *De Regimine* was a standard book in
Chaucer's day, when it was translated into English, probably
by John Trevisa.[6] Hence it is Giles ('Egidio eremita') not
Aristotle whom Dante cites in the *Convivio* as an authority
on the ages of man, alongside Virgil (the *Aeneid* allegorically
interpreted) and Cicero (*De Senectute* and *De Officiis*).[7]
Giles presents a version of the ages quite unlike that found in
sermons and moral poems. Being concerned with princely
rule, he considers the ages from a purely secular point of view.
The difference may be seen in the treatment of middle age.
In homiletic writings, the worldly preoccupations associated

---

[5] B text XII. 3-9. See my essay, 'Langland *Nel Mezzo del Cammin*', in P. L.
Heyworth (ed.), *Medieval Studies for J. A. W. Bennett* (Oxford, 1981), pp. 21-41.
[6] The standard Latin translation of Aristotle's *Rhetoric* was made about 1270
by William of Moerbeke. Giles of Rome wrote a commentary on it *c.*1280. His
De Regimine was written *c.*1285. I have used the 1482 Rome edition. The Middle
English translation ascribed to Trevisa survives only in Bodleian MS Digby 233.
[7] *Convivio*, IV. xxiv. 9.

with this age naturally win it a low moral grading; but in
Giles's scheme it figures as the best age for a ruler, because it
strikes the ideal mean between the opposite extremes of
youth and age. From Aristotle's brilliant paragraphs, Giles
laboriously extracts six good and six bad points of youth
(generosity and modesty, for instance, but on the other hand
lack of moderation and instability), and similarly for age
(temperate desires on the one hand, scepticism and pusillanimity on the other); but, like Aristotle, he sees in the
middle age no faults at all:

For those who are in the prime of life, holding a middle position between
the old and the young, as the Philosopher has it in the second book of
the *Rhetoric*, possess the praiseworthy qualities of both old and young.
For being neither too hot like the young nor too cold like the old, they
are neither as spirited and precipitate [as the young] nor as timid and
pusillanimous as the old, but something in between: they are afraid
only when there is really something to fear, and daring only where
daring has an object.[8]

From this worldly point of view, middle age is not the age
furthest from God, but, as Dante says, the 'colmo de la
nostra vita'—the high point of the noble life.[9]

I

The idea that the hero of a story should be young prevails in
European narrative especially from the twelfth century; and
the *Knight's Tale*, like most Middle English romances, follows
this convention. Its heroes are Palamon and Arcite, two young
scions of the royal house of Thebes. Their youth is never in
doubt from the moment when they are first discovered on
the battlefield:

> Two yonge knyghtes liggynge by and by,
> Bothe in oon armes, wroght ful richely. (1011–12)

---

[8] Ed. cit., I. iv. 4. Aristotle makes the same point more concisely: 'All the
valuable qualities that youth and age divide between them are united in the prime
of life, while all their excesses or defects are replaced by moderation and fitness'
(*Rhet.* II. 14).

[9] *Convivio*, IV. xxiv. 3.

It is true that the time-references in the poem, if gathered together and totalled up, show that the events of the story must cover more than a decade;[10] but one does not need to invoke Arcite's references, made shortly before his death, to his own 'youthe' (2379, 2393) to establish that the passage of time has in this poem a purely ethical significance. The long-suffering fidelity of the courtly lover is a commonplace, and the many years spent by Palamon and Arcite in the service of Emily have significance only as proof of that fidelity. Again, the 'lengthe of certeyn yeres' which elapses between Arcite's death and the concluding marriage serves only to show the sincerity of everyone's grief, the strength of Palamon's loyalty to his dead cousin, and above all the decency of Emily's widowhood. She is the moral antithesis of the Wife of Bath, who at the very funeral of her dead husband is already spotting his successor. But then, of course, the Wife of Bath does grow old, whereas Emily is still at the very end of the poem a radiant young heroine, with a lifetime of happiness still to share with Palamon. Time in the *Knight's Tale* is not like time in Stendhal's *Charterhouse of Parma*, where the period spent by Fabrice imprisoned in the tower is real time. Clelia is still young enough to be able to spare it, but the Duchess is not; and part of the latter's eagerness to engineer Fabrice's escape springs, we feel, from an awareness that she cannot remain attractive to him for much longer. Such pathos is quite alien to Chaucer's poem, which presents what is essentially a static tableau of the three ages. It begins and ends with a wedding; but in between these two great *rites de passage*, which initiate first Theseus and finally Palamon and Emily into full maturity, the age-status of the various characters does not seem to change at all. Brooks and Fowler speak of the poem as presenting 'a symbolic representation of character-development'; but it is hard to see any such development on the literal level of the story.[11]

Several critics have claimed to find differences between the two young heroes; but no such distinctions need to be made

---

[10] Taking together lines 1033, 1426, 1452, 1850, 2967. The action in Boccaccio's *Teseida* occupies less time: P. Boitani, *Chaucer and Boccaccio*, Medium Aevum Monographs, n.s. viii (Oxford, 1977), p. 127.

[11] Brooks and Fowler, p. 138.

for purposes of the present discussion, if indeed they can be made at all. Brooks and Fowler see Palamon and Arcite as representing different ages, the first and second respectively, in a four-age scheme: the age of Venus must be succeeded by the second age, that of Mars, just as Palamon must yield in the tournament to Arcite; but that age of Mars, represented by Arcite's champion Emetreus, must itself in turn give way to the third of the four ages, that of Saturn, which is represented by Palamon's champion, the mature, Saturnian Lygurge.[12] These complications arise, I think, from a mistaken attempt by Brooks and Fowler to trace the humoral and planetary patterns associated with the four and the seven ages in a poem which recognizes only three.[13] By contrast, it is easy to see why Venus and Mars should, in a simpler three-age context, represent both together the activities and pre-occupations characteristic of young noblemen such as Palamon and Arcite. For their first age is given over to just that life of armed adventure in the service of love which is epitomized mythologically in the image, invoked by Arcite, of Mars enjoying the beauty of Venus (2383-92). The two young men both suffer, travel, and fight, not (after the first battle at Thebes) for reasons of state, but for love. This is the essence of their youthful existence, manifest above all in the great tournament which settles their rival claims to Emily. Although Chaucer's Knight has, we know, his own quite different reasons for taking up arms, he looks with a benevolent paternal eye upon this activity:

> For if ther fille tomorwe swich a cas,
> Ye knowen wel that every lusty knyght
> That loveth paramours and hath his myght,
> Were it in Engelond or elleswhere,
> They wolde, hir thankes, wilnen to be there, —
> To fighte for a lady, *benedicitee*!   (2110-15)

---

[12] Brooks and Fowler, pp. 130-9.

[13] The planetary associations cited by Brooks and Fowler are as follows: Four Ages: I Jupiter (and Venus), II Mars, III Saturn, IV Moon (and Venus); Seven Ages: I Moon, II Mercury, III Venus, IV Sun, V Mars, VI Jupiter, VII Saturn. The latter is the most common set, based on the order of planets in increasing distance from the earth. In the case of triadic schemes, there are too few ages to allow a full set of planetary parallels.

'To fighte for a lady': the idea that nobility of soul, as
Dante would say, manifests itself during youth in the pursuit
of love and prowess in arms is too familiar to require much
illustration. The courtly figure of Youthe in the *Parlement of
the Thre Ages* is described thus:

He was yonge and yape and yernynge to armes,
And pleynede hym one paramours and peteuosely syghede.
                                                    (171-2)

This conjunction of *armes* and *paramours* easily called to
mind the corresponding mythological pair, Mars and Venus,
as can be seen, for instance, in the official biography of King
Henry V, written by the Italian scholar Tito Livio in 1438.
Here we read that young Henry, while his father was still
alive, 'delighted in music, and pursued in moderation the
feats of Venus and of Mars, and the other things which
pleasure has to offer to young knights'.[14] The concise Latin
of the humanist, *veneria et martialia*, sums up the life of
Prince Hal in terms equally applicable, *mutatis mutandis*, to
Chaucer's young heroes. It may be noted here that Tito Livio
regards the service of Venus and Mars—in moderation,
mediocriter—as requiring no particular comment or excuse
in a spirited young heir to the throne; and when he comes to
the famous story of how Hal changed his way of life on
becoming king, he seems to consider the course of events as
eminently right and proper. Allowance has to be made here
for the layer of whitewash proper to official biographies; but
by contrast with later, more problematic accounts (one
thinks of the rejection of Falstaff), Tito's narrative of Henry's
conversion seems to rest on a calm acceptance of the principle
stated by that stern moralist Dante in his *Convivio*: 'Our
nature, when good and straight, follows a seasonable procedure

---

[14] *Titi Livii Foro-Juliensis Vita Henrici Quinti*, ed. T. Hearne (Oxford, 1716),
pp. 4-5: 'musicis delectabatur, veneria et martialia mediocriter secutus, et alia
quae militaribus [adolescentibus] licentia praebere solet'. Cf. the anonymous
English translation, *The First English Life of King Henry the Fifth*, ed. C. L. Kings-
ford (Oxford, 1911), p. 17: 'he exercised meanelie the feates of Venus and of Mars'.
At the beginning of *Teseida*, Boccaccio invokes Mars, Venus, and Cupid (I. 3), and he
frequently mentions Mars and Venus in connection with the adventures of Palemone
and Arcita (e.g. V. 75): *Teseida*, ed. A. Limentani, in *Tutte le Opere di Giovanni
Boccaccio*, ed. V. Branca, Vol. ii (Milan, 1964).

in us, as we see the nature of plants doing in them; and therefore different ways and different deportment are suitable at
one age rather than at others, wherein the noble soul proceeds
in due order, on one simple path, exercising its acts in their
times and ages according as they are ordained for its ultimate
fruit.'[15]

The fact that Palamon prays to Venus and Arcite to Mars
may seem to suggest, nevertheless, that the two men are to
be distinguished, if not in maturity, then at least in their
preferences as between *veneria* and *martialia*; but the story
strenuously resists such a conclusion. As fighters the cousins
are so evenly matched that neither can defeat the other in
single combat; and in the tournament Palamon is overcome
only by the united efforts of twenty adversaries—the sort of
thing which could happen to anyone, just like Arcite's fall
from his horse, as the Knight himself observes in a carefully
balanced comment (2719–30). Nor, certainly, is Arcite any
less in love with Emily than Palamon is:

> if that Palamon was wounded sore,
> Arcite is hurt as muche as he, or moore. (1115–16)

It is Arcite, after all, who nearly dies of the lover's malady
of *hereos*. Indeed, the story seems to insist that the two
knights are so exactly equal both in love and in prowess that
distinction can be made between them only by means of
quibbling and equivocation. We see this already in the first
scene in prison, where Palamon insists that he saw Emily first
and Arcite retorts by claiming that Palamon thought she was
a goddess, not a woman. The latter argument surely does not
show that Arcite is less romantic than his friend; it represents
rather, exactly like Palamon's argument, a desperate attempt
to establish distinctions where none exist. In the end the
dilemma can be resolved only by the more effective equivoca-
tions of the gods, who customarily 'speken in amphibologies'
(*Troilus*, IV. 1406).[16] When Saturn grants Arcite's prayer to
Mars, 'Yif me victorie, I aske thee namoore', by indeed giving

---

[15] *Convivio*, IV. xxiv. 8.
[16] See A. J. Minnis, *Chaucer and Pagan Antiquity* (Woodbridge, 1982), pp. 135–
43. Compare Mercury's promise to Arcite of 'an end to his woe' in Athens (1392).

him victory and no more, he is not giving Arcite what he really wants; for what Arcite wants is Emily, just as much as Palamon ('or moore'). Saturn is simply taking advantage of a quibble to resolve an otherwise insoluble problem.

Emily herself is the other main representative of youth in the *Knight's Tale*. In Boccaccio's *Teseida*, Emilia is only fifteen years old (XII. 64); and the Knight's heroine need be no older. She is, in any case, plainly a female type of that youthful nobility characterized by Dante in the canzone which occasions his discussion of the ages in the *Convivio*:

> Ubidente, soave e vergognosa
> è ne la prima etate,
> e sua persona adorna di bieltate.[17]

She is obedient, sweet, bashful and beautiful. In particular, her service of Diana, goddess of chastity, symbolizes that species of *vergogna* which Dante calls *pudore*.[18] It is her 'shamefast chastitee' (2055) which leads her to pray Diana that she may 'ben a mayden al my lyf'. In this she outdoes even the blushing lady eagle in the *Parliament of Fowls* (652-3) who, faced with some equally well-matched suitors, expresses only the determination not to serve Venus and Cupid 'as yit'. One modern reaction to such female behaviour is to see in it an implied criticism of anaemic courtly womanhood; to which the learned historical critic may reply by recalling the respect accorded by the Medieval Mind to virginity as the highest order of life, nobler than widowhood or marriage. As sometimes happens, both naïve and learned readings miss the point. We have only to recall the Temple of Venus in the *Parliament of Fowls*, its walls decorated with the broken bows of young damsels who set out to serve Diana in the wild woods, but succumbed to her rival Venus when the time came. Emily's 'shamefast chastitee' is in fact, as modern parents would say, a 'phase'. Or, to put the matter in Dante's terms, it forms a proper stage in the 'due order' of the development of the noble soul. One should not be

---

[17] 'It [the noble soul] is obedient, sweet and bashful in its first age, and adorns its person with beauty', *Convivio*, IV, Canzone Terza 125-7.

[18] *Convivio*, IV. xxv. 7.

surprised, and indeed most readers are not surprised, when
Emily settles down to married bliss with Palamon at the end
of the poem. Like Helena in *All's Well that Ends Well*, she
must now renounce her service of the Virgin huntress:

> Now, Dian, from thy altar do I fly,
> And to imperial Love, that god most high,
> Do my sighs stream.[19]

II

Neuse suggests that the second of the three ages in the
Knight's Tale, its middle generation, is represented by Duke
Theseus. In fact, Chaucer says nothing about the actual age
of his Theseus; but the Duke's position in the age-structure of
the Tale is sufficiently clear. Boccaccio speaks of his Teseo as
being in his first age or 'età primeva' (*Teseida*, II. 5); but this
would not be appropriate to the English Theseus. He is the
son of aged Egeus; but he is also the husband of Hippolita,
the former queen of the Amazons and elder sister to young
Emily. The seniority to Emily, and to Palamon and Arcite,
implied in the latter relationship may not seem very marked;
but it is in fact strongly felt in the *Knight's Tale*, as it is not
in the *Teseida*. Thus, Theseus stands in a relationship to
Venus, Mars, and Diana significantly different from that of
the three young principals. When he is said to serve Diana
(1682), the triform goddess is to be understood as patroness
not of maiden bashfulness but of manly hunting. He also
serves Mars (1682) and displays his image on the banner
which he raises against Thebes (975); but he engages in
martialia, and also in *veneria*, on terms which distinguish him
from the two younger men.[20]

[19] Brooks and Fowler point out (p. 127) that 'virginity is . . . only one of the
stages of female life over which [Diana] presides'. She is also Lucina, goddess of
childbirth, represented in the temple by a woman calling for her help in travail
(2083-6).

[20] See Chauncey Wood, *Chaucer and the Country of the Stars* (Princeton, NJ,
1970), pp. 72-5. Like several others, Wood pays no attention to distinctions of
age and sees Theseus as simply the moral superior of Palamon, Arcite, and Emily
(whose service of Diana he dismisses as 'the product of self-indulgence'). Cf. D. W.
Robertson, *A Preface to Chaucer* (Princeton, NJ, 1963), pp. 260-6. Brooks and
Fowler (pp. 140-2) present Theseus as a man in the process of transition from the

Theseus' relation to the romantic love which Venus represents for both Palamon and Arcite is most clearly displayed in the speech which he addresses to the two noble kinsmen when he comes upon them fighting in a grove outside Athens for the love of Emily. This speech, beginning 'The god of love, a, *benedicite*!', falls into two movements. In the first (1785-1810), the Duke remarks incredulously on the fact that Palamon and Arcite, both of whom could by now have been living comfortably in Thebes, have been forced by the power of love to risk their lives in enemy territory:

> Now looketh, is nat that an heigh folye?
> Who may been a fool, but if he love?

But in the second movement (1811-25), he expresses understanding and even forgiveness:

> But all moot ben assayed, hoot and coold;
> A man moot ben a fool, or yong or oold, —
> I woot it by myself ful yore agon,
> For in my tyme a servant was I oon.

Theseus has himself been a 'servant' or lover in his time and has experienced the pain of love (the reader may recall his famous amour with Ariadne); but now he is a settled, married man. The mixture of sympathy and detachment is finely conveyed. It is a speech of sterling sense and bantering humour. Something like the same tone may be heard in *A Midsummer Night's Dream*, where the attitude of Shakespeare's Theseus to the young lovers owes a good deal to Chaucer:

> Lovers and madmen have such seething brains,
> Such shaping fantasies, that apprehend
> More than cool reason ever comprehends.

The contrast between Theseus and the two young men in the matter of *martialia* takes a similar form. As has already been

---

fifth age of Mars to the sixth age of Jupiter. Here as elsewhere their use of the seven planets / seven ages scheme creates more problems than it solves; but their discussion of Theseus is nevertheless very penetrating.

observed, Palamon and Arcite, though first discovered wounded in the cause of Creon's Thebes, thereafter take up arms only in the cause of Emily, first in the grove and then in the great tournament. Theseus, on the other hand, fights for public causes. He is a great *conquerour*, and his most recent conquest, that of the Amazons, is presented as an act of state policy.[21] The fact that he wins a wife in the process seems almost accidental. When, on the occasion of his triumphant return to Athens, he leaves his newly won bride to do justice on Creon, the action shows how for him public concerns must take precedence over private ones. When he later lays down strict rules to prevent bloodshed at the tournament, these rules mark clearly the distinction between mortal battle, such as he himself waged against the Theban tyrant, and a tourney undertaken 'for a lady'.

The great image of the Duke seated at a window before all the people, 'arrayed right as he were a god in trone', proclaiming his decrees through his herald, vividly expresses the essential fact about Theseus: he is 'lord and governour' of Athens (861), 'the grete Theseus' (2523). His middle position in the age-structure of the Tale properly qualifies him for his ducal role. He is not 'middle-aged' in the drab sense of that expression, still less parsimonious and petty-minded like Medill Elde in the *Parlement of the Thre Ages*. Rather, as Giles of Rome prescribes, he combines the positive qualities of both age and youth. In Theseus, however, this is a dynamic and sometimes unstable combination, rather than a continuously equable moderation or 'mesure'. He displays a fiery impetuosity of temperament when he responds to the pleas of the Theban widows, and also when he comes upon Palamon and Arcite fighting in the grove ('Ye shal be deed, by myghty Mars the rede!'); but this does not lead him into acts of youthful folly. Nor does the lavish generosity of his arrangements for the tournament (the lists) and for Arcite's funeral (the pyre) represent mere youthful extravagance.[22] These occasions all, in their different ways, represent the greatness

---

[21] On the term *conquerour*, see P. M. Kean, *Chaucer and the Making of English Poetry* (London, 1972), vol. ii, pp. 6–7.

[22] Chaucer refers to Theseus' 'dispence' over the lists (1882) and to the 'grete cost' of temples and theatre (2090, cf. 1900–1, 1908).

of soul, the 'magnanimity', proper to a great ruler, which is as far from the recklessness of the young as it is from what Giles calls the 'timidity and pusillanimity' of the old.[23] Above all, Theseus proves himself as a 'trewe juge' (2657), who can be both just and merciful. It is Theseus who condemns Palamon and Arcite to perpetual prison for their association with the monstrous crimes of Creon, Theseus who releases Arcite and banishes him from Athens, Theseus who decrees, regulates, and judges the tournament. Such things are among the proper duties of a noble man in the prime of life. Thus Dante notes that *lealtade* is one manifestation of nobility in the second, mature age: '*Lealtade* is the following out and putting into action of that which the laws dictate; and this is most especially fitting for one in the prime of life.'[24] Dante goes on to cite an example of this mature *lealtade* from Virgil's *Aeneid*—interpreted, in accordance with ancient tradition, as an allegory of the ages of man.[25] At the funeral games in Book V, he remarks, Aeneas 'loyally gave to each of the victors what he had promised for the victory, as was their ancient usage'. Theseus' conduct of the tournament is another example of the same quality.

The part played by Theseus in the last scene of the poem has sometimes been misunderstood. Some years after Arcite's death, Theseus summons Palamon, still in mourning for his dead cousin, to a parliament. The Duke's oration at the parliament begins on a high philosophical note with its reference to the 'firste moevere of the cause above', and it continues with a lofty Boethian exposition of the order of created things, in which death, change, and decay are inescapable facts. He even speaks of life as a 'foul prisoun'. But it should be noted that this strikingly eremetical phrase occurs

---

[23] 'Timidi et pusillanimes', I. iv. 3. The English translation says that old men are 'pusillanymes and ferful' because 'they ben ibrought lowe in the lyf. For by cause of longe levynge thei ben brought lowe and faylen. Thanne as in hem faillen humours and lif, so in hem faillen [*sic*] the herte of confort' (fo. 56 a–b).

[24] *Convivio*, IV. xxvi. 14.

[25] Cf. *Convivio*, IV. xxiv. 9: 'Io figurato che di questo diverso processo de l'etadi tiene Virgilio ne lo Eneida'. There are two chief authorities: Fulgentius, *Expositio Virgilianae Continentiae*, translated in A. Preminger, O. B. Hardison, and K. Kerrane (eds.), *Classical and Medieval Literary Criticism* (New York, 1974), pp. 324–40; and Bernardus Silvestris (?), *The Commentary on the First Six Books of the 'Aeneid'*, translated J. W. and E. F. Jones (Lincoln, Neb., 1977).

as part of a conventional *consolatio mortis* (Arcite is better off where he is). What is more, the Boethian exposition of universal changefulness proves to have been directed towards a practical and positive conclusion. All things have an end; therefore the period of mourning for Arcite must itself come to an end. Theseus even allows himself a mildly humorous observation, recalling the bantering manner of his God of Love speech, where he remarked that Emily would feel no gratitude to the young lovers since she was quite unaware of their passion: she 'kan hem therfore as muche thank as me' (1808). So here he comments on the folly of the long mourning of Palamon and Emily for Arcite: 'Kan he hem thank? Nay, God woot, never a deel' (3064). His conclusion follows:

> What may I conclude of this longe serye,
> But after wo I rede us to be merye,
> And thanken Juppiter of al his grace?
> And er that we departen from this place
> I rede that we make of sorwes two
> O parfit joye, lastynge everemo.   (3067–72)

The proposal is that Emily should marry Palamon and live happily ever after. It is an astonishing conclusion to a speech which began by demonstrating that no earthly joy could last for ever. Not, of course, that one takes Theseus' talk of a perfect and everlasting joy too seriously either. He speaks neither as a grave philosopher nor as a romantic idealist. His so-called 'sermonyng' serves to dignify and ease the always awkward transition from mourning to remarriage; and the marriage itself concerns him, in part at least, for reasons of state: to 'have fully of Thebans obeisaunce' (2974). Theseus is most himself when he speaks as a lord and governor, whose business it is to make the best of difficult and painful situations:

> Thanne is it wysdom, as it thynketh me,
> To maken vertu of necessitee,
> And take it weel that we may nat eschue.[26]

---

[26] I agree with Ian Robinson, *Chaucer and the English Tradition* (Cambridge, 1972), that Neuse (pp. 249–50) overstresses Theseus' politicking. See also Ian Bishop, 'Chaucer and the Rhetoric of Consolation', *Medium Aevum* 52 (1983), 38–50. For a different view of the limits of Theseus' wisdom, see Minnis, pp. 125–31.

In the course of his oration Theseus twice refers to the god Jupiter; once, in the lines quoted above, as a source of grace, and a second time as 'Juppiter the kyng' (3035). Though Theseus is elsewhere said to serve both Diana and Mars, many critics now agree that his special relationship is with Jupiter.[27] In the poem's age-structure, as Neuse saw, the son of Egeus occupies the same middle position as the son of Saturn. In seven-age schemes, Jupiter (the last-but-one planet counting outwards from the earth) represents the sixth age, *senectus*, with only decrepitude (Saturn) beyond it; but here as elsewhere other traditions are more relevant. Astrologically considered, as Dante observes, 'Jove is a star of temperate composition between the cold of Saturn and the heat of Mars'; and this consorts well with Giles's account of middle life as a temperate condition between the 'calor' of youth and the 'frigiditas' of age.[28] Mythologically considered, 'Juppiter the kyng' is the ruler of the gods; and he is also commonly regarded as representing the ruler's virtue, justice. In Dante's *Paradiso*, Jupiter's is the sphere of the just. Hence it is not hard to see why the astrologer Michael Scot, in his *Liber Introductorius*, should picture Jupiter as a man in the prime of life: 'He has full and regular features, with all appropriate colouring, like a man of forty years, with flaxen hair and the beard a little grown after shaving.'[29] The description could serve well enough for Chaucer's Theseus.

Yet Jupiter cannot be called a commanding or central figure in the world of the *Knight's Tale*, and this despite the fact that Arcite, like Theseus, twice refers to him in terms which would suggest to a Christian reader the one true god who really rules the universe (2786, 2792). He has no temple in Athens, and his one intervention in the action is brief and inconclusive, when Mars and Venus quarrel so fiercely on behalf of their devotees that 'Juppiter was bisy it to stente'

[27] Neuse, p. 249; Brooks and Fowler, pp. 125-6; Kean, vol. ii, p. 3; A. T. Gaylord, *Chaucer Review* 8 (1974), 182-3; Minnis, pp. 117-20. Minnis notes that the description of Theseus seated 'right as he were a god in trone' (2529) may recall the iconography of Jupiter 'in trono eburneo in sua mayestate sedens'.

[28] *Convivio*, II. xiii. 25; *De Regimine Principum*, I. iv. 4.

[29] Cited from F. Saxl, *Der Islam* 3 (1912), 175. Klibansky, Panofsky, and Saxl see astrologers such as Michael Scot as important in determining late medieval views of the gods: *Saturn and Melancholy*, pp. 191-3.

(2442). The decisive intervention of Jupiter's father Saturn at this difficult moment may call to mind the one moment in the poem when Theseus is at a loss, or at least in distress, and has to look for comfort to his father Egeus; but Egeus, unlike his son, appears dim and ineffective by comparison with his Olympian counterpart.

III

Comparison with Chaucer's source, the *Teseida*, reveals that Chaucer took some pains to sharpen the distinction between Duke Theseus and his old father. Boccaccio speaks of his Egeo as 're d'Attene' (I. 6), of Athens as still the 'regno d'Egeo' (IV. 12), and of Duke Teseo as reigning jointly with his father ('col padre insiememente regna', VII. 20). In the *Knight's Tale*, on the other hand, Egeus has evidently passed all power on to Theseus, who reigns supreme. We see the old man only twice: once when he walks with Theseus by Arcite's bier in the funeral procession, and otherwise only in that scene where he counsels his son and comforts him:

> No man myghte gladen Theseus,
> Savynge his olde fader Egeus,
> That knew this worldes transmutacioun,
> As he hadde seyn it chaunge bothe up and doun,
> Joye after wo, and wo after gladnesse,
> And shewed hem ensamples and liknesse.
> 'Right as ther dyed nevere man,' quod he,
> 'That he ne lyvede in erthe in some degree,
> Right so ther lyvede never man,' he seyde,
> 'In al this world, that som tyme he ne deyde.
> This world nys but a thurghfare ful of wo,
> And we been pilgrymes, passynge to and fro.
> Deeth is an ende of every worldly soore'.   (2837–49)

At the same point in the *Teseida*, Egeo is reported as speaking philosophically of the inevitability of deaths and changes ('morti e' mutamenti', XI. 11); but Boccaccio does not give his actual words.[30] For these, Chaucer drew on the opening

---

[30] Egeo is addressing not Teseo but Palemone, as also at XI. 33, where he speaks of 'la vita d'esto mondo reo'.

of the speech made later by Boccaccio's Teseo when he proposes the marriage of Palemone and Emilia (*Knight's Tale*,
2843-6, *Teseida* XII. 6. 1-3). At that later point in the
Knight's Tale, as we have seen, Chaucer's Theseus also makes
a consolatory reference to the miseries of life; but the English
poet evidently thought extended reflections on this topic
more appropriate to old Egeus.[31]

Some modern readers see Egeus' speech as representing no
more than the threadbare platitude of senility—'Polonius-like
wisdom', as one puts it. To this, a historical critic may reply
with talk of Pope Innocent's *De Contemptu Mundi* and the
other-worldly Medieval World Picture. But again both readings miss the point. Egeus' remarks do display the pessimism
which Giles, following Aristotle, attributes to the old; but
they are not meant to seem ridiculous.[32] Rather, they
represent the time-honoured wisdom of old age, just like the
speeches of Elde in the *Parlement of the Thre Ages*. Yet what
Egeus says does not, on the other hand, represent the prevail-
ing truth of the *Knight's Tale*, as references to medieval
contemptus mundi will suggest. In the *Parlement*, Elde
occupies a commanding position. He has the last word. But
in Chaucer's poem, the last word belongs with Theseus; and
by the end Egeus remains in the reader's mind, if at all,
merely as a representative of what Boccaccio calls 'oscura
vecchiezza', dim old age (*Teseida* XII. 8).

Not so the corresponding figure among the gods. There is no
mention of Saturn anywhere in the *Teseida*; but in Chaucer's
poem it is he who determines the outcome of the story,
finding a 'remedie' for the strife between Mars and Venus and
making an unforgettable speech in the process. Saturn has
no oratory in Athens, nor does Egeus ever mention him; so
the correspondence between them, noted by several critics,
rests mainly on the simple fact that Saturn is the god, or
planet, of old age and of wisdom.[33] The relevant traditions
are amply documented in the study by Klibansky, Saxl, and

---

[31] See Kean, vol. ii, p. 40.

[32] The old are 'of evel hope and have non good hope and trist' (English translation of *De Regimine*, fo. 56 b).

[33] On the Egeus-Saturn correspondence, see Neuse, pp. 248-9; Brooks and
Fowler, p. 126; Kean, vol. ii, pp. 3, 40-1.

Panofsky, *Saturn and Melancholy*.[34] But there is no need to cite authorities here, since Chaucer himself makes the associations clear:

> the pale Saturnus the colde,
> That knew so manye of aventures olde,
> Foond in his olde experience an art
> That he ful soone hath plesed every part.
> As sooth is seyd, elde hath greet avantage;
> In elde is bothe wysdom and usage;
> Men may the olde atrenne, and noght atrede.
>
> (2443-9)

The parallel with old Egeus, 'that knew this worldes transmutacioun', seems sufficiently clear, if rather general. But there is also a more specific parallel. Saturn is the father of Jupiter, as Egeus is the father of Theseus; and Theseus has superseded Egeus as ruler of Athens (in Chaucer) just as Jupiter superseded Saturn as ruler of Olympus. Both are 'deiectus imperio', as Manilius says of Saturn.[35]

However, with Saturn the argument reaches a point beyond which it is no longer possible to go on considering the gods simply as celestial analogues of human society, representing the natural characteristics of its three generations. The reader has no doubt already noticed that the preceding discussions of Mars, Venus, and Diana as representing the adventurousness, amorousness, and bashfulness of the young have glossed over the fact that, in all three temples, Chaucer emphasizes the human suffering and 'wo' that each of these divinities causes.[36] With Saturn, this theme

---

[34] See also Kean, vol. ii, pp. 30-3. Typical are Pierre Bersuire's observations on Saturn: 'Senex est eciam et maturus per discrecionem et racionem' ('He is also old and ripe in knowledge and discernment'); 'Senio gravari dicitur pro eo quod prudencia magis habundat in senibus; unde etiam, ut ait, Saturnus grece dicitur Cronos, quod est tempus latine, pro eo quod prudencia indiget tempore, id est deliberacione et competentibus dilacionibus' ('He is said to be weighed down by age because prudence prevails especially in the old; and that is why, as [Remigius] says, Saturn is called Chronos in Greek, which is "tempus" in Latin, because prudence depends upon time, that is, due time for deliberation'). Ed. J. Engels, *Reductorium Morale, Liber XV: Ovidius Moralizatus, Cap. i, De Formis Figurisque Deorum*, Werkmateriaal iii (Utrecht, 1966), pp. 8, 9.

[35] Cf. *Saturn and Melancholy*, p. 141.

[36] Especially in the description of the temple of Mars (astrologically disas-

comes to a head, in the speech which the old god addresses
to his granddaughter Venus:

> Myn is the drenchyng in the see so wan;
> Myn is the prison in the derke cote;
> Myn is the stranglyng and hangyng by the throte . . .

This speech and the ensuing death of Arcite, so painfully
described, make it quite impossible to regard Saturn simply
as a type of 'wysdom and usage' in old age; nor does it seem
helpful to invoke here alternative traditions of old age as a
time of envy and spite, though such may be found.[37] In their
study of Saturn, Klibansky, Saxl, and Panofsky make it
abundantly clear that Chaucer's Saturn is by no means alone
in exhibiting his unnerving combination of wisdom and
malignancy. On the contrary, this can be traced right back to
the original Greek conception of Chronos, which was 'distinguished by a marked internal contradiction or ambivalence'
of just this sort.[38] But the historical evidence does not help
to explain what in this poem Saturn's 'ambivalence' (and
indeed that of all the other gods, except Jupiter) means.

IV

In the foregoing discussion of the three ages of gods and men
in the *Knight's Tale*, it has become clear that the poem does
not, as Neuse's scheme might suggest, present a balanced or
neutral view of the matter, giving each age its due and equal
place in a natural order which embraces both Athens and
Olympus. Among both gods and men there are imbalances
and distortions; and these give rise to asymmetries between
the two orders. Among the gods, Saturn is given prominence
at the expense of Jupiter, the most unfortunate planet at the
expense of the most fortunate. Accordingly we find a general
emphasis (except in the case of Jupiter himself) on the many

trous): 1995-2050. But in the temples of Venus and Diana, too, the stress falls
on 'care and wo' (2072, cf. 1952).

[37] In *Parlement of the Thre Ages*, Elde is 'envyous and angrye' (163). Cf. 'olde
Creon' (*Knight's Tale* 938), where *old* is a dyslogistic epithet, as often in Middle
English.

[38] *Saturn and Melancholy*, p. 134.

human sorrows and disasters which the god-planets represent. Among men, on the other hand, Theseus is given prominence at the expense of Egeus. Indeed, like Hans Sachs in Wagner's *Mastersingers of Nuremberg*, Theseus dominates the *Knight's Tale* in a way that is at odds, somewhat mysteriously, with his ancillary role in the main story of young love. 'The *Knight's Tale*', as Boitani observes, 'is much more of a "Teseida" than the *Teseida* itself.'[39] Accordingly, at the end of the poem, where we see men making the best of what the gods have left them, it is Theseus on the one side who confronts Saturn on the other.

It is a problem in parallax to identify the point of view which will explain both these different distortions at once; but the position of the observer is not in this case a matter of pure speculation. The Tale, we know, is told by the pilgrim Knight; and the Knight has his own position in the scheme of generations, defined by his relationship to his son, the young Squire who accompanies him on the road to Canterbury. This relationship, as others have suggested, may be seen as corresponding to that between Theseus and the two young lovers in the Tale.[40] Whereas the Knight has been at fifteen mortal battles 'and foughten for oure feith at Tramyssene', the twenty-year-old Squire has seen action of a different sort:

> he hadde been somtyme in chyvachie
> In Flaundres, in Artoys, and Pycardie,
> And born hym weel, as of so litel space,
> In hope to stonden in his lady grace.

This is the same youthful blend of romantic *veneria* and adventurous *martialia* already noticed in the life of Palamon and Arcite; and the Knight narrator, we may now add, takes very much the same attitude to the two young heroes of his story as does his surrogate in it, Duke Theseus. Boccaccio's *Teseida* is, as Boitani points out, very much a young man's poem.[41] The poet's own point of view seems to coincide with

[39] *Chaucer and Boccaccio*, p. 147.
[40] Neuse, pp. 259-60; B. F. Huppé, *A Reading of the Canterbury Tales* (Albany, NY, 1964), pp. 54-5.
[41] *Chaucer and Boccaccio*, pp. 187-9.

that of the young lovers; indeed he suggests, in his letter to
Fiammetta, that he is to be identified with one of them. In
the *Knight's Tale*, on the other hand, the narrator's attitude
to the lovers, though by no means unsympathetic, is detached
and at times humorous:

> Whan that Arcite hadde romed al his fille,
> And songen al the roundel lustily,
> Into a studie he fil sodeynly,
> As doon thise loveres in hir queynte geres,
> Now in the crope, now doun in the breres,
> Now up, now doun, as boket in a welle.
>
> (1528-33)

The tone and imagery of these lines (hardly thinkable in
Boccaccio's poem) associate them closely with Theseus's
bantering speech on the God of Love.

If then we define the narratorial point of view in the
Knight's Tale as exhibiting a bias towards that middle position occupied by both the Knight and Duke Theseus in the
scheme of the three ages, why is the corresponding deity,
Jupiter, so overshadowed by Saturn? Perhaps the best answer
to this difficult question is that the Knight's vision of 'middle
age' requires that it should be confronted by a universe of
hostile circumstances. For the necessities of which Theseus
strives to make a virtue are harsh necessities: passion (Venus),
conflict (Mars), and death (Saturn). These are facts of life
which it is the business of the 'governour' to humanize and
control. Dead bodies cannot be left for the dogs, they must
be cremated with the proper obsequies. Men cannot be left
to fight in the woods like animals, they must settle their
differences like gentlemen in the tourney. And sexual passion
must eventually submit to 'the bond that highte matrimoigne
or mariage'. The ceremonies of matrimony, tournament, and
funeral, all presided over by Theseus, together allow the Tale
to arrive at its own kind of happy ending—an ending which,
while not minimizing the Saturnian facts of life, Jovially
affirms the obligation of not dwelling unduly upon them. As
the Knight himself says later in the *Tales*, when he interrupts the Monk's long series of tragedies, 'litel hevynesse / Is

right ynough to muche folk, I gesse' (VII. 2769-70). Life must go on. It is, in a sense more specific than Matthew Arnold's, 'a central, a truly human point of view'; and it commands the admiration of the whole company of pilgrims, whose diversity is specified, here for the only time in the *Tales*, in terms of age:

> Whan that the Knyght had thus his tale ytoold,
> In al the route nas ther yong ne oold
> That he ne seyde it was a noble storie,
> And worthy for to drawen to memorie.

3. IRONY IN THE *MERCHANT'S TALE* *

The *Merchant's Tale* is usually classed as a 'fabliau tale', and the classification has its point. But it has perhaps drawn attention away from those qualities which distinguish the *Merchant's Tale* from the rest of Chaucer's fabliaux. These are qualities which it shares, not with the comic tales of the Miller or the Summoner, but with the moral fable of the Pardoner—the persistent irony, the seriousness which informs even the farcical climax. This climax (the gulling of January in the 'pear-tree episode') is no more simply comic than the death of the Pardoner's rioters. It is much more closely realized than, for example, the denouement of the *Miller's Tale*; and Chaucer, in filling out the fabliau form in this way, makes something new. The French fabliaux may be cruel, but they are also casual—one generally gets just enough about, for example, the duped husband to make the joke, and no more. The comic effect depends on the preservation of the skeletal bareness of the story. The reader is never allowed to get near enough, as it were, to be seriously involved. In contrast, the *Merchant's Tale* is full of 'close-ups':

> . . . Januarie hath faste in armes take
> His fresshe May, his paradys, his make.
> He lulleth hire, he kisseth hire ful ofte,
> With thikke brustles of his berd unsofte,
> Lyk to the skyn of houndfyssh, sharp as brere —
> For he was shave al newe in his manere.   (IV. 1821-6)

The clarity of the observation is given a sharp point, here, by the simile of the dogfish, and by the ironic comment in the last line. The reader is forced to visualize the scene, as rarely in the French fabliau, to grasp its human reality; and in the process the moral issues, with which the French authors were not concerned (Bédier called them 'amoral'), come alive.

Unlike the other fabliau tales, but like the *Pardoner's Tale*, the story of January and May faces up to the moral issues it

---

* First published in *Anglia* 75 (1957), 199-208.

raises. This involves a radical modification of the fabliau
method. The treatment of January's dream life (his 'fantasye')
recalls, not the carpenter or the miller, but the Pardoner's
rioters with their dreams of wealth:

> This yongeste, which that wente to the toun,
> Ful ofte in herte he rolleth up and doun
> The beautee of thise floryns newe and brighte.
>
> (VI. 837-9)

> Heigh fantasye and curious bisynesse
> Fro day to day gan in the soule impresse
> Of Januarie aboute his mariage.
> Many fair shap and many a fair visage
> Ther passeth thurgh his herte nyght by nyght.
>
> (IV. 1577-81)

But it is the distinguishing characteristic of the *Merchant's
Tale* that the ironic contrast between the dream and the
reality, the self-centred and insecure 'heigh fantasye' of the
old knight and the predictable course of his marriage, should
be pointed insistently at every turn. In the *Pardoner's Tale*
there is a strong general dramatic irony. The rioters pursue
their own downfall; and they ignore the old man, as January
ignores Justinus. But there is nothing like the accumulation
of local irony which marks the *Merchant's Tale*.

Take, for example, the opening passage of the poem (lines
1245-1398) where January, in what is really an internal
monologue, persuades himself that he will find permanent
'joy and blisse' in marriage with a young wife. The general
irony of this is clear. The mistake would have been as obvious
to a medieval reader as the rioters' mistake about the gold
('But myghte this gold be caried fro this place . . . Thanne
were we in heigh felicitee'). But the point is made more
heavily—January's dotage is much more ridiculous than anything in the *Pardoner's Tale*. He turns proverbial and biblical
lore inside out in a way that places him decisively in the
moral scheme of the poem—'Oold fissh and yong flessh
wolde I have ful fayn', 'Do alwey so as wommen wol thee
rede'. These lines, and lines like them, suggest the proverbs of

which they are distortions (elsewhere in Chaucer—'Wom-
mennes conseils been ful ofte colde', 'Men sholde wedden
after hire estaat, / For youthe and elde is often at debaat').
One more quotation will illustrate the tone of the poem's
opening:

> Alle othere manere yiftes hardily,
> As londes, rentes, pasture, or commune,
> Or moebles, alle been yiftes of Fortune,
> That passen as a shadwe upon a wal.
> But drede nat, if pleynly speke I shal,
> A wyf wol laste, and in thyn hous endure,
> Wel lenger than thee list, paraventure.
>
> (IV. 1312-18)

The last line makes a joke out of what is obviously a philosophical blunder. It is interpolated into the sequence of
January's thoughts to point the irony, like an aside in an
Elizabethan play. January is subjected to the most unblinking
scrutiny throughout the poem. His fantastic thoughts and
desires, his slack skin and his bristles, are all rendered in un-
sparing detail; and every detail carries a point, strengthening
the general with a local irony:

> Adoun by olde Januarie she lay,
> That sleep til that the coughe hath hym awaked.
>
> (IV. 1956-7)

(This technique is familiar from the *General Prologue*, where
the poetry is all detail—of behaviour or dress or appearance—
and the ironies depend on the implications of the details.)
The insistent irony, and the answering choice of detail,
expose the characters of the poem in a brilliant light, which
makes the *Pardoner's Tale* feel almost kindly by comparison.

Now, although Chaucer was by no means always 'gentle
Chaucer', he was not characteristically a destructive poet. His
irony, as in the portrait of the Prioress, is often so fleeting as
to be genuinely ambiguous, at least to the modern reader; his
tone is most often that of Theseus in the *Knight's Tale*—'The
god of love, a, *benedicite*! / How myghty and how greet a
lord is he!'—and can modulate easily, as in the same speech
of Theseus, into a sympathetic generalization—'A man moot

ben a fool, or yong or oold, — / I woot it by myself ful yore
agon'. It is an irony which does justice to its victims; the
destructive or critical impulse does not work unchecked. Of
course, there is no a priori reason why the *Merchant's Tale*
should not be an exception to this generalization; it might be
argued that a ruthless almost hysterical story was called for at
this point in the 'Marriage Group' from the disillusioned
Merchant. But I want to suggest that the 'corrosive, destructive, even hopeless quality' which Patch, and other
critics, found in this poem, and with which I have so far been
concerned, is not the whole story; and that, if it were, the
poem would not be as good as it is. The *Merchant's Tale* is
not only a poem of clarity, critical observation, and disgust—
a medieval *Madame Bovary*. There is an opposing impulse, an
impulse to approach and understand, which appears in a
tendency to *generalize*. This I consider to be a feature of all
Chaucer's best narrative poetry.

Take one line from the description of January's marriage
—'tendre youthe hath wedded stoupyng age'. The point is a
critical one again (it is the old fish and young flesh theme)
but there is no mistaking the genuine lyrical note. There is
generalization, but it is not the dry generalization of a
proverb inside out. A generosity about the line contrasts
sharply with the nagging irony we have been noting. The
gentle contrast between 'stoupyng' and 'tendre' is not like
the sharp and disgusting physical contrast between January's
bristly chin and May's 'tendre face' in the description of the
wedding night from which a passage has already been quoted.
There is a generous lyrical note about the line, which we find
again in the introduction of Bacchus and Venus into the
wedding festivities:

> Bacus the wyn hem shynketh al aboute,
> And Venus laugheth upon every wight,
> For Januarie was bicome hir knyght,
> And wolde bothe assayen his corage
> In libertee, and eek in mariage;
> And with hire fyrbrond in hire hand aboute
> Daunceth biforn the bryde and al the route.
>   (IV. 1722-8)

There is malice in the equating of liberty with marriage; but hardly, it seems, any mock-heroic effect in the introduction of Bacchus and Venus. January's marriage takes on a festal dignity in the archaic 'shynketh', and the last buoyant couplet. There is another finer couplet on this theme a little later:

> So soore hath Venus hurt hym with hire brond,
> As that she bar it daunsynge in hire hond.
>
> (IV. 1777-8)

(Here the 'daunsynge' can refer either to Venus, or to the torch; it effectively goes with both.) The effect of such lines as these is to dignify the emotions involved by setting them in the general context of human feelings represented by the gods. It will be clear from these examples that there is nothing thin or abstract about the generalization. It is done concretely, and is felt as a sort of lyrical expansiveness in the verse (an effect I do not find in the *Pardoner's Tale*).

There is, further, a perceptible drift towards allegory in the poem. The names January and May, Justinus and Placebo, suggest this. At one point there is a significant reference to what for Chaucer was the allegory *par excellence*, the *Romance of the Rose*:

> He made a gardyn, walled al with stoon;
> So fair a gardyn woot I nowher noon.
> For, out of doute, I verraily suppose
> That he that wroot the Romance of the Rose
> Ne koude of it the beautee wel devyse . . .
>
> (IV. 2029-33)

The garden, which is here being introduced, plays an important part in the poem. As it serves to dignify and strengthen January's feelings by generalizing them, and to counter the corrosive irony to which they are exposed, it may fittingly be considered here.

January's desire for a young wife is presented from the start as 'fantasye'—self-deception (the word is a favourite of Chaucer's, occurring very frequently in *Troilus and Criseyde*).

But it is associated equally, in a series of contexts at the beginning of the poem, with the image of the earthly paradise, the general fantasy of the great good place. 'Wedlok', January thinks, 'is so esy and so clene, / That in this world it is a paradys ... wyf is mannes help and his confort, / His paradys terrestre, and his disport'. Then at the wedding 'Januarie hath faste in armes take / His fresshe May, his paradys, his make'. Marriage is like the earthly paradise quite specifically in being at once 'esy' and 'clene'—delightful and morally irreproachable. Desire and duty are at one in marriage, as January points out to May on their wedding night—'blessed be the yok that we been inne, / For in oure actes we mowe do no synne'.

It is true that January's 'heigh fantasye' is made to look ridiculous in the poem. When he worries lest he should have 'myn hevene in erthe heere' and pay for it later, Justinus remarks:

> Dispeire yow noght, but have in youre memorie,
> Paraunter she may be youre purgatorie!
> She may be Goddes meene and Goddes whippe;
> Thanne shal youre soule up to hevene skippe
> Swifter than dooth an arwe out of a bowe.
>
> (IV. 1669–73)

But it is not only ridiculous. It draws strength from association with the image of the earthly paradise (or the garden of Genesis, as is clear from lines 1325–32). January's 'fantasye' is broadened by these allusions to include a general human fantasy; it is not only the delusion of a besotted *senex amans*. Here again the generalizing lends dignity and significance to the action of the poem, contributing to the reader's sense of an intelligible and meaningful narrative progression.

It seems clear that in this progression January's garden in the second part of the poem takes over from the image of the 'paradys terrestre' in the first. It is in fact the paradys of his sexual fantasy realized; in the poem the garden has something approaching a symbolic status (as gardens often have in medieval literature). The opening of the description has already been quoted. It goes on:

> Ne Priapus ne myghte nat suffise,
> Though he be god of gardyns, for to telle
> The beautee of the gardyn and the welle,
> That stood under a laurer alwey grene.
>
> (IV. 2034-7)

The *Romance of the Rose* has already been explicitly introduced into the description, and the well under the laurel is
certainly meant to recall the well in the garden of the *Romance*
which, in Chaucer's translation, lies 'under a tree, / Which
tree in Fraunce men cal a pyn'. The laurel must have been
substituted for the pine to link the garden with January's
erotic fantasies. It is meant to recall his earlier boast:

> Though I be hoor, I fare as dooth a tree
> That blosmeth er that fruyt ywoxen bee;
> And blosmy tree nys neither drye ne deed.
> I feele me nowhere hoor but on myn heed;
> Myn herte and alle my lymes been as grene
> As laurer thurgh the yeer is for to sene.
>
> (IV. 1461-6)

This suggests that Chaucer is considering more than the
narrative necessities in organizing the detail of the tale. There
is a further suggestion of the sexual significance of the garden
in the introduction of Priapus here. The repetition through
the opening description (2029-37) of the words 'garden' and
'beauty' gives to the lines an emphatic, almost incantatory,
ring, which disposes the reader to look for meanings, as if it
were the garden of the *Parlement* or of Dante's *Purgatorio*. It
is in this garden of love, for such it clearly seems to be, that
January 'payes his wyf hir dette'. He guards it as jealously as
if it were May herself, and walls it off, like the garden of
Guillaume Lorris, with stone.

January goes blind, and the extravagance of his jealousy
(it is 'outrageous') is noted in the best fabliau manner—although not without gestures of sympathy ('O Januarie, what
myghte it thee availle, / Thogh thou myghte se as fer as
shippes saille?'). His fantasy, no longer associated with the
solid and persuasive ideal image of the fertile garden of love,

becomes almost imbecile ('He nolde suffre hire for to ryde or go, / But if that he had hond on hire alway'). But, with the opening of the final scene in the garden, the tone changes again:

> . . . in a morwe unto his May seith he:
> 'Rys up, my wyf, my love, my lady free!
> The turtles voys is herd, my dowve sweete;
> The wynter is goon with alle his reynes weete.
> Com forth now, with thyne eyen columbyn!
> How fairer been thy brestes than is wyn!
> The gardyn is enclosed al aboute;
> Com forth, my white spouse! . . .'   (IV. 2137–44)

This very striking passage, as Skeat pointed out, is a mosaic of phrases from the Song of Solomon. It is beautifully timed. The strong impersonal lyric note re-establishes January's passion, bringing out the essential intelligibility of his behaviour, making sense of him again after the fabliau comedy of the preceding passage. And the garden, the symbolic home of his ideal of fertility and privacy, gains a further reference. 'The gardyn is enclosed al aboute' recalls, from the Song of Solomon: 'A garden enclosed is my sister, my spouse; a spring shut up, a fountain sealed'. Chaucer has turned this metaphor into a literal statement about January's walled garden, and it might seem that the resulting line would sit oddly in the middle of the passage, which in general preserves the elaborately metaphoric style of the biblical original. That it seems quite natural suggests how the literal garden of Chaucer's poem has itself gathered a kind of metaphorical significance.

This is not to deny that there is meant to be some kind of mock-heroic effect in the passage, although I think it is faint. The passage primarily works in the other direction, resisting the 'corrosive' irony. Chaucer certainly damps the Solomon passage down with his comment 'Swiche olde lewed wordes used he' (where 'lewed' seems to mean 'lecherous' rather than 'ignorant'). But the final effect is rather of pathos than of irony. As January speaks, Damyan slips in through the gate and hides behind a bush; and January, 'blynd as is a stoon', follows him in with May. He *is* presented as pathetic, absurd, and repulsive (there is more pathos in him as the poem progresses, though this never involves any sort of moral concession towards him on the author's part). But he is not only the object of ironic sympathy and contempt. Chaucer makes out of his sexual 'fantasye' something that the reader can feel is real and intelligible, by extending the poem's field of reference beyond the range of its narrative particularities, drawing on the common literary experience of his culture. The *Romance of the Rose* and the Bible were the obvious common points of reference (knowledge of the Italian poets was much more restricted), and these works are very much present in the *Merchant's Tale*.

This width of reference seems to me to be a general characteristic of Chaucer's best poetry. It is this which marks the *Merchant's Tale* off from the two other fabliau tales which are sometimes associated with it—the *Friar's Tale* and the *Summoner's Tale*. These poems have in common with the *Merchant's Tale* a quality of destructive wit (which appears at its best in the ironically observed speeches of the Friar to Thomas) and of farcical popular humour (which appears in the denouements of the poems). The anecdotes are filled out with ironic detail. The Friar comes to see Thomas:

> . . . fro the bench he droof awey the cat,
> And leyde adoun his potente and his hat,
> And eek his scrippe, and sette hym softe adoun.
>
> (III. 1775-7)

The Friar's smooth impudence is superbly conveyed in the rhythm and even the rhyme of these lines. It is comedy—more obviously comedy than the close-up of January sitting up in bed which was quoted earlier. The first part of the *Summoner's Tale* is brilliantly successful. But if we compare the poem as a whole with the *Merchant's Tale* we may feel that it lacks solidity. The Friar is taken at his face value—the common satiric type of the corrupt cleric. The tone of the poem never modulates from the ironic and critical; the method is exclusively mimetic. It is 'poetry of the surface'. We find these qualities in the *Merchant's Tale* too. But January's behaviour is not only observed, it is explored (the key word, I have suggested, is 'fantasye'). It is traced back to a compelling sexual fantasy, which is linked, through the garden, with the fantasies of the Earthly Paradise, the Song of Solomon, and the *Romance of the Rose*. There is a lyrical expansiveness ('tendre youthe hath wedded stoupyng age') in the poem, where the anecdote is being generalized in this way. The particularity of the *Summoner's Tale* is invigorating (at least in the earlier part); but in the end the poem does not add up to much. It remains an extended anecdote.

It seems obvious that the quality in the *Merchant's Tale* which is being described bears some relation to allegory. The allegorical suggestions of the names January and May, Placebo and Justinus, are apparent enough. The reader of *Piers Plowman* will recognize in the system of cross-references which links January's garden with other gardens, and all these gardens with the theme of sexual fantasy, a familiar technique. It bears little relation to the strict allegorical method, which some critics detect in *Piers*—the method of four-level meaning deriving from biblical interpretation; but neither does most medieval allegory. Usually the technique is loose, flexible, and intermittent. The equations may for a time seem very fixed and clear ('Petrus id est Christus'); but they may equally well amount to nothing more than a casual cross-reference. Only on a too rigid definition could the part played by the allegorical method in the *Merchant's Tale* be ignored. Its story is not in itself allegorical; neither is the story of the Eighteenth Passus of *Piers Plowman* (the story of the crucifixion and resurrection) with which, technically, the poem has something in common. In both, allegory is at work generalizing and equating (Christ is Light is Piers; January is Age, his garden is Adam's and Solomon's and Lorris's). In both, allegorical figures can enter the story without anomaly (Mercy, Peace, Truth, and Righteousness; Venus and Bacchus).

The point here is that this generalizing impulse (characteristic of allegory) exists side by side, in Chaucer, with the ironic or satiric impulse (characteristic of the fabliau), which tends to isolate its object and particularize it. It is this dual impulse which makes the *Merchant's Tale* a saner and more balanced poem than the conventional account might suggest.

It is unlike the *Summoner's Tale* in having a significance beyond its anecdotal content, in having a meaning. The irony is controlled (and this is surely characteristic of Chaucer) by a recognition that January's case illustrates general human weakness—a suggestion that is rigidly excluded in the treatment of the Summoner's Friar. It is a knowledge of 'fantasye' which informs the poem and gives it its moral framework within which the irony works. This knowledge appears in the unobtrusively allegorical treatment of the story, notably of the garden. The poem owes as much to the allegory as to the fabliau, bringing to the anecdotal clarity of the latter a scope and significance which belong to the former tradition. This seems to be one of the secrets of Chaucer's best narrative poems. They grow in the mind without losing the precision of their outline.

4. FOUR NOTES ON CHAUCER'S
SIR THOPAS

The first of these notes draws attention to a small but striking
instance of the inertia to which editors, like lexicographers,
are subject. William Caxton happened to set the text of the
first printed *Canterbury Tales* (*c*.1478) from an inferior
manuscript which had lost one of the text-divisions in *Sir
Thopas*; and editors ever since have followed him in dividing
the poem into only two sections or 'fits', despite evidence
both in the text itself and in well-known manuscripts such as
Ellesmere and Hengwrt that it should be divided into three—a
division which more clearly displays the poem's peculiar
structure. Explanatory annotations to Chaucer's text have
also suffered from the same inertia. Commentators too often
confine their attentions to those places where their predecessors have found something to comment on, as if all the difficulties had already been spotted, if not solved, by W. W.
Skeat and F. N. Robinson. So the explication of individual
words and lines has failed to keep pace with the general
progress of Chaucer criticism; and discussion of Chaucer's
poetic language, lacking a regular diet of detailed word-studies,
suffers from chronic malnutrition. With the most notable
exception of E. T. Donaldson, Chaucer scholars have commonly failed to pay sufficient attention to individual words.
Yet a little investigation in the standard dictionaries and con-
cordances is often enough to recover significant patterns of
usage and nuances of meaning, as the remaining three notes
here attempt to demonstrate. They are devoted to three
expressions in Chaucer's burlesque, each of which represents
a calculated departure from his normal usage: the word
listeth, the honorific *sir* prefixed to a knight's name, and the
form *worly*. *Sir Thopas* is a ridiculous piece, but even here we
can see how sedulously this author attended to the minute
details of his work. Like those engravers of small seal-rings to
whom he elsewhere refers, Chaucer practised an art whose
products deserve to be examined closely and under a strong
light.

I. AN AGONY IN THREE FITS*

Towards the end of *Sir Thopas*, before the stanza beginning at VII. 891, many editions of the *Canterbury Tales* have a heading: 'The Second Fit'.[1] No such headings appear in any of the manuscripts. However, the existence of a fit-division at this point is established by the lines which end the preceding stanza:

> Loo, lordes myne, heere is a fit!
> If ye wol any moore of it,
> To telle it wol I fonde.   (VII. 888-90)[2]

There is also manuscript evidence, though not in the form of headings. The new fit begins with the line:

> Now holde youre mouth, *par charitee.*

Several manuscripts distinguish this line, either by initial letters of unusual size, form, or colour, or by paragraph signs in the margin beside it, or by a combination of both.[3] Bo*1* and its twin Ph*2* have a paragraph sign together with either *Now* (Bo*1*) or *Now holde* (Ph*2*) in heavy, flourished letters. Six manuscripts have an illuminated, or large, initial *N*: El, Ha*4*, He, Ld*1*, Ne, Se; and the scribe of Hg leaves space for an illuminated capital which was not made.[4] In five other manuscripts,[5] the scribes place a small, cursive paragraph mark

---

* First published in *Review of English Studies* n.s. 22 (1971), 54-8.

[1] Thus Skeat, the Globe editors, Manly (1928), Robinson, Donaldson, Baugh.

[2] 'Here is a fit', meaning 'this is the end of a fit', is also found in the ballad 'Adam Bell, Clim of the Clough, and William of Cloudesly', stanzas 51 ('Her is a fit of Cloudesli') and 97 ('Here is a fytte of these wyght yongemen').

[3] I have used the complete set of rotographs of *Canterbury Tales* manuscripts in the British Library. The set was assembled by Manly and Rickert for their *Text of the Canterbury Tales* and presented to the Library by the University of Chicago.

[4] En*1* is a doubtful case. Its *N* is not large or ornamented, but seems to depart from the normal form.

[5] Not counting manuscripts which set out to distinguish every stanza with a paragraph mark (e.g. En*2*, Ln, Ry*2*). The cursive paragraph mark is that described by Jenkinson as deriving from the capital C sign: H. Jenkinson, *The Later Court Hands in England* (Cambridge, 1927), p. 102 (I owe this reference to Mr M. B. Parkes). It is not always easy to see in Manly and Rickert's rotographs, owing to their numbering of lines in ink down the margins. Thus Ma might possibly also have a mark at this point.

beside the line: Cn, Ch, Dd, Ph^1, To. Thus, of the 47 manuscripts which have the line in question, 14 (including several of the most important) accord it some distinguishing mark.[6]

Further examination of the manuscripts, however, suggests that it is not the *second* fit which begins at line 891. There are two places earlier in *Sir Thopas* where, once the evidence of all the manuscripts is collected and tabulated, paragraph signs and distinctive initials cluster in what appears to be a significant way.[7] At line 748, Ph^2 has a paragraph sign together with *And so bifel* in heavy, flourished letters; Cp and Ma have paragraph signs; and La has an elaborated capital. No fit-division is called for here, however, after only six stanzas of the Tale. These scribes are simply marking the end of the introductory description of Sir Thopas and the beginning of the action:

> And so bifel upon a day,
> For sothe, as I yow telle may,
>   Sire Thopas wolde out ride.   (748–50)

The case is different at line 833. For one thing, the cluster of paragraph markings and distinctive letters at this point in the manuscripts is almost as dense as at 891. Ph^2 has a paragraph sign together with *Yet listeth* in heavy, flourished letters. Six manuscripts have an illuminated, or large, initial *Y*: Ad^1, El, Ha^3, He, Hg, Se. It is particularly striking that Ellesmere and Hengwrt agree (as do He and Se) in placing special capitals at both 833 and 891, and only in those two places. Five other manuscripts have a small scribal paragraph mark beside the line: Cn, Ch, Ma, Ph^1, To. Of these, Cn, Ch and To agree in placing marks only at 833 and 891. Thus, in the case of line 833, 12 out of the 48 manuscripts which have the line distinguish it in some way, as compared with 14 out of 47 in the case of line 891.[8]

The manuscript evidence alone does not prove that a fit-division was intended at 833 as well as 891. Not all divisions

---

[6] In addition, Mc and Ra^1 break off their text at line 890, and Ry^1 has 891–918 in a new hand.

[7] No significance can be attached to Fi's paragraph sign at 888, Ln's signs at 810 and 830, or Ph^1's at 918.

[8] Fi's omission of 833–87 is specially interesting in the present context.

are fit-divisions; and the scribes may, in any case, have been following a bad tradition. But the nature of the passage centring on 833 goes far to establish that this line does indeed mark the beginning of a new fit: the true 'Second Fit'.

The stanza before line 833 describes how the giant Olifaunt bombarded Thopas with stones, and concludes with general reflections on the hero's fortunate escape from danger:

> But faire escapeth child Thopas,
> And al it was thurgh Goddes gras,
> And thurgh his fair berynge.   (830-2)

That sounds quite like the ending of a fit; but the next stanza sounds even more like the beginning of a new one:

> Yet listeth, lordes, to my tale
> Murier than the nightyngale,
> For now I wol yow rowne
> How sir Thopas, with sydes smale,
> Prikyng over hill and dale,
> Is comen agayn to towne.   (833-8)

The first three lines of this stanza are modelled on the first three lines of the tail-rhyme romance *Beves of Hamtoun*.[9] The stanza is also closely parallel to those with which Chaucer begins the first and last fits of his poem (712-17, 891-6). In each case, there is an appeal for attention: 'Listeth, lordes, in good entent' (712), 'Yet listeth, lordes, to my tale' (833), 'Now holde youre mouth, *par charitee*, . . . And herkneth to my spelle' (891, 893). This appeal is followed by an announcement of subject: 'I wol telle . . .' (713), 'I wol yow rowne . . .' (835), 'I wol yow telle . . .' (896). It seems reasonable, in view of the manuscript evidence, to conclude that each of these three passages of appeal and announcement (there are no others in the Tale)[10] is to be associated with the beginning of a fit.

[9] In the Auchinleck Manuscript, *Beves* begins thus: 'Lordinges, herkneth to me tale / Is merier than the nightingale / That y schel singe'. See L. H. Loomis in W. F. Bryan and G. Dempster (eds.), *Sources and Analogues of Chaucer's Canterbury Tales* (London, 1958), p. 498.

[10] The only other minstrelish addresses to the audience are three casual asseverations in the First Fit: 728, 749, 758.

The custom of dividing *Sir Thopas* only at VII. 891 has a long history in printed editions of Chaucer. William Caxton's editions (c.1478 and c.1484) have a single special capital at that line,[11] as do the much-studied editions of Thomas Speght (1598 and 1602, reissued 1687).[12] But modern editors are wrong to follow this tradition. The poem should be divided as it is divided in the Ellesmere and Hengwrt manuscripts—not to mention witnesses of less authority—into three fits: 712-832, 833-90, 891-918.

The division newly proposed here throws light upon the distribution of stanza-forms in *Sir Thopas*, and also upon the poem's structure.

Since Chaucer is a poet who elsewhere shows complete mastery of his stanza-forms, the apparently random distribution of varying tail-rhyme forms in *Thopas* demands explanation. One puzzling feature is explained by the proposed fit-divisions. The most common type of stanza in the poem is a six-liner rhyming aa^baa^b. Of $31\frac{1}{2}$ stanzas in all, 18 (or $18\frac{1}{2}$)[13] belong to this type. The poem opens, in fact, with a solid block of 13 such stanzas. There follow 5 stanzas exhibiting various other forms. Then comes another, smaller block of 4 stanzas of the common type, again followed by a series of variants (which includes, however, a single isolated stanza of the common type). This sequence appears very arbitrary until we notice that the beginning of the second, smaller block coincides with the beginning of the second, smaller fit. Thus, the two completed fits of *Thopas* exhibit the same basic pattern: each begins with a string of regular or common stanzas and ends with a burst of inventive variation.

It is noteworthy that, of the three fits distinguished here, the first has 18 stanzas, the second 9, and the third $4\frac{1}{2}$. The ratios 4 : 2 : 1 do not hold for the line-totals, because of variation in the number of lines per stanza,[14] but they can

---

[11] Caxton was no doubt following his manuscripts here. Ne, which is closely related to Cx^1, is one of the five manuscripts (Bo^1, Dd, Ha^4, Ld^1, Ne) which divide *Thopas* at line 891 only, in the way favoured by Caxton and (less excusably) modern editors.

[12] Speght was followed by Urry (1721), but not by Tyrwhitt (1775-8), who has no divisions.

[13] If the interrupted last line was intended to continue '— it so bifel', as seems only too likely (compare 748), the last stanza would have belonged to the common type.　　　[14] The line-totals are 121, 58, and $27\frac{1}{2}$.

hardly, in my opinion, be ascribed to coincidence. Rather, these ratios are the formal, mathematical expressions of a principle of progressive diminution, a principle which appears more obviously in the distributing of narrative material between the three fits. The First Fit is relatively eventful, incorporating the whole basic pattern of romance adventure: the hero sets out from home for strange countries, encounters a dangerous adversary, and returns home safely (though in this case somewhat ignominiously). The Second Fit, by contrast, is almost entirely devoted to a laboriously detailed account of how Thopas dons his armour in preparation for his second encounter with Olifaunt; and in the Third Fit, the hero only has time to mount his good steed and set off once more to find the giant before Harry Bailey interrupts: 'Namoore of this, for Goddes dignitee'. Thus the poem seems to narrow away, section by section, towards nothingness—like Alice's idea, in Lewis Carroll, of the 'long sad tale' told by the Mouse.

The basic ratio 2 : 1 is one of those singled out by Macrobius in his commentary on 'Tullyus of the Drem of Scipioun' as being productive of harmony.[15] In music, the ratio produces an octave or 'diapason'; and it was thought by many to produce a similarly harmonious effect in poetry.[16] Even the fragmentary Third Fit of *Sir Thopas* is concordant in so far as it stands an 'octave above' the Second, just as the Second stands an octave above the First. Harry Bailey unwittingly interrupts Chaucer at a point, almost exactly half-way through the fifth stanza of his Third Fit, which allows the Tale, despite its apparent raggedness, to achieve a harmonious resolution. Such mathematical harmony of form is quite uncharacteristic of the minstrel and ballad poetry which *Thopas* appears to represent. If Chaucer meant it to be perceived at all, it could only be by his more 'philosophical' readers, the Gowers and the Strodes, who, unlike poor Harry Bailey, knew what he was capable of. It would form part of the secret, not to say 'superior', joke.

[15] *Commentary on the Dream of Scipio*, trans. W. H. Stahl (New York, 1952), Book II, Chapter I. On Chaucer's knowledge of this work, see Stahl's Introduction, pp. 52-5.

[16] Examples of the octave proportion in later English poetry are given in *Triumphal Forms* (Cambridge, 1970) by Dr A. D. S. Fowler, to whom I am indebted for his help in this matter.

II. 'LISTETH, LORDES'*

Chaucer's *Tale of Sir Thopas* opens with a call for the attention of the audience:

> Listeth, lordes, in good entent,
> And I wol telle verrayment
> Of myrthe and of solas   (VII. 712-14)

According to the *Index of Middle English Verse* and its *Supplement*, this coupling of *list* (or *listen*) with *lord* (or *lord(l)ing*) occurs in the opening lines of no less than thirty-three Middle English poems.[1] Chaucer is imitating, humorously, one of the favourite alliterating collocations in the poetry of his day; and just to make sure of the joke, he repeats the phrase a hundred lines later:

> Yet listeth, lordes, to my tale
> Murier than the nightyngale.   (VII. 833-4)

Here 'yet listeth', which means 'keep on listening', strikes a fresh note of comic anxiety.

But Chaucer's joke has more to it than this. It is a remarkable fact that neither the word *list* nor its synonym *listen* occurs anywhere else in his writings. The *Chaucer Concordance*, which is based on the text of the Globe edition, records only the two uses in *Sir Thopas* of *list* and none at all of *listen*—as against fifteen examples of *hark* and a hundred of *hearken* (including one in *Thopas* itself). One stray example of *listen* does occur in the text of the currently standard edition by Robinson; but this arises from an editorial misjudgement. At the beginning of Book II of the *House of Fame*, Robinson reads as follows:

> Now herkeneth, every maner man
> That Englissh understonde kan,
> And listeneth of my drem to lere.   (509-11)

---

* First published in *Notes and Queries* 213 (1968), 326-7.

[1] The accepted reading *listeth* at the beginning of *Sir Thopas* rests on the authority of six manuscripts (including Ellesmere and Hengwrt). Forty-four manuscripts read *listeneth*. In view of this uncertainty (which exists also at line 833), I have not made a, perhaps necessary, distinction between the two words in what follows.

Listeneth is the reading of both manuscripts in Robinson's preferred *alpha* group (Bodley 638 and Fairfax 16) and of Caxton's print; but two of the three authorities in the *beta* group (from which Robinson says he takes 'a good many readings'), Pepys 2006 and Thynne's print, read *listeth*. This reading, which was adopted by Skeat as well as by the Globe editor (and hence the *Concordance*), gives distinctly better sense (taking *list* in its usual Chaucerian sense of 'desire'): 'Now pay attention, everyone who knows English and desires to learn about my dream'. One might compare *Canterbury Tales*, VIII. 1056, as well as I. 3176 etc.

The contrast between the 115 examples of *hark/hearken* and the two examples (both in parodic contexts) of *list/ listen* is striking enough to require explanation. The statistics presented by A. Rynell, in his *Rivalry of Scandinavian and Native Synonyms in Middle English* (Lund, 1948), show clearly that *hearken* was more common than *list/listen* in Northern literary texts (30 : 12 in *Cursor Mundi*, 24 : 7 in *York Plays*, 43 : 2 in *Towneley Plays*);[2] and, according to the *Dictionary of the Older Scottish Tongue*, *list* is found in Scotland not at all and *listen* 'only in early [i.e. fourteenth- and fifteenth-century] verse'. Such evidence suggests that *hearken* was strengthening against *list/listen* in the North in Chaucer's time and after. But outside Northern texts (which are all relatively late) the picture is less clear. Some of the earlier Southern texts studied by Rynell show a distinct preference for *list/listen* over *hark/hearken*—26 : 1 in *Trinity College Homilies* (twelfth century, SE Midland), 12 : 0 in *Owl and Nightingale* (c.1200, Southern), 14 : 2 in Mannyng's *Handlyng Synne* (1303, Lincs.). In the course of the fourteenth and fifteenth centuries *list/listen* does seem to have lost ground in many places; but the great majority of authors continue to use it, side by side with *hark/hearken*. Thus we find both types of word in the poems of Gower and of Lydgate.[3] But there is one notable exception, besides Chaucer himself, to this generalization. A reading of the complete

---

[2] *Hark*, *hearken*, *list*, and *listen* are all native words (OE **heorcian, heorcnian, hlystan*, and ONorth. *lysna*). The 'rivalry' which concerns Rynell is between them and *lithe* (cf. OIcel. *hlýða*).

[3] Rynell does not give proportions for these authors, and I have not attempted to arrive at any.

works of Hoccleve (in the three-volume Early English Text Society edition) reveals twenty-one uses of *hearken* and none of *list/listen*. Now Hoccleve is closer to the usage of Chaucer, in many respects, than any other Middle English author—closer, certainly, than Gower or Lydgate. Professor M. L. Samuels classes him with Chaucer as a representative of the London English of about 1400—as against the earlier 'East Anglian' type of London speech represented by the main scribe of the Auchinleck Manuscript, on the one hand, and the 'Chancery Standard' of the fifteenth century, on the other.[4] It may be, then, that the complete avoidance of *list/listen* was a feature of metropolitan English round about 1400.

Professor Samuels contends that this type of London speech evolved out of the earlier 'East Anglian' type found in the Auchinleck Manuscript under the influence of Central Midland and (more indirectly) Northern dialects. Influences from these areas might explain, perhaps, why Chaucer and his fellow-citizens came to feel that *list/listen* was no longer acceptable.[5]

Mrs L. H. Loomis has argued very convincingly that Chaucer was acquainted with the Auchinleck Manuscript, and that, in his second address to the audience in *Sir Thopas*, he was imitating the opening of the Auchinleck *Beves of Hamtoun* (which is written in the hand of the main scribe):

> Lordinges, herkneþ to me tale
> Is merier þan þe niȝtingale . . .
> > (Beves [Auch.], 1-2)

> Yet listeth, lordes, to my tale
> Murier than the nightyngale . . .
> > (*Thopas*, 833-4)[6]

[4] M. L. Samuels, 'Some Applications of Middle English Dialectology', *English Studies* 44 (1963), 81-94. The documents (in Chambers and Daunt, *London English*, and Furnivall, *Earliest English Wills*) cited by Samuels along with Chaucer and Hoccleve do not appear to contain examples either of *list/listen* or of *hark/hearken*.

[5] The 'Central Midland Standard', through which Northern influences chiefly operated on London speakers, according to Samuels, is represented principally by Wycliffite writings. The glossaries to the four volumes so far published of Conrad Lindberg's edition of the Bodley 959 text of the Early Version of the Wycliffite Bible record eight uses of *hearken* and none of *list/listen*. Is this typical?

[6] L. H. Loomis, 'Chaucer and the Auchinleck MS: *Thopas* and *Guy of*

Like the majority of Middle English speakers, this Auchinleck scribe shows himself ready elsewhere to accept *list/listen*. London usage in his day was not yet exclusive in this matter; nor, on the hypothesis suggested in the preceding paragraph, would we expect it to have been so. But in this particular passage the scribe happened to write *herkneþ*; so it was left for Chaucer to strike what must have been to him the right jarring note.

III. THE TITLE 'SIR'

In the opening stanza of *Sir Thopas*, Chaucer signals the peculiar character of the tale which is to follow with a cluster of lexical oddities: *listeth* (for *herkneth*), *entent* (for *entente*), *verrayment* (only here in his work), and *gent* (usually *gentil*).[1] One other departure from his normal usage has so far escaped detection, hidden in the stanza's simple last line: 'His name was sire Thopas'.

Many readers besides Shakespeare ('Sir Topas, Sir Topas, good Sir Topas, go to my lady') must have noticed how persistently Chaucer harps on the title *sir* in this tale. The hero is named nine times, always with a title of honour prefixed to his name. Once he is 'child Thopas' (VII. 830); but eight times he is 'sir(e) Thopas' (717, 724, 750, 772, 778, 827, 836, 901).[2] Chaucer also refers to 'sir Gy' (899), 'sir Lybeux' (900) and 'sire Percyvell' (916). Even the giant is called 'sire Olifaunt' (808). The absurdity of a knighted giant is obvious; but the other eleven uses may seem to err merely by excessive frequency—suggesting, perhaps, the work of a minstrel romancer over-keen to bestow knightly status on everyone he mentions. The evidence of the *Concordance* suggests, however, that this may not be the whole story, for it reveals that Chaucer does not prefix *sir* to a knight's name anywhere else

Warwick', *Essays and Studies in Honor of Carleton Brown* (New York, 1940), pp. 111-28, esp. p. 114 n. 10.

[1] On *listeth*, see the previous essay; on *gent*, see E. T. Donaldson, *Speaking of Chaucer* (London, 1970), p. 22.

[2] In view of the argument which follows, it may be noted that Chaucer uses *child* as a title of honour in conjunction with a proper name only here and in *Thopas* 898 ('Horn child').

in his work.[3] The word itself is common enough in his work. It can mean 'master', 'husband' or 'father'; and it is also frequently used as a form of polite address, either by itself or in combination with some common noun denoting occupation and standing ('sir knight', 'sir man of law', 'sir parish priest'). In the *Romaunt of the Rose* it is prefixed, for no apparent reason, to two allegorical names ('sir Myrthe', 614 etc.; 'sir Daunger', 3549); but there are only five places, outside *Thopas*, where the title is used with a true proper name. Two of these clearly represent the old custom, still followed by Malvolio in *Twelfth Night*, of applying the title to a priest: the Nun's Priest is addressed by the Host and referred to by the poet as 'sir John' (VII. 2810, 2820). Two other cases most probably represent the same custom. The Friar describes in his tale how a corrupt summoner's wenches report to him the names of men who have slept with them: 'sir Robert or sir Huwe, / Or Jakke, or Rauf' (III. 1356-57). The summoner's high-handed treatment of these victims ('pile the man, and lete the wenche go') makes it unlikely that Sir Robert and Sir Hugh are knights, and most editors suppose them to be priests, no doubt rightly. The remaining case occurs in the *Physician's Tale*, where a judge is addressed as 'sire Apius', presumably out of respect for his learning in the law (VI. 178).

The fact that *sir + knight's name* occurs twelve times in *Sir Thopas* and not once elsewhere in the works of a poet who had so many other occasions to name knights ancient and modern suggests the surprising possibility that it is to be numbered among those non-U expressions which Chaucer confines to burlesque contexts. Admittedly, many of the characters described in his work as 'knights' belong to the ancient world of Troy, Greece, and Rome. The *Oxford English Dictionary* (s.v. *Sir* sb. 2) gives several Middle English examples of the title 'applied retrospectively to notable personages of ancient, especially sacred or classical, history', and it is easy to find others: 'sir Achilles', 'sir Ulixes', and 'sir Anthenor' in Lydgate's *Troy Book*, for instance.[4] The absence

---

[3] J. S. P. Tatlock and A. G. Kennedy, *A Concordance of the Complete Works of Geoffrey Chaucer* (Washington, 1927), s.v. *Sir* and *Sire*. The distinction between these two forms can be ignored for present purposes.

[4] *Lydgate's Troy Book*, ed. H. Bergen, EETS e.s. 97, 103, 106, 126 (1906-20), III. 3875, IV. 1810, IV. 4659.

of such expressions from *Troilus*, the *Legend of Good Women*, the *Knight's Tale*, and the rest may be explained simply by supposing that Chaucer thought them ridiculously anachronistic; yet there is so much 'medievalization' elsewhere in these poems that this explanation seems less than adequate. Chaucer did not balk at 'Sir Appius'. Why should he so consistently have balked at 'Sir Troilus', 'Sir Hector', 'Sir Palamon', or 'Sir Theseus'? It must be admitted, however, that the other pieces of negative evidence, though less numerous, carry more individual weight. Chaucer does not often refer by name to Arthurian knights outside *Thopas* (the Wife of Bath's hero is never named), but when he does they are always *sir*-less. On the one hand we find 'sir Lybeux' and 'sire Percyvell' in *Thopas*, on the other 'Gawayn' and 'Launcelot' in the *Squire's Tale* (V. 95, 287), 'Launcelot de Lake' in the *Nun's Priest's Tale* (VII. 3212), and 'Tristram' in *Parliament of Fowls* 290 and in *Rosemounde* 20, all without the title of honour. Unlike Froissart, to whom we shall return, Chaucer was also sparing in his references to the knights of his own day. On the two occasions when he does name a living knight, however, he again fails to use *sir*. Sir Otes de Graunson is referred to simply as 'Graunson' in the *Complaint of Venus*; and in *Lenvoy to Bukton*, the poet addresses his friend, thought to be either Sir Peter or Sir Robert, as 'my maister Bukton'.[5]

The explanation of these facts is to be found, I suggest, in the French usage of Chaucer's day. In a remarkable study entitled 'Sire, Messire', published in five parts in *Romania* and extending to no less than 231 pages, Lucien Foulet has traced in great detail the history of *sire* and related French titles of honour from the beginnings up to the late fourteenth century.[6] His findings, so far as they are relevant here, may

[5] *Venus* 82, *Bukton* 1. Robinson, note ad loc., observes that 'Bukton is possibly addressed as *maister* because he was a lawyer', citing Rickert. But see *OED* s.v. *Master* sb.¹ 21a: 'Prefixed to a surname or a Christian name. Down to the 16th c. or a little later, *master* could be prefixed to the name of a knight or a bishop'. Perhaps this was Chaucer's normal English usage when addressing or referring to a knight, on those occasions where the sophisticated plainness of 'Graunson' was not appropriate. He may have regarded it as the English equivalent of the (etymologically unrelated) French *messire*, discussed below.

[6] *Romania* 71 (1950), 1-48, 180-221; 72 (1951), 31-77, 324-67, 479-528. I am grateful to Dr Elspeth Kennedy for drawing my attention to this study.

be summarized as follows. *Sire* is commonly prefixed to knights' names in the earliest French texts ('Sire Rollant, e vos, sire Oliver', *Roland* 1740), and it remains frequent in this use until about the middle of the thirteenth century. At that time, however, it was superseded by the rival term *messire* as the correct title of honour for a knight (though expressions of the type *li sires de Nigrepont* remained acceptable). Foulet thinks that *sire* had been too frequently associated with unworthy names and so became tainted with vulgarity. 'Les nobles', he writes, 'vont se lasser de cette communauté d'appellation, et ils laisseront définitivement le *sire*, à leurs yeux déprécié, aux bourgeois qui le garderont longtemps.'[7] However this may be, his evidence shows decisively that in the latter part of the thirteenth century and throughout the fourteenth, French writers, employing *messire* as the proper prefixed title for knights, regularly reserved *sire* + *name* for the upper bourgeoisie. Foulet's discussion of Froissart's usage in this respect, based on a substantial sample of the *Chronicles*, is of particular interest to the student of Chaucer, since Froissart was a near contemporary of the English poet and quite possibly an acquaintance at the court of Edward III and his queen.[8] In the *Chronicles* of Froissart the proper honorific for a knight is *messire* (oblique case *monseigneur*): 'messire Huon', 'messire Jehan', 'monsigneur Philippe'. *Sire* (oblique case *seigneur*) continues as a general term of respectful address, as in Chaucer; and it is also used to designate noble possessors of a fief, in expressions of the type *li sires de Nigrepont*. But *sire* + *name* is not used by Froissart of knights: 'Il demeure et demeurera bien des années encore l'apanage de la bourgeoisie . . . Tout au cours de ses *Chroniques* nous rencontrons des bourgeois ainsi désignés.'[9] Foulet cites numerous examples of this usage, which he calls 'le "sire" bourgeois'. Froissart refers to the famous burghers of Calais as 'sire Eustache de Saint-Pierre', 'sire Jaques de Vissant', and so on; a rich man from Montpellier is called 'sire Berengier Oste'; 'sire Ghisebert Grute' and 'sire

    [7] *Romania* 71 (1950), 182.
    [8] Foulet's discussion of Froissart, from which all my examples are taken, is to be found in *Romania* 72 (1951), 333–67, 479–509.
    [9] *Romania* 72 (1951), 347.

Simon Bete' are two rich citizens of Ghent; and the comman-
der of a Flemish fleet which met an English fleet commanded
by 'messires Guis de Briane' in 1372 is named as 'sires Jehans
Pietresone'. On this last example Foulet comments: *'Messire*
contre *sire*, voilà qui peint assez bien une lutte des seigneurs
d'Angleterre contre la bourgeoisie de Flandres.'[10]

This observation brings us back to *Sir Thopas*. Chaucer's
hero was born in the Flemish town of Poperinge. His father
is described in exalted terms as 'a man ful free' and 'lord . . .
of that contree', and Thopas himself is twice referred to as a
knight (VII. 715, 909); but his birthplace also associates him
inescapably with 'la bourgeoisie de Flandres'. Hence, Chaucer's
repeated *'sir* Thopas', contrasting as it does with his usage
elsewhere, would have a particular aptness for any English
reader acquainted with the niceties of polite usage in contemporary French—and that would surely include any reader
with a footing in the court of Richard II, where French was
still a living language of chivalry. It may be noted in this connection that Chaucer's own testimony before the Court of
Chivalry, when he was called as a deponent in the Scrope-
Grosvenor case, was delivered or at least recorded in French,
and that the poet is reported as having referred to the principals, Sir Richard Scrope and Sir Robert Grosvenor, as
'Monsieur [= Messire] Richard Lescrop' and 'Monsieur
Robert Grovenour'.[11]

There is, so far as I know, no study which does for medieval
English honorifics what Foulet's does for the French; but it
seems clear that the general reaction against *sire .+ knight's
name* which took place in thirteenth-century French was not
followed in English, at that or any other time. The usage has,
after all, as Foulet reminds his French readers, actually
survived to the present day in England, 'où se conservent tant
de souvenirs du passé'. The *Oxford English Dictionary* (s.v.
Sire) records it first in Laȝamon's *Brut*, and all readers of
later Middle English literature will recognize the frequency of
its occurrence there, not only in romances of the popular
type imitated in *Sir Thopas*, but also in works such as *Sir*

[10] *Romania* 72 (1951), 348.
[11] M. M. Crow and C. C. Olson (eds.), *Chaucer Life-Records* (Oxford, 1966),
pp. 370-1.

Gawain and the Green Knight and Malory's *Morte Darthur*. The continued currency of *sir + knight's name* in English after the thirteenth century is too obvious, in fact, to need documenting. What would better repay investigation is the possibility that some English authors besides Chaucer may have followed French practice in avoiding the usage—Gower, perhaps, or Hoccleve. In the mean time, it may be suggested that Chaucer's use of *sir* in *Sir Thopas* is to be understood as a coterie joke—unobtrusively divisive of its audience, like many of the jokes in the poem. Excluded readers see nothing except, perhaps, an excessively insistent use of a normal honorific; but the favoured few wince at the honorific itself and also see, in its application to Thopas, a hidden felicity. For according to current French usage, such a title would mark the hero as precisely the kind of man that his birth in Poperinge would lead one to expect: a 'sire bourgeois'.

IV. 'WORLY UNDER WEDE'*

In Robinson's edition (1957), Chaucer's *Sir Thopas* ends as follows:

> Hymself drank water of the well,
> As dide the knyght sire Percyvell
>   So worthy under wede,
> Til on a day—   (VII. 915-18)

The immediate cause of the Host's interruption at this point ('Namoore of this, for Goddes dignitee') may be found in the predictability of the next rhyme word: Chaucer has already had 'And so bifel upon a day' (748), and on this occasion he must intend 'Til on a day it so bifel'. The rhyme is already bad, in any case, since *well* appears as a disyllable *welle* (OE *wiella*) in all the thirty-two other places where it rhymes in Chaucer's work, and so will not go with *Percyvell* (itself an authentic English form). The one remaining line of the unfinished stanza, 'So worthy under wede', is also offensive, though for a different reason. Alliterative phrases of the fair-under-garment type ('lovely under linen', ' seemly under sark',

* First published in *Chaucer Review* 3 (1969), 170-3.

'comely under kell', etc.) are among the most overworked clichés of Middle English poetry; and 'worthy under weed' (or more commonly 'in weed') is itself found in tail-rhyme romances such as *Emaré* and *Amis and Amiloun*, in alliterative poems such as *Golagros and Gawain*, and in many other places. Chaucer does not use such collocations anywhere else in his writings. He no doubt intended 'worthy under weed' as a crowning infelicity for an unhappy stanza.

But Robinson's text does not tell the whole story. His reading 'worthy under wede' is that of the majority of editors since Thynne in the sixteenth century: Speght, Urry, Tyrwhitt, Wright, Bell, Skeat, Pollard, Baugh. The chief dissentients (apart from Caxton, who has *worthily*) are J. M. Manly and E. T. Donaldson. The former, in his 1928 edition of the *Canterbury Tales*, printed 'worly under wede' without comment or gloss; but in *The Text of the Canterbury Tales*, produced with Edith Rickert in 1940, he changed his mind so far as to conclude that the common ancestor of all surviving manuscripts read *worthy*, remarking that *worly* 'is a spelling slip (unless it is the original form)' (ii. 365). In 1958, *worly* was once more adopted by Donaldson, in his *Chaucer's Poetry: An Anthology for the Modern Reader*. I want to show that Manly (1928) and Donaldson are probably right, and that *worly* yields a better joke than *worthy*.

There are thirty-seven witnesses for the line in question. Four read *worly*: Ch El Hg Ph[1]. Five read *worthily*: Cp[2] Cx[1] Dl Mm Ne. Six read *worthly*:[1] Ad[3] Ha[2] Ht Ld[1] Ph[3] Pw. Twenty-two read *worthy*: Ad[1] Bo[1] Bo[2] Cn Dd Ds En[1] En[3] Gl Ha[3] Ha[4] Ii Ln[2] Ma Nl Ox Ph[2] Py Ra[3] Ry[1] Se To.

It is difficult to explain why, if the received text is correct, these variants should have arisen at all. The Chaucerian adjective is elsewhere always (and very frequently) *worthy*; and I can find no other place in Chaucer where this familiar word gives rise to variant readings like those in the present passage. If the original was damaged or illegible at this point, scribes would certainly have guessed *worthy* rather than any of the rarer variants. The only explanation available to

---

[1] Ha[2] Ht Ld[1] Ph[3] Pw have forms with medial -e- (*worthely*). Manly and Rickert treat these MSS as supporting the reading *worthily*; but *worthely* is best regarded as a fifteenth-century spelling of *worthly* (see *OED* under *Worthly*).

defenders of the received reading, it would seem, is that some scribes tried to improve Chaucer's joke by introducing non-Chaucerian forms; and this runs counter to the usual habit of scribes, which is to regularize irregularities, not to create new ones.[2]

It therefore seems most probable that *worthy* represents a scribal normalization of some irregular (i.e. non-Chaucerian) form in the original. The three irregular forms in the manuscripts seem to exhaust all the possibilities of restoration. They are all genuine forms (not 'spelling slips'), and all are found elsewhere in combination with *weed*. *Worthily* is recorded (as an adjective) by *OED* in late Middle English alliterative poetry only; but it also occurs in the tail-rhyme *Sir Perceval of Galles*: 'those worthily in wede' (1606). This example is of special interest, because *worthily* here occurs with *weed* in the very romance which probably suggested to Chaucer his bad rhyme *Percyvell / well*.[3] *Worthly* is a much more common adjective, with a direct descent from OE 'weorþlic', and is found in Middle English both in verse and in prose. It occurs with *weed* in the poems of Minot (see *OED* under *Worthly*), and in at least two tail-rhyme romances: *Amis and Amiloun* (Auchinleck MS) 138 ('worþliest in wede'), also 443, 453, 467, 1430;[4] and *Guy of Warwick* (Auchinleck MS) 10. 9 ('þat worþly were in wede').[5] *Worly* is an altogether rarer form, not recorded in *OED*. It developed from *worthly* by loss of [th] between [r] and a following consonant.[6] It occurs four times (in the forms *wurh-liche*, *worhliche*, and *worly*) in the lyrics of MS Harley

---

[2] Compare J. R. R. Tolkien's study of the scribes' handling of Northern dialect forms in the *Reeve's Tale*: 'Chaucer as a Philologist: the *Reeve's Tale*', *Transactions of the Philological Society* (1934), 1-70.

[3] 'His righte name was Percyuell, / He was ffosterde in the felle, / He dranke water of þe welle', *Sir Perceval* 5-7, in *Middle English Metrical Romances*, ed. W. H. French and C. B. Hale (New York, 1930).

[4] Ed. McE. Leach, EETS o.s. 203 (1937). In lines 443, 453, and 467, the other MSS read *worthy*.

[5] Ed. J. Zupitza, EETS e.s. 42, 49, 59 (1883-91). Evidence that Chaucer was acquainted with the Auchinleck MS is collected by L. H. Loomis, 'Chaucer and the Auchinleck MS: *Thopas* and *Guy of Warwick*', *Essays and Studies in Honor of Carleton Brown* (New York, 1940), pp. 111-28.

[6] See E. J. Dobson, *English Pronunciation 1500-1700* (Oxford, 1957), vol. ii, par. 408, giving evidence for loss of [th] in *earthly*. *Worship* (OE *wurþscipe*) shows forms without [th] from the thirteenth century in *OED*.

2253;[7] once in another lyric;[8] twice in the alliterative *William of Palerne*;[9] twice in the *Pistill of Susan*;[10] and five times in the *Awntyrs off Arthure*.[11] The last two poems, which survive in more than one manuscript, show variants very similar to those in our passage. In both places in *Susan* it is the two oldest and (according to their editor) best manuscripts which read *worly*, as against *worthy* or *worthily* in the later copies. In the *Awntyrs* the Ireland Manuscript has all five occurrences of *worly*, with *worthy*, *worthly*, and *worthily* all appearing as variants in the other three manuscripts. This same Ireland Manuscript has the unique text of the tail-rhyme *Avowing of Arthur*; and it is here that we find *worly* with *weed*:

> Þen þe lady wex drede,
> Worlyke in wede.[12]

The same collocation occurs in the dramatic fragment *Dux Moraud*: 'I am dowty in dede, / I am worly in wede, / I am semly on stede' (36–8).[13] This passage well illustrates the conventional nature of the phrase.

It is not easy to determine which of these three forms Chaucer actually used. The variant readings in *Amis and Amiloun*, the *Pistill of Susan*, and the *Awntyrs off Arthure* suggest that *worthly*, *worly*, and *worthily* formed, with *worthy*, a lexical group within which scribal substitutions

[7] *The Harley Lyrics*, ed. G. L. Brook (Manchester, 1948), No. 12, line 10, 13. 31 (*worli wede*), 14. 9 and 14. 42.

[8] 'A Midsummer Day's Dance', line 12. No. 28 in R. H. Robbins (ed.), *Secular Lyrics of the XIVth and XVth Centuries*, 2nd edn. (Oxford, 1955).

[9] Ed. W. W. Skeat, EETS e.s. 1 (1867), lines 138 and 2700. *Worthy*, *worthly*, and *worthily* all occur as adjs. elsewhere in this text.

[10] Ed. F. J. Amours, *Scottish Alliterative Poems*, Scottish Text Society, 27, 38 (Edinburgh, 1892–7), lines 54 (Add. and Vern. MSS) and 134 (Add. and Vern. MSS).

[11] Ireland MS, ed. J. Robson, *Three Early English Metrical Romances*, Camden Society (London, 1842), XIII. 3, XXVIII. 10, XXIX. 1, XXXII. 2, XXXVIII. 6. For readings of two other MSS see Amours, ed. cit.

[12] Ed. French and Hale, *Middle English Metrical Romances*, 851–2. The editors' gloss 'prudent one' for *worlyke* rests on an identification with ME *warly* which is phonologically impossible.

[13] Ed. N. Davis, *Non-Cycle Plays and Fragments*, EETS s.s. 1 (1970). The form *worly* occurs three times elsewhere in *Moraud* (55, 79, 160): see Davis's Introduction, p. cviii.

were likely to occur easily and often. Hence the interrelations of the variants in the *Canterbury Tales* manuscripts may well be very complex. *Worthly* is least likely to have been the original reading (despite its occurrence in the Auchinleck manuscript) because it is a rather common word, sometimes found in prose. *Worthily* is a more likely candidate, both because it is a rare, poetic form, and because it occurs in a poem which Chaucer seems to have used elsewhere in this very stanza. But it seems most probable that the main line of tradition ran from an original *worly* through the expanded form *worthly* to *worthily*, with *worthy* readings branching off at all three points. The chief virtue of this hypothesis is that it explains how the very unusual *worly* form came to be the reading of the Ellesmere, Hengwrt, and Christ Church manuscripts. These are three carefully spelt manuscripts of high authority which have very few errors in common in this tale and are regarded by Manly and Rickert as belonging to independent lines of descent.[14]

The distribution of *worly*, in lyrics, alliterative poems, and metrical romances, shows that it belongs to that general stock of well-worn native poetic words and forms which Chaucer picks over elsewhere in *Sir Thopas*, and also in the *Miller's Tale*.[15] Such a word, and in such a collocation, might well persuade the Host that he had heard enough.

[14] Manly and Rickert (ii. 361–8) distinguish 7 lines of descent in this tale.
[15] See E. T. Donaldson, 'Idiom of Popular Poetry in the *Miller's Tale*', *English Institute Essays 1950*, 116–40, reprinted in *Speaking of Chaucer* (London, 1970), pp. 13–29.

5. THE ACTION OF LANGLAND'S SECOND VISION*

I

The second of the ten visions in the B version of *Piers Plowman* contains some of the poem's most famous episodes. It has the confession of the Seven Deadly Sins in Passus V, the ploughing of the half-acre in Passus VI, and the tearing of the pardon in Passus VII. Critics have devoted a good deal of attention to these episodes; but they have generally failed to see them as parts of that whole to which they most immediately belong—the action, that is, of the second vision. I hope to show that, so far as its action is concerned, this vision *is* a whole, and that its more difficult episodes make better sense if we see them as parts of it. This is in the general belief that readers and critics of Langland have made too little of his vision-structure. I suppose that many people do not even know that the B version has ten visions.

One cannot appreciate the wholeness of the second vision if one starts from the three famous episodes just mentioned. It may be worth recalling what Aristotle says about wholeness: 'A whole is that which has beginning, middle, and end. A beginning is that which is not itself necessarily after anything else, and which has naturally something else after it; an end is that which is naturally after something itself, either as its necessary or usual consequent, and with nothing else after it; and a middle, that which is by nature after one thing and has also another after it. A well-constructed plot, therefore, cannot either begin or end at any point one likes' (*Poetics*, translated Bywater, ch. 7). But an action which begins with a confession, proceeds with a ploughing, and ends with a pardon can hardly be called usual or natural, let alone necessary. On the contrary, it seems quite arbitrary. One feels one could extend it indefinitely, with masses, sea-voyages, community singing, and the like, 'beginning and ending at any point one likes'.

* First published in *Essays in Criticism* 15 (1965), 247–68.

The feeling that the whole thing could be otherwise is not unfamiliar to readers of *Piers Plowman*, perhaps; but in the second vision at least there is a well-constructed plot, however incoherent our usual memories of it may be. The parts of this plot are not confession, ploughing, and pardon, but sermon, confession, pilgrimage, and pardon.

This series may itself seem somewhat arbitrary; but Langland wrote for readers who would appreciate its coherence. A sinful man hears a SERMON. This is the beginning of the action: it is 'not itself necessarily after anything else'; but it 'has naturally something else after it' in so far as it moves its hearer to contrition, and so sends him on to CONFESSION. This is a middle, not an end, because the priest's absolution, though it wipes away the guilt ('culpa') and the eternal punishment, leaves a debt of temporal punishment to be paid. Hence penance necessarily follows confession; and a usual form of penance, in hard cases, is PILGRIMAGE. But a pilgrimage is not an end either, for it is not normally thought sufficient in itself to pay off the whole debt of temporal punishment. This is done by the plenary PARDON (or indulgence), the usual object of major fourteenth-century pilgrimages. The pardon is a true end, both because it follows the pilgrimage as its 'usual consequent', and because it requires nothing else after it. By its power the penitent is freed from the last consequences of his sin; and the arc of penitential action is therefore complete.

Before going on to examine what Langland does with this plot, let me briefly suggest a reason why he chose it for this particular vision. The story of Lady Meed, in the first vision, concludes with the triumph of Conscience and Reason in the King's court at Westminster. This represents a major reformation of society—the reformation of law; but Conscience's response to the King's enthusiasm suggests that it is not enough. The King says:

'I wole have leaute in lawe, and lete be al youre jangling,
And as moost folk witnesseth wel, Wrong shal be demed';

to which Conscience replies:

'But the commune wole assente,
It is ful hard, by myn heed, herto to brynge it,
And alle youre lige leodes to lede thus evene.'

(Passus IV. 180-4)[1]

This is the cue for the second vision: the 'commune'—that is,
the whole of the community, not just the King and his judges
—must assent to the rule of Reason. What Langland has in
mind here is not a total, apocalyptic transformation of
society: that event, prophesied by Conscience in Passus III
(284 ff.), is placed in the future, out of the range of the Visio.
He means rather to show the kind of change, or conversion,
that can be expected of people here, now, and in England.
His problem was to find some form of action which would
represent such a change. This cannot have been easy; and the
course of the second vision, as we shall see, suggests that the
solution he adopted caused him some misgivings. But the
sermon-confession-pilgrimage-pardon sequence had definite
advantages. It was a familiar and at the same time a dramatic
way of turning from sin to righteousness; and it was a way
which a whole society—or at least a representative 'thousand
of men'—could plausibly be shown as taking.

One should realize that it was quite common in the Middle
Ages for great public sermons to be followed by mass confession and a mass pilgrimage in search of pardon. An early
example is the First Crusade (1095). After the Pope's sermon
at Clermont, the audience knelt, recited the Confiteor, and
undertook an armed pilgrimage to Jerusalem, the Pope
promising plenary pardon to all who took part. Norman
Cohn, in his book *The Pursuit of the Millennium*, discusses
this and many other examples of what he calls the 'collective
quest for salvation'. The quest was often associated, as in the
case of the First Crusade, with a period of natural calamity.
People were specially ready at such times to 'cluster in
devotional and penitential groups'—just like Langland's
thousand men—and set out on crusades, or on other more
pacific kinds of pilgrimage. It is perhaps worth noticing here
that the very calamities referred to by Langland's Reason in

---

[1] All quotations from the B version are from A. V. C. Schmidt's edition (London, 1978).

his sermon—the winds and pestilences of 1361-2—provoked just such a reaction. John of Bridlington, a contemporary of Langland's, reports that on account of the pestilence certain English lords received the sign of the Cross to go to the Holy Land.[2] Such movements were less frequent in England than on the Continent, where 'hordes' of penitential pilgrims seem to have been almost commonplace; but Langland must have known about them. For his presentation of the conversion of the 'commune' as a collective or horde response to natural calamity implies knowledge, if not approval.

II

The plot described in the last section provides the essential ground-plan of the second vision: unless one perceives it the whole structure will remain unintelligible. But it is no more than the ground-plan. The vision does not give a straight, literal account of a collective quest for salvation. Langland, rather, uses the customary sequence of events as a base from which to derive his allegorical action. The reader must know the original sequence, obviously; but most of the interest lies in the process of cut, addition, and substitution by which it is transformed. In the case of the second vision, as I hope to show, it is specially important to attend to the substitutions. Since these do not become really interesting until we reach the third and fourth stages of the story, I shall deal with the sermon and the confession rather briefly.

The vision begins with Reason's sermon to the 'commune' (identified with the 'feeld ful of folk' of the Prologue). Reason preaches to 'al the reaume', with a cross, and in the King's presence. These details suggest a great episcopal occasion, rather than an ordinary parochial one; and the character of the sermon itself rather supports this impression. It is a 'sermo ad diversos status hominum', such as fourteenth-century bishops are known to have preached on special occasions—an address to the various 'states' of men, calling upon husbands, fathers, priests, etc. to amend their ways. Yet the preacher is Reason, not a fourteenth-century bishop; and

[2] See *Political Poems and Songs*, ed. Thomas Wright, Rolls Series (London, 1859-61), vol. i, p. 183.

his homely tone suggests the personification rather than the parson:

> 'My sire seide so to me, and so dide my dame,
> That the levere child the moore loore bihoveth;
> And Salamon seide the same, that Sapience made—
>   *"Qui parcit virge odit filium*:
> Whoso spareth the spryng spilleth hise children."'
>
> (V. 37-40)

This represents what any man's reason will tell him about his duties; and it is this reasoning with oneself, rather than any grand public preaching, which Langland sees as the beginning of the conversion of the folk of the field. People have only to take thought to see that all is not as it should be. Yet we should note, in view of developments later in the vision, that the substitution of Reason for the usual priest or bishop is not polemical. Langland, that is, does not seem concerned to score points off the priests and bishops by suggesting that self-examination is *better* than sermon-going.

There is a like absence of polemic in the second stage of the action—the confession. Here Langland substitutes the personifications of the Seven Deadly Sins (representing the sins of the folk) for the penitents, and the personification of Repentance for the confessor. The latter substitution is not an altogether happy one: 'confessing to Repentance', unlike 'listening to Reason', makes little sense when one tries to convert it into literal terms. But the general point of the episode is quite clear. Once a man has taken thought and recognized his imperfections, he must then repent and confess. It must be admitted that Langland is vague about the externals of the confession. For example, Repentance speaks, in the manner of a confessor, of absolving the Sins individually (V. 184 and 272); but his actual absolution, which must be looked for in V. 479-506, is of a purely general and supplicatory character. He simply prays that God may have mercy on them all. The fact that this prayer ends with Hope blowing his horn of *'Deus tu conversus vivificabis nos'* (507) suggests that Langland is here thinking of public liturgical, rather than private sacramental, penance; for this verse from the Psalms occurs after the Confiteor and the absolution-prayer Misereatur in the Mass.[3] But such inconsistencies are typically Langlandian. We do not conclude that he thought sacramental absolution unnecessary or *merely* external.

It is, I want now to argue, exactly because he did think this way about pilgrimages that the third stage of his action presented him with a special challenge. The fact is beyond dispute. Langland, to put it bluntly, though he believed in sermons and confessions, did not believe in pilgrimages. His opinion of pilgrims is clearly stated in the Prologue:

> Pilgrymes and palmeres plighten hem togidere
> For to seken Seint Jame and seintes at Rome;
> Wenten forth in hire wey with many wise tales,
> And hadden leve to lyen al hire lif after.   (Prol. 46-9)

Later in the first vision Reason says that, in his ideal society, St. James would be sought 'there I shal assigne' (IV. 126). The point of this enigmatic remark is made clear in the C text, where Reason requires that

> 'Seynt Iame be souht ther poure syke lyggen,
> In prisons and in poore cotes for pilgrymages to Rome'.
> (C V. 122-3)

Reason, in other words, tells us that it is better to do good works at home than to travel abroad on pilgrimages. The B text has a very similar passage later on, when Anima, speaking of Charity, says that it is his custom

> 'to wenden on pilgrymages
> Ther poore men and prisons liggeth, hir pardon to have'.
> (XV. 182-3)

Good works *instead* of pilgrimage: this is surely also the point of the pilgrimage to Truth proclaimed by Reason at the end of his sermon in the second vision:

---

[3] I owe this information to Fr. S. Tugwell, who also points out that the source of the verse (wrongly given by Skeat) is Psalm 84: 7 (Vulgate).

'And ye that seke Seynt James and seyntes of Rome,
Seketh Seynt Truthe, for he may save yow alle'.

(V. 56-7)

Seeking St. James and the saints of Rome is not an acceptable
form of penance—the echo of the Prologue is sufficient proof
of that. So the substitution of St. Truth (i.e. God) for these
saints, unlike the substitutions of Reason and Repentance for
preacher and confessor, *is* polemical. There is a new tension
here between the allegorical action and that which it signifies.
The pilgrimage proposed by Reason signifies, one might
almost say, *anything but* actual pilgrimage.

Langland makes this point dramatically in the last part of
his long fifth passus. After the confession of the Sins and
Repentance's great prayer, a thousand men from the field full
of folk cluster (Langland uses the word 'thrungen') into a
devotional and penitential group, and set out on the expiatory
pilgrimage proclaimed by Reason. But they are not yet real
pilgrims by any standards—Langland's or the world's—for
they have no sense of where they are going. So they just
roam about like a herd of animals, until they meet the
Palmer:

> blustreden forth as beestes over baches and hilles,
> Til late was and longe, that thei a leode mette
> Apparailled as a paynym in pilgrymes wyse.

(V. 514-16)

The Palmer is a pure grotesque, embodying everything Langland most hated in the pilgrims of his day—the worldliness,
the meaningless rigmarole of place-names and keepsakes, and
above all the bland complacency:

> 'Ye may se by my signes that sitten on myn hatte
> That I have walked ful wide in weet and in drye
> And sought goode Seintes for my soule helthe'.

(V. 529-31)

The Palmer knows all the 'good saints', it appears, except
Truth. He represents the business of worldly pilgrimage, and

so stands to be contrasted with Piers, the representative of the true or spiritual pilgrimage, who 'puts forth his head' for the first time at this point in the poem. The contrast is boldly stated, and there is no need to enlarge upon it. Piers knows Truth well, and he knows the way to his place. It leads through Meekness, Conscience, Love of God, Love of Neighbour, and the Ten Commandments.

By the end of the fifth passus, then, Langland has established his third substitution—that of St. Truth for St. James and the saints of Rome—and has made sure, one would have thought, that the reader sees its polemical point. So we have every reason to expect, as we begin the sixth passus, that he will proceed with the account of the conversion of the commune by showing them following the road described by Piers, reaching Truth's shrine, and receiving his pardon. The actual course of events in the sixth passus is therefore disturbing—and, I think, deliberately so.

The opening of the passus gives no particular cause for alarm. Piers offers to guide the people on the way to Truth; but first he has a 'half acre . . . by the heighe weye' to plough and sow. One may not quite see the point of this interruption; but it does not seem to matter very much. Ploughing and sowing a single half-acre cannot take very long—it seems in fact to have been no more than a customary 'long morning's work'[4]—and the land is right 'by the heighe weye', the road which the pilgrims are to travel (described in the C text as the 'alta via ad fidelitatem'). So one expects the company to resume its journey very shortly. True, when Piers enlists the help of the pilgrims and instructs them in their various duties —the ladies to sew church vestments, the common women to spin and weave, the knight to hunt and fight, etc.—he seems to be treating the long morning's interruption in the half-acre as if it were a lifetime in the world; but we are comforted by his repeated assurances that he will lead the pilgrims on shortly, as soon as he is ready:

> 'Hadde I eryed this half acre and sowen it after,
> I wolde wende with yow and the wey teche' (VI. 5–6)

---

[4] See G. C. Homans, *English Villagers of the Thirteenth Century* (Cambridge, Mass., 1941), p. 49.

'And I shal apparaille me,' quod Perkyn, 'in
    pilgrymes wise
And wende with yow I wile til we fynde Truthe'
                                        (57-8)

'For I wol sowe it myself, and sithenes wol I wende
To pilgrymage as palmeres doon, pardon for to have'
                                        (63-4)

'To penaunce and to pilgrimage I wol passe with
    thise othere;
Forthi I wole er I wende do write my bequeste'.
                                        (84-5)

The 'bequest', or will, which these last lines introduce
seems at first to provide further reassurance; for the making
of a will was a customary part of the preparations for a pilgrimage, it being necessary to set one's house in order in case
one did not get back safely. Surely, we feel, Piers *is* going to set
out on the journey. Yet it is the will which, in its closing passage, first positively suggests that this is not so. After bequeath-
ing his soul to God, his body to the Church, and his lawful
winnings to his wife and children, Piers speaks of what is left:

'And with the residue and the remenaunt, by the Rode
    of Lukes!
I wol worshipe therwith Truthe by my lyve,
And ben His pilgrym atte plow for povere mennes sake.
My plowpote shal be my pikstaf, and picche atwo the
    rotes,
And helpe my cultour to kerve and clense the furwes'.
                                        (VI. 100-4)

This noble passage strongly suggests that Langland has in
mind, however bewilderingly, a second polemical substitution.
The opening lines recall a bit of anti-pilgrimage polemic in
the confession of Sloth in the previous passus (a parallel
which is even closer in the A text where Piers refers, like
Sloth, to the rood of Chester):

'And with the residue and the remenaunt, bi the
    Rode of Chestre,
I shal seken truthe erst er I se Rome!'   (V. 460-1)

But the present passage goes further than that. Having substituted the pilgrimage to Truth, proclaimed by Reason and
described by Piers, for the false and meaningless Rome-
running represented by the Palmer, Langland now has Piers
talk of a 'pilgrimage at the plough', as if the ploughing of
the half-acre was to be substituted for the pilgrimage to
Truth.

The rest of the sixth passus, together with the beginning
of the seventh, seems to me to provide decisive evidence that
this was indeed Langland's intention, despite the opinion of
several good critics (T. P. Dunning and R. W. Frank among
them) to the contrary. The main point to note in Passus Six
is the disintegration of the time-scheme proposed in its opening passage. The long morning's work stretches out to a
whole year. The action of the passus begins round about
Michaelmas, at the beginning of the husbandman's year, with
the ploughing and sowing of the winter corn field—Piers's
half-acre. Then, after the intervention of Hunger, there
follows a threshing:

> Faitours for fere herof flowen into bernes,
> And flapten on with flailes fro morwe til even.
>
> (VI. 183-4)

This comes in its right place, for, as Homans observes in his
excellent account of the medieval farming year, 'after the
sowing of the winter corn field, the husbandman would be
likely to turn from the land to the barn, where he would
busy himself with the sheaves of the last harvest' (op. cit.,
p. 356). There follows the discussion between Piers and
Hunger about poor-relief, after which we learn from Piers
that the people are to live sparsely until Lammas (1st August).

> 'And by that I hope to have hervest in my croft'.
>
> (290)

Then, with dream-like suddenness, 'hervest' or autumn (the
period between Lammas and Michaelmas) approaches once
more, bringing the wheel round in a full circle:

By that it neghed neer hervest and newe corn cam to
  chepyng;
Thanne was folk fayn, and fedde Hunger with the beste.

(299-300)

So the people, it would seem, are no longer merely pausing
by the highway on their pilgrimage to Truth. They are living,
under Piers's guidance, through the whole yearly cycle of
dearth and abundance which determined the everyday life of
the medieval 'commune'.

But the decisive indication that the pilgrimage is not to be
resumed comes at the beginning of the following passus:

Treuthe herde telle herof, and to Piers sente
To taken his teme and tilien the erthe,
And purchaced hym a pardoun *a pena et a culpa*
For hym and for hise heires for everemoore after;
And bad hym holde hym at home and erien hise leyes,
And alle that holpen hym to erye, to sette or to sowe,
Or any maner mestier that myghte Piers availe—
Pardon with Piers Plowman Truthe hath ygraunted.

(VII. 1-8)

Two things, for the moment, are particularly to be noticed in
this passage. First, Truth sends a message to Piers telling him
to 'holde hym at home' and plough his lands once more—in
preparation for another year of sowing and reaping. This
surely means that on one level—the literal level—the pilgrimage
is abandoned. For St. Truth himself, the very object of the
proposed pilgrimage, commands his servant to stay at home.
At the same time, the fact that Truth obtains a plenary
pardon for Piers, his heirs, and his helpers, suggests equally
clearly that the pilgrimage is, in another sense, completed.
Critics have not generally drawn this inference; but it seems
quite unavoidable. Piers himself said, towards the beginning
of the sixth passus, that he would go

'To pilgrymage as palmeres doon, *pardon for to have*'.

(VI. 64)

Truth's pardon is the object of the pilgrimage to Truth; so the granting of it can only mean that the object of the pilgrimage has been attained. There seems no alternative to this simple explanation of why the pardon comes at this point in the action. We are forced to recognize a second substitution. Piers will not lead the folk on a pilgrimage 'as palmeres doon'. *His* pike-staff is a 'plowpote', *his* scrip a seed-hopper, and *his* pilgrimage a pilgrimage at the plough.

In the third stage of his action, then, Langland first substitutes an allegorical pilgrimage for a real one, and then substitutes for that allegorical pilgrimage something which is not a pilgrimage at all, even in the allegorical action. Pilgrimage first becomes an allegorical form or 'vehicle', then dwindles into a mere metaphor. The point of both transformations is essentially the same; but the second involves a more explicit emphasis on the idea of 'holding oneself at home'.

In the forty-fifth chapter of Rabelais's *Gargantua*, Grangousier addresses the following 'good words' to a company of pilgrims recently swallowed by Gargantua in a salad: 'Go your ways, poor men, in the name of God the Creator, to whom I pray to guide you perpetually; and henceforward be not so ready to undertake these idle and unprofitable journeys. Look to your families, labour every man in his vocation, instruct your children, and live as the good Apostle St. Paul directeth you: in doing whereof God, his angels and sancts, will guard and protect you, and no evil or plague at any time shall befall you.' This view of pilgrimage—which is exactly Langland's—can be traced right back to the Fathers. Typical statements are to be found in Jerome—'the palace of heaven can be reached as well from Britain as from Jerusalem; for the Kingdom of God is within you'—and in Augustine—'one must travel to Him who is everywhere present and everywhere all, not with one's feet but with one's conduct (*non pedibus, sed moribus*)'. In another passage, Augustine finds scriptural authority for the idea in the words of Christ to the woman of Samaria: 'Woman, believe me, the hour cometh, when ye shall neither in this mountain, nor yet at Jerusalem, worship the Father. . . . God is a Spirit: and they that worship him must worship him in spirit and in truth' (John 4: 21 and 24).

This biblical antithesis between worshipping God 'at Jerusalem' (interpreted by Augustine, evidently, as a reference to
pilgrimages) and worshipping him 'in spirit and in truth' is
particularly close, I believe, to Langland's thought in the
fifth and sixth passus. We must recall that in Passus I Holy
Church uses the word 'truth' not only of God ('Truth' with
a capital T), but also of a way of life. The word has a sub-
jective reference to conduct, as well as an objective one to
supernatural reality. She also says that the life of truth is
the best way of reaching Truth. I think that Langland intended
the experiences of Piers and his pilgrims to illustrate this very
biblical paradox ('I am the way, the truth, and the life').

This implies that the life of the half-acre is to be identified
with the life of truth, as defined by Holy Church. There are
two main arguments in support of this identification. Both
Passus I and Passus VI stress the importance of labouring
honestly ('truly') in one's vocation: compare, for example,
the discussions of a knight's vocation in I. 94–7 and VI. 27 ff.
Again, both passus are much concerned with charity. Piers's
concern for his 'blody bretheren',

> 'Truthe taughte me ones to loven hem ech one
> And to helpen hem of alle thyng, ay as hem nedeth',
>
> (VI. 208–9)

recalls the teaching of Holy Church in such passages as I. 179–
84. It is true that charity takes a somewhat mundane form in
the half-acre, where it is a question of those who can labour
in their vocations helping those of their neighbours who cannot (or will not); but this is quite proper, for the half-acre
represents the life of truth as it is lived 'day by day' (see
VII. 191).

I hold, then, that Piers and his faithful followers—'alle
kynne crafty men that konne lyven in truthe'—are on the
highway to Truth, 'non pedibus, sed moribus', when they
stay at home labouring in their vocations and helping their
neighbours, since this is the way of truth which Truth himself
taught. They are worshipping him not in Jerusalem but in
spirit—'by their lives' as Piers says (VI. 101). It is therefore

not surprising that they win his pardon. Holy Church promised that they would:

> Ac tho that werche wel as Holy Writ telleth,
> And enden as I er seide in truthe, that is the beste,
> Mowe be siker that hire soules shul wende to hevene,
> Ther Treuthe is in Trinitee and troneth hem alle'.
>
> (I. 130–3)

III

I believe that many of the difficulties in the controversial fourth stage of the vision, to which I now turn, will disappear once we realize that Langland handles the pardon in very much the same ways as he handled the pilgrimage. In each case there is a tension between the literal action and that which it signifies; and in each case Langland eases this tension by a twice-repeated gesture of substitution.

It cannot be said of pardons, as of pilgrimages, that Langland simply did not believe in them. In the epilogue to the second vision he goes out of his way to assert that the Pope *has* power to grant pardon:

> And so I leve leelly (Lord forbede ellis!)
> That pardon and penaunce and preieres doon save
> Soules that have synned seven sithes dedly.
>
> (VII. 177–9)

The protestation is doubtless sincere; yet it seems clear that Langland's deepest feelings on the matter are represented in the following lines (where 'triennals', despite Skeat's note, probably refers to pardons):

> Ac to trust on thise triennals—trewly, me
>   thynketh,
> It is noght so siker for the soule, certes, as is
>   Dowel.   (180–1)

Langland's fear, as so often, is that the external form or institution—even though it is acceptable in itself—may come to

usurp the place of the inner spiritual reality. It is this fear
which determines his treatment of the pardon in Passus VII.
His chosen action required that the final reward for the converted members of the commune should take the form of a
pardon. But this was no more than a 'form', embodying the
spiritual truth, stated by Holy Church in the first vision and
spelt out in the epilogue to the second, that those who turn
from their wickedness and do well will receive their reward
in heaven. And Langland explicitly says that this Dowel—
represented, again, in the life of the half-acre[5]—is more 'siker
for the soule' than any pardon. So Truth's pardon, like his
pilgrimage, is not—emphatically not—to be taken literally. It
is in his anxiety to make this point that Langland resorts
once more to a somewhat bewildering double transformation
of his primary action.

The first of these transformations is basically quite straightforward, in that it follows directly from the substitution of
St. Truth for St. James and the saints of Rome as the object
of the pilgrimage. But it led Langland into certain complications, to understand which the reader must know that a
pardon involves three parties—a producer, a distributor, and
a consumer. The producers are Christ and the saints, who by
their lives and deaths have accumulated a 'treasury of merit'
which is available to the faithful. The distributor is the Pope,
who as God's vicar alone has the power—though he can delegate
it—of distributing the treasure by the grant of pardons. The
consumers are those who obtain such grants. Now Langland's original intention, if that is what the A text represents,
was simply to introduce Truth as the saint who by his life
and death 'purchased' the pardon which the penitent commune obtain. This works out well, since Truth is God, and
God did purchase a pardon for the faithful in the redemption.
Christ founded the treasury of merit. So the A text has

[5] See Nevill Coghill, 'The Character of Piers Plowman', *Medium Aevum* 2
(1933), 108-35, *passim*. Several critics have disputed Coghill's contention that
Dowel is represented in the half-acre. But the second vision is (among other
things) a story of how some people, instead of going on a pilgrimage to win an
indulgence, stay at home and win salvation there; and I cannot see why Langland
should draw from this the conclusion that Dowel surpasses indulgences unless he
meant 'Dowel' to refer to the people's life at home. Subsequent definitions of
Dowel, especially VIII. 81-4, IX. 108-9, and XII. 32 ff., support this view. Passus
VI does not say the last word on Dowel; but this is another matter.

Truth 'purchase' the pardon (A VIII. 3) and the Pope 'grant' it (A VIII. 8 and 21). This is entirely consistent; but the B author was apparently not satisfied with it, for he substituted (if our text is to be trusted) Truth for the Pope in line 8. This also works out, since Truth/God not only purchased man's pardon in the person of Christ, he also grants it through his vicar the Pope (compare XIX. 183 ff.). It was left for C to regularize the alliteration of line 8 (where B has 'Pardon with Piers Plowman Truthe hath ygraunted') and make the corresponding change, neglected by B, in A VIII. 21—thus eliminating the Pope altogether and creating a new unmetrical line.

This comparison between the three texts is of interest because it allows one a glimpse, seemingly, of Langland—or his atelier—actually at work on the kind of substitution with which this essay is largely concerned. But the changes in question are of relatively minor importance. The main points are the same in all three versions: that the pardon is purchased by St. Truth, and that it is available (whoever actually 'grants' it) to all who help Piers:

> Alle that holpen hym to erye, to sette or to sowe,
> Or any maner mestier that myghte Piers availe—
> Pardon with Piers Plowman Truthe hath ygraunted.

The essence of the first substitution is here. This is not an ordinary saint's pardon, such as could be obtained at any registered shrine; it is *Truth's* pardon.

After a longish passage (VII. 9–104) specifying the various benefits the pardon brings for various classes of men—kings, knights, bishops, merchants, etc.—Langland proceeds to dramatize his point by confronting Piers with a representative of ordinary pardons: the Priest. There have been considerable differences of opinion about this character, whom Langland seems rather to have taken for granted; but I would agree with Nevill Coghill that he is 'a sophist who understands the letter but not the spirit'.[6] Those who share this view will see here a notable parallel between the third and fourth stages of

---

[6] See 'The Pardon of Piers Plowman', *Proceedings of the British Academy* 30 (1944), p. 319.

the action. The Priest stands to Piers with respect to the pardon exactly as the Palmer stands to Piers with respect to the pilgrimage. In each case a representative of the un-substituted, literal institution challenges the spiritual version for which Piers stands. The Palmer does not recognize the pilgrimage to Truth:

> 'I seigh nevere palmere with pyk ne with scrippe
> Asken after hym er now in this place';   (V. 535-6)

and the Priest does not recognize Truth's pardon:

> 'Peter!' quod the priest tho, 'I kan no pardon
>   fynde
> But "Do wel and have wel, and God shal have thi
>   soule,"
> And "Do yvel and have yvel, and hope thow noon
>   oother
> That after thi deeth day the devel shal have thi
>   soule!"'   (VII. 111-14)

It is natural that a priest should want to see the pardon, since priests were responsible for seeing that false pardons were not distributed in their parishes. But this priest, it would seem, is so much concerned with proper drafting and proper sealing that he does not recognize the word of God.

Some critics have held that the Priest's attack on the pardon is supported by the author; but I cannot believe that this is right. The pardon is 'purchased' by Truth/God, and, in the B and C texts, 'granted' by him too; and it carries a message from the Athanasian Creed:

> 'Et qui bona egerunt ibunt in vitam eternam;
> Qui vero mala, in ignem eternum'.

This recalls the words of Holy Church in Passus I (128-33, quoted in part above), and harmonizes with the whole argu-ment of the second vision, especially Passus VI. Those who 'werche wel' (live the life of truth, do well, 'bona egerunt') will, by the grace of God, be saved; those who don't, won't.

It is true that the message is very simple, and can be reduced, as the Priest reduces it, to a common proverb: 'Do well and have well . . .' ('est notandum quod proverbialiter solet dici, "bene fac et bene habe"', Brunton, 1376). But Langland respected proverbs and admired simplicity.

In the C text the second vision ends with the Priest's attack on the pardon. This is a possible, if not a very satisfactory, ending. What Imaginative later calls God's 'gret mede to truthe' (XII. 292) has, notwithstanding the Priest's misguided objections, been demonstrated by the pardon. The arc of penitential action is complete. But in the A and B texts the vision continues for another twenty odd lines (B VII. 115–39) before the dreamer wakes. This closing passage, cut by the C poet, requires some discussion here.

First, Piers responds to the Priest's attack on the pardon by tearing it up:

> And Piers for pure tene pulled it atweyne.

This is, of course, the most notorious crux in the whole vision. If I treat it rather briefly here, it is because I believe that R. W. Frank, in his article on the pardon scene in *Speculum* xxvi (1951), to which I refer the reader, has already made the essential points better than I can. I can claim only that the argument of this essay provides new support for his case. Frank believes, as I do, that the pardon is valid and that Piers does not reject it. He explains the tearing in terms of a 'clash between form and content' (on pages 322–3 of his essay). The pardon, he argues, 'contains a message which is by implication an attack on pardons and which does in fact lead to such an attack by the Dreamer' (in the epilogue). It is definitely not an ordinary pardon. Indeed, 'in trusting its message, Piers is *rejecting* bulls with seals. In tearing the parchment, Piers is symbolically tearing paper pardons from Rome.' So the tearing, 'because of the special character of the pardon, was intended by Langland as a sign that Piers had rejected indulgences and accepted the command to do well. Unfortunately, it was a very confusing sign'.

This reading enables us to see a clear parallel between the tearing of the pardon and the shelving of the pilgrimage. The 'clash between form and content' is the same in each case; for the pilgrimage, like the pardon, contains a message which is by implication an attack on itself. And in each case Langland responds in the same fashion. First he allegorizes the 'form' polemically (pilgrimage to *Truth*, *Truth's* pardon); then, as if not content with this, he has Piers turn against even the allegorized version. And the significance of this 'second substitution' is the same in each case. Piers does not reject the 'content' of Truth's pardon (Dowel etc.) when he tears it up, any more than he rejects the content of Truth's pilgrimage (Meekness, Conscience, etc.) when he distracts the folk from that. He is demonstrating angrily ('for pure tene'), and on Langland's behalf, against the 'form'.

What makes the pardon-tearing a somewhat obscure demonstration, however, is that in this case Langland could find nothing concrete or dramatic—no vehicle, form, objective correlative, or what you will—to convey positively what was to be substituted *for* pardon-mongering, as the ploughing of the half-acre conveys what is to be substituted for pilgrimage. It is one thing to show Piers living 'truly' at home, quite another to show—really *show*—him trusting in Dowel. Trust in Dowel is an idea not easy to present dramatically. In the event, Langland was content to follow the tearing with a single quotation from the Psalms:

> And Piers for pure tene pulled it atweyne,
> And seide, '*Si ambulavero in medio umbre mortis*
> *Non timebo mala, quoniam tu mecum es*'.
>
> (VII. 115–17)

Langland, I think, cuts a corner here. I would suggest that he is trying to convey in a single verse Piers's trust in the saving power of Dowel or Truth. The evidence for this is that Imaginative expresses the same trust with the very same verse at the end of Passus XII:

> 'Ne wolde nevere trewe God but trewe truthe were
>   allowed.
> And wheither it worth or noght worth, the bileve is
>   gret of truthe,

> And an hope hangynge therinne to have a mede for
>   his truthe;
> For *Deus dicitur quasi dans vitam eternam suis,*
>   *hoc est fidelibus.*
> *Et alibi, Si ambulavero in medio umbre mortis etc.*
> The glose graunteth upon that vers a gret mede to
>   truthe.'   (XII. 288–92)

The relevant passage from Psalm 23 runs as follows: 'He
leadeth me in the paths of righteousness for his name's sake.
Yea, though I walk through the valley of the shadow of
death, I will fear no evil: for thou art with me'. Peter Lom-
bard, author of the most widely used commentary ('glose')
on the Psalms, takes 'thou art with me', following Augustine,
to refer to the reward enjoyed after death by the man who
walks 'in the paths of righteousness'.[7] The 'gret mede to
truthe' is God's company in heaven. This, surely, is the point
of Piers's enigmatic quotation: that righteousness ('truth')
can be trusted, as pardons cannot, to win the reward of
eternal life.

The remainder of Piers's speech (VII. 118–30) raises
questions which reach beyond the scope of this essay, for it
points forward from the Visio to the Vita de Dowel, Dobet &
Dobest. Langland seems to be trying to link Visio and Vita
by starting issues for the one at the end of the other:

> 'I shal cessen of my sowyng,' quod Piers, 'and
>   swynke noght so harde,
> Ne aboute my bely joye so bisy be na moore;
> Of preieres and of penaunce my plough shal ben
>   herafter,
> And wepen whan I sholde slepe, though whete breed
>   me faille'.

These lines open up new perspectives; but the reader of the
second vision should be familiar at least with the *movement*
of the thought. 'Of preieres and of penaunce my plough shal
ben herafter': this is the movement of substitution which
Langland uses so often when he is in the process of advancing,

---

[7] See Frank's article cited in the text, p. 96, for quotation and references.

serpent-like, from something which is, or may be, no more than an externality towards a more inward statement of his theme. So in Passus VI he advanced from the pilgrimage to Truth—itself representing an advance on real-life pilgrimage, but seen in retrospect as itself 'formal'—to the pilgrimage at the plough: 'My plowpote shal be my pikstaf'. That is, essentially, as far as the second vision takes us; but in the lines quoted above Langland is preparing for a further advance. As a substitute for the pilgrimage, the ploughing of the half-acre is sufficient to embody Dowel; but it too can be seen critically, in retrospect, as just 'a way of putting it—not very satisfactory'. Langland certainly did believe that the life of labour and love could be trusted to save a man's soul—that is the main message of the second vision. Yet the action of the half-acre cannot adequately represent that life without an indeterminate degree of metaphor and metonymy. A 'bisy' ploughman may, after all, be little better than a busy palmer. So the plough comes to figure, in the context of Piers's new resolution, as another externality, like the pike-staff; and it suffers the same fate: 'Of preieres and of penaunce my plough shal ben herafter'. It is as if the images which carry Langland along are consumed in the process.

IV

Perhaps the most peculiar and perplexing feature of the second vision, as I have described it, is the degree of interference on the literal level of the allegory. This is sufficiently common in Langland's work to be considered characteristic. It contributes to the general 'lack of a sustained literal level' noted by Miss Woolf among the chief 'non-medieval qualities' of *Piers Plowman*.[8] A good example, to add to the shelving of the pilgrimage and the tearing of the pardon, is provided by Passus XVIII. By the beginning of this passus Langland has already made quite elaborate preparations for presenting the passion as a joust between Jesus and the powers of evil. Jesus is a young knight, instructed by Piers and wearing his mentor's armour, who rides into Jerusalem, announced by

[8] 'Some Non-Medieval Qualities of *Piers Plowman*', *Essays in Criticism* 12 (1962), p. 112.

the herald Faith, to do battle with his enemies in a joust presided over by Pilate. Langland could easily have sustained this allegory, as other medieval writers, such as Bozon, had done before him. Instead, he allows such interference from the Bible story that the joust is almost forgotten. There are references to the apocryphal story of Longinus, the blind knight who 'jousted' with the dead body of Jesus (see XVIII. 78–91); but the joust between Jesus and Satan, the expected climax of the action, simply never takes place. The few remaining references to the matter (e.g. in line 368) therefore strike the reader as sustaining a metaphor rather than carrying on an allegory.

Serious objections can undoubtedly be raised against this mode of proceeding. It is foreign, one might say, not only to the 'typical medieval allegories' of which Miss Woolf speaks, but also to the very nature of allegory itself. An allegorical story is, in one very simple way, unlike a metaphor. A metaphor, however long it may be sustained, has no exclusive rights: the author is always free to dispense with it whenever he feels that his real subject would be better served that way. An allegorical story, on the other hand, has itself a kind of 'reality'—the reality of the literal level—and for that reason the author, however much he may digress and delay, cannot simply dispense with it. If he chooses to represent the good life allegorically as a pilgrimage or the passion as a joust, one might say, he must stand by his choice. A full-scale allegorical action can perhaps never be in all its parts equally congruous with, or adequate to, its creator's intended meanings; so an author who wants to write allegory at all must be prepared just to tolerate some incongruity and inadequacy. Otherwise, if he allows his intended meanings to interfere with the course of his chosen action whenever it suits him, he may well fail to communicate altogether. When the discarded parts of his allegory return to haunt him in the shape of metaphors, for example, his literal level may become hopelessly confused. For as Eliot says in his essay on Dante, 'allegory and metaphor do not get on well together'.

It cannot be denied that Langland's two interferences with the chosen action of his second vision have both given rise to confusions of this sort among his modern readers; and the

C poet's omission of the tearing of the pardon suggests that one of them at least puzzled his contemporaries too. Clearly there has been some failure of communication here. Yet it seems to me equally clear that the vision would be a poorer thing if Langland had *not* interfered as he did. I fear that this paradoxical opinion needs more justification than I have been able to find for it. Perhaps it is partly that the gradual super-session of the pilgrimage and the sudden tearing of the pardon are both, in their different ways, such authentically dream-like inventions. Langland's visions do, as Miss Woolf contends, have a greater sense of true dream about them than most medieval visions; and that is a good reason for valuing them. But more important, perhaps, is that the two inventions in question represent so powerfully, in their dream-like way, that peculiar movement of Langland's thought which I have already tried to describe as a 'serpent-like' movement towards more inward statements. This mode of movement, as the case of the second vision shows, runs counter to the demands of the 'sustained literal level'; but it seems essential to the progress of Langland's poem. Without the tearing of the pardon, the second vision would in itself be a more perfect whole; but it would, after all, stop the poem dead.

6. THE AUDIENCE OF *PIERS PLOWMAN* *

It is sometimes said that the medieval poet, writing before the invention of printing, worked for a strictly local audience. He had in mind, not a national reading public (there was no such thing), but whatever public his immediate environment offered—whether the household of a great lord, or a gathering of peasants 'yn gamys and festys and at the ale'.[1] The spread of a poet's reputation beyond the immediate circle of his listeners was a very slow and uncertain process, depending upon personal contacts and recommendations, and limited by the expense and rarity of manuscripts. Only the wandering minstrel, it is suggested, could hope for a wide reputation in his lifetime.

This account, highly simplified and selective as it is, applies well enough to some of the poets of the fourteenth-century Alliterative Revival. The Revival itself was a local affair, centred on the West and North-West. The romance *William of Palerne* was translated from the French by a local poet at the command of a local magnate;[2] and poems like *Gawain* and the *Morte Arthure* were perhaps produced in one or other of the baronial courts of the region.[3] The line 'fill freschely and faste, for here a fit endes', with which each section of *Wynnere and Wastoure* is concluded, testifies to the intimate closeness of the circle for which such a poem was composed; and there is no evidence that any of these poems reached a wider public. The testimony of manuscripts is treacherous—losses can never be calculated—but it seems more than chance that so many of the alliterative poems survive in only one manuscript (*Gawain*, *Pearl*, *Patience* and *Cleanness*, *Morte Arthure*, *Destruction of Troy*, *Wynnere and Wastoure*, etc.),

---

* First published in *Anglia* 75 (1957), 373–84; reprinted here with corrections and a new Postscript.

[1] Robert Mannyng of Brunne, *Handlyng Synne*, ed. F. J. Furnivall, EETS o.s. 119, 122 (1901, 1903), l. 47.

[2] Sir Humphrey de Bohun. See the poet's own statement, *William of Palerne*, ed. W. W. Skeat, EETS e.s. 1 (1867), ll. 163–9.

[3] See the interesting essay of J. R. Hulbert, 'A Hypothesis Concerning the Alliterative Revival', *Modern Philology* 28 (1931), 405–22.

where the *Canterbury Tales* survive in over eighty, and *Piers Plowman* in over fifty.

The contrast, in the matter of surviving manuscripts, between *Piers* and the other poems of the Revival is suggestive. The argument that religious and didactic works stood a better chance of survival than secular ones no more explains the many manuscripts of *Piers* than it explains the eighty-two copies of the *Tales*. The other religious and didactic works of the Revival fare little better than the romances and chronicles. It seems that *Piers* had an extensive popularity among some class of the community not normally reached by alliterative poetry. This was the contemporary audience of *Piers Plowman*, whose significance I wish to consider.

The first question is: What kind of person owned and read copies of the poem in the fourteenth century? Three pieces of contemporary evidence suggest an answer. First, a copy is once mentioned in a fourteenth-century will. In 1396 Walter de Bruge, a wealthy canon of York Minster, bequeathed 'unum librum vocatum Pers Plewman' to Dominus Johannes Wormyngton[4] (the next mention of the poem in a will comes some forty years later when John Wyndhill, Rector of Arncliffe, left a copy to one John Kendale[5]). Second, there is the mention of 'Peres Plouhman' in the letter of the priest John Ball to the peasants of Essex during the rising of 1381. This in itself might prove nothing. It is quite possible that Piers was an established traditional figure before Langland introduced him into his poem—or at least that the name Piers was conventional for a ploughman. But the veiled reference at the end of the letter to 'do wel and bettre' seems to establish that Ball knew Langland's poem—and that he knew it well enough to draw on its terminology in a moment of crisis. It does not prove that he assumed a knowledge of the poem in his peasant audience; only that he himself, a priest, knew it.[6]

---

[4] *Testamenta Eboracensia*, Surtees Society, vol. i (London, 1836), p. 209. See Greta Hort, *Piers Plowman and Contemporary Religious Thought* (London, 1939), pp. 156–7, for a brief discussion of Langland's audience in the light of the wills. See also *Piers Plowman*, ed. W. W. Skeat, Part IV, EETS o.s. 81 (1884), p. 864 (Index IX, 'Notices of *Piers Plowman*').

[5] *Testamenta Eboracensia*, vol. ii (London, 1855), p. 34.

[6] For the text of Ball's letter, see K. Sisam, *Fourteenth Century Verse and Prose* (Oxford, 1921), p. 160.

The third piece of evidence is afforded by the fourteenth-
century manuscripts of the poem. From their general quality,
which is inferior to the often very elaborately decorated
copies of Chaucer's works, they seem not to have circulated
among the rich patrons and bibliophiles of the court. More
positive evidence is provided by one of the fourteenth-
century copies of the A version of the poem—the Vernon
Manuscript, from which Skeat printed his A text. This manuscript is a thick miscellany of religious prose and verse, dating
from round about 1385. *Piers* rubs shoulders with the *Ancren
Riwle*, Rolle's *Form of Perfect Living* and the *Treatise of the
Active and Contemplative Life*, with the *Prick of Conscience*
and the *Northern Homily Collection*. The occurrence of *Piers*
so early in such a collection is suggestive, particularly when
there is reason to think that it once had a place in at least one
other miscellany of the same kind—the imperfectly preserved
Simeon Manuscript (BL MS Add. 22283). This manuscript
reproduces almost exactly the contents of the Vernon Manuscript up to a point where an unknown number of leaves is
missing. *Piers* occurs towards the end of the Vernon collection; and it is almost certain that the Simeon Manuscript,
continuing to reproduce the Vernon contents, included a text
of the poem in its missing leaves.

The nature of the contents of these miscellanies leaves no
doubt that they were intended for the clergy. More specifically,
they seem to belong with the many other manuscripts of this
period which formed part of the general movement in the
Church to combat the ignorance of the parish priests and
lower clergy. W. A. Pantin refers to the part played in this
movement by 'miscellaneous collections of short didactic
treatises', quoting a manuscript (Bodley 110) whose contents
resemble those of the Vernon and Simeon collections.[7] This
may be a mere coincidence; but the presumption that our
manuscripts belong, at least, somewhere within the Church
is very strong.

Piers, then, owned by a Yorkshire canon, known if not
owned by an Essex priest, included—probably—in at least two
religious miscellanies, seems, on surviving contemporary

[7] W. A. Pantin, *The English Church in the Fourteenth Century* (Cambridge,
1955), pp. 277–80. On Vernon and Simeon, see also Postscript below.

evidence, established among the clerks. Nothing supports the view, sometimes put forward or implied, that Langland was a popular poet, writing to such an audience as was reached by the tribe of Sir Thopas. The complexity and allusiveness of the poem's content (the knowledge it assumes of traditional biblical interpretation, for example) make this unlikely anyway.[8]

It seems from surviving evidence that *Piers* was unusual among alliterative poems in attaining this sort of currency among the clerks. This would explain why it alone survives in so many manuscripts, for the audience of clerks was, and always had been in medieval England, one which cut across local boundaries. For centuries, indeed, it had been the one national audience—though not, until the late Middle English period, an audience for writing in English. The taste of the clerks, at a time when they were coming to read devotional works in the vernacular rather than in French or Latin, is well represented in the Vernon and Simeon collections. It can hardly be said, on this showing, that they were the right audience for a native poet. Their almost exclusive interest in didactic content encouraged the hack versifier. Nearly all the Vernon contents which must, on formal grounds, be classified as poetry, are nothing more than treatises in verse (the *Northern Homily Collection*, for example). The authors used certain elementary verse forms because they make the material memorable and easy to read. Their work belongs to didactic, not to literary, tradition. With the exception only of the group of lyrics printed by Carleton Brown in his *Religious Lyrics of the Fourteenth Century*, *Piers* is the only poem in the collection which offers more than the didactic value of its content to the reader. It is unique in drawing on the living literary traditions of the Revival for what might be called a national public with specialized, non-literary interests. This helps towards understanding the peculiar place of *Piers* in the Revival. But first, a further factor must be taken into account.

The picture of the national audience of clerks and the local audiences of laymen needs, at least by the fourteenth century,

---

[8] See D. W. Robertson and B. F. Huppé, *Piers Plowman and Scriptural Tradition* (Princeton, NJ, 1951).

considerable modification to fit the facts. There was growing up, during Langland's lifetime, a new kind of lay public, independent, like the audience of clerks, of any specific locality —the original, it might be said, of the modern reading public. This public was recruited from the growing class of men, outside the Church, who had enough money to buy manuscripts, and enough education to read them—such men as members of the rising bourgeoisie. By the fifteenth century, vernacular manuscripts to satisfy the demands of this public were being produced on a large scale, as the machinery of commercial book production and distribution took shape. It is clear that these developments reach well back into the fourteenth century, when the existence of 'stationarii' or book dealers is well attested. The commercial trade in manuscripts originated, as might be expected, in London and the two university towns; but by the end of the century it seems to have been working —albeit haphazardly—on something like a national scale. The rapid spread of Chaucer's reputation cannot be ascribed simply to the force of his genius. A system of literary intercommunications was being established by commercial interests, putting the layman in the picture, making him less and less dependent upon wandering minstrels and local poets for his listening and reading.[9]

Although this new public consisted of well-to-do laymen, it is clear that its demands were not restricted to secular literature. For the merchant or the small landowner, Piers was as acceptable a hero as Troilus. Indeed, among bequests of vernacular books in the fifteenth century, didactic and devotional works are much more numerous than secular ones. The new public for which the book-dealers catered seems, in fact, to have been highly conservative, preserving the pattern of traditional tastes. Chronicles and saints' lives, devotional works and romances alike were produced in separate, often unbound, manuscripts, or in thick miscellanies ('grete bokes'), for men like John Paston. The readers of the fifteenth century

---

[9] See, on the developing commercial book trade and the public for which it catered: L. H. Loomis, 'The Auchinleck Manuscript and a possible London Bookshop of 1330-1340', *PMLA* 57 (1942), 595-627; H. S. Bennett, 'The Production and Dissemination of Vernacular Manuscripts in the Fifteenth Century', *Library* 5th Series 1 (1947), 167-78; and the same author's *Chaucer and the Fifteenth Century* (Oxford, 1947), ch. V 'The Author and his Public'.

fed off the authors of the fourteenth. There was no patronage for a new movement here, no stimulus for authors to try and express the changing ideals of the time. Manuscripts of Chaucer and Langland multiplied. *Piers* finds a place in books written for this market side by side with Mandeville's *Travels* and chronicles of England. Certainly there is no question, by the fifteenth century, of *Piers* being read only by priests. The inventory of the books of a member of Lincoln's Inn in 1459 includes Langland's poem side by side with the *Canterbury Tales*, *Beves of Hamtoun*, and the *Siege of Troy*,[10] and there seems no reason to deny that such men were reading the poem during Langland's lifetime.

We must think, then, of *Piers Plowman* reaching two kinds of audience—the old audience of clerks, and the new one of prosperous, literate laymen. It is not necessary for the present purpose, nor is the evidence sufficient, to assess the relative importance of these two kinds of reader. The point is that both were equally unlike, and unlike in the same way, the groups of local listeners for which *Sir Gawain* or most other alliterative poems were written. In *Piers* we see, uniquely, alliterative poetry adapting itself, its conventions of language and structure, to the demands of this new situation—to an audience of heterogeneous literary experience and expectations, reached not through oral recitation but through the dissemination of manuscripts. I believe that many features of *Piers Plowman* can profitably be considered from this point of view—as products of such an adaptation. A poetic tradition must in some way be modified in the face of such new conditions of production as I have outlined above. Alliterative poetry had always demanded an unusually high degree of co-operation between the poet and his audience. It depended on shared literary experience—most obviously, on a knowledge of a specialized kind of poetic language. Such knowledge was, by the fourteenth century, effectively limited to certain parts of England—the areas to the north and west normally associated with the Alliterative Revival. Within these areas alliterative poetry could function as it had always functioned—before local audiences acquainted with, and delighted by,

[10] J. M. Manly and E. Rickert, *The Text of the Canterbury Tales* (Chicago, 1940), vol. i, p. 610.

its traditions. But Langland—himself, if we accept the conventional account, living in distant London—could depend on no such sympathetic audience of initiates. Why should John Ball, or Walter de Bruge, have known anything more than Chaucer of the ways of 'rum, ram, ruf'?

To suggest the kind of modifications to which the traditions of alliterative poetry were subject under such conditions, we may consider very briefly Langland's handling of the inherited poetic language.

Let us take, for the purposes of comparison, the two poems of the Revival most closely related in many ways to *Piers—Wynnere and Wastoure* and *The Parlement of the Thre Ages*. These poems may fairly be taken as representing the staple alliterative type for our purposes. They bear all the marks of having been produced for the older kind of local audience—for example, the line already quoted from *Wynnere and Wastoure*, 'fill freschely and faste, for here a fit endes', makes no sense in any other context—and there is no evidence to suggest that they achieved the kind of wide currency which we have noted in the case of *Piers*. A comparison between the language of these poems and that of Langland's poem will suggest the significance of this contrast.

Here, then, is a passage to illustrate the common poetic language of these poems—the beginning of the description of Youth, from the *Parlement of the Thre Ages*:

> The firste was a ferse freke, fayrere than thies
>   othire,
> A bolde beryn one a blonke bownne for to ryde,
> A hathelle on ane heghe horse with hauke appon hande.
> He was balghe in the breste and brode in the scholdirs.
>   (109–12)[11]

This fairly, though not too flatteringly, represents the poetic language of the Revival. There are, according to the lists given in J. P. Oakden's *Alliterative Poetry in Middle English*, three

[11] Ed. M. Y. Offord, EETS o.s. 246 (1959).

'chiefly alliterative' poetic words in these lines—*hathelle*, *blonke*, and *balghe*—and two more widely used poetic synonyms for man—*freke* and *beryn*. These words are deployed by the poet in emphatic parallel phrases ('ferse freke . . . bolde beryn one a blonke . . . hathelle on ane heghe horse') which here clog the development of the description—the first half of the second and third lines hardly does more than recapitulate the sense of the line before on a new alliterative letter. We are told three times that Youth was a man, twice that he was warlike, twice that he sat on a horse, and once that he intended to ride it. Alliterative poetry does not always press its points so hard; but it can hardly be denied that diffuseness of this kind is the characteristic fault of the poets of the Revival. They seem to rely on the intrinsic interest of the alliterative line and language to hold the audience's attention, as if, sometimes, the mere display of the words were enough. The sense is continually being forced to eddy back in order to include another synonym.

I do not find in Langland's poem this kind of primary pleasure in the alliterative poetic language. Langland often is diffuse; but his diffuseness is not of the kind illustrated above. His arguments may sometimes go round in circles; but this is not because they are being driven off their course in search of poetic synonyms. It would be impossible to find a passage like the one quoted above in *Piers Plowman*. *Piers* is distinguished within the Revival by the extreme economy with which the alliterative poetic diction is used—Oakden distinguishes only ten 'characteristically alliterative' words in the whole poem. I suggest that this feature of the poem is not fortuitous. A poetic language flourishes where it is a common language—this is true, at any rate, of the Middle Ages—shared in a given community by the poet and his audience. The naïve pleasure in alliterative words and phrases, indefinitely repeated, which marks some of the long narrative poems of the Revival, testifies to such a situation. It was not Langland's situation.

Significantly, where we do find 'characteristically alliterative' words and phrases used in *Piers Plowman*, it is in a new way—for secondary, ironical effects. Langland seems to be using the traditional language as a point of literary reference,

as it were from outside. Here is an example from Passus III.
Lady Mede has been arrested and brought before the king:

> Curteisly the clerk thanne, as the Kyng highte,
> Took Mede bi the myddel and broghte hire into
>   chambre.
> Ac ther was murthe and mynstralcie Mede to plese;
> That wonyeth in Westmynstre worshipeth hire alle.
> Gentilliche with joye the justices somme
> Busked hem to the bour ther the burde dwellede.
>
> (9–14)

Mede is being treated courteously, like a guest in a castle,
(Edward III was much admired for treating prisoners in this
way). The disingenuous politeness of the Westminster household is ironically pointed by the use of the language of the
alliterative romances. 'Murthe and mynstralcie' is a phrase
which occurs often in such poems (see for example *Gawain*
1952–3; 'With merthe and mynstralsye, wyth metez at hor
wylle, / Thay maden as mery as any men moghten'). It is
used again ironically by Langland in X. 48; and here, together
with the phrase 'busked hem to the bour', it serves to evoke
the genuine romance ideal of courtesy for a kind of mock-
courtly effect. Here, too, for the only time, the poetic word
'burde' is used of Lady Mede, implying the same kind of
ironical contrast with the heroine of an alliterative romance.[12]

This oblique use of the alliterative diction for an effect of
literary irony is not easy to parallel elsewhere in the poems of
the Revival. It is quite unlike the simple primary use illustrated from *The Parlement of the Thre Ages*; and it suggests
a more sophisticated and disengaged relation to the tradition,
such as might be expected from a poet writing for a heterogeneous and impersonal audience. Certainly it might be
expected from such a poet that he would play down the
traditional poetic language, if only for the practical reason
that many of the words would not be understood by many of
his readers; and we find Langland doing this. If the language

---

[12] For further instances of Langland's use of alliterative diction for ironical
purposes, see my *Ricardian Poetry* (London, 1971), pp. 34–5.

of *Piers Plowman* seems less remote from modern English than that of most of the alliterative poems, this is not only because of its dialect. It is because Langland was, from this point of view, on the edge of the alliterative tradition, little concerned with reproducing its peculiar linguistic effects. The contrast between his work and the verbal extravagances of the *Pearl* is striking.

In this respect, Langland is, of all the poets of the Revival, nearest to modern taste. He is least infected by the pernicious medieval idea of amplification 'longius ut sit opus' (the phrase is from Geoffrey of Vinsauf). He can be accused of 'circumcogitatio' but not of 'circumlocutio' or gratuitous poeticism. His impatience with such superfluous elaboration can be seen if we compare the opening of his poem with that of *Wynnere and Wastoure*. The convention of the allegorical dream had become part of the alliterative poet's stock-in-trade, and with it the convention of the dream prologue, explaining how and where the poet fell asleep. This usually involved some kind of formal description of a pleasant landscape ('locus amoenus') built up, perhaps, according to the precepts of the rhetoricians. Such a set piece occurs at the beginning of *Wynnere and Wastoure*:

Fele floures gan folde ther my fote steppede.
I layde myn hede one ane hill, ane hawthorne besyde,
The throstills full throly they threpen togedire,
Hipped up heghwalles fro heselis tyll othire,
Bernacles with thayre billes one barkes they roungen,
The jay janglede one heghe, jarmede the foles,
The bourne full bremely rane the bankes bytwene.

(35–41)[13]

This is very medieval. The author, who refers to poets as 'makers of myrthes that matirs couthe fynde' in the course of the prologue, builds up the piece by an accumulation of detail which conforms exactly to his description of the poet as 'finding matter' (the vernacular equivalent of the rhetorician's

[13] Ed. T. Turville-Petre, in B. Ford (ed.), *Medieval Literature: Chaucer and the Alliterative Tradition* (Harmondsworth, 1982).

'inventio'). The corresponding passage in *Piers Plowman* is quite different:

> I was wery forwandred and wente me to reste
> Under a brood bank by a bourne syde;
> And as I lay and lenede and loked on the watres,
> I slombred into a slepyng, it sweyed so murye.
>
> (Prol. 7–10)

Here the vision prologue is stripped down to its bare essentials. All we are given in the opening lines of the poem is the sun, the bank, and the brook, and the dream begins. For Langland, the dream is a structural device; and he does not exploit its decorative possibilities in the manner of *Wynnere and Wastoure*, *The Parlement of the Thre Ages*, or *Pearl*.

Here, as in the matter of the alliterative diction, the comparison goes in Langland's favour. Certainly he falls victim to a hypertrophied poetic language, a conventional automatism of style and treatment, much less frequently than most poets of the Revival. I suggest that this was, at least partly, because Langland did not belong to, or write exclusively for, those regional groups to whom such predictable effects were as acceptable as the equally predictable course of a church service. *Piers Plowman* would have been impossible, of course, without the alliterative tradition; but we must recognize Langland's special relation to this tradition. It is a relation which permits our talking of his originality much more freely than we would of any other poet of the Revival. His handling of the vision form itself is a case in point (the use, in the B version, of ten visions, with a very definite structural function, cannot be paralleled elsewhere in medieval literature). Langland's originality, the special characteristics which his poem presents when we compare it with other poems of the Revival, bear, I suggest, some relation to his unique situation with regard to his audience. Langland's was the modern situation—more modern than Chaucer's. His poem was destined for an audience as variegated as our reading public; and this, at the least, freed him from some of the exact pressure exerted on an author by a close familiarity with his readers and their tastes. Very few medieval authors were as free as Langland of such pressures; certainly none of the alliterative poets. When we compare *Piers Plowman* with *Sir Gawain* we will be aware both of gains and losses. The proportion of gain to loss is another subject. The differences are indisputable. It has been argued in this paper that an understanding of the unique nature of Langland's audience helps in the discussion of such points—and they are points which demand discussion if the Alliterative Revival is to be brought into any sharper focus.

POSTSCRIPT

Since the preceding essay was published in 1957, much has been done to bring the Alliterative Revival into sharper focus, as may be seen in Thorlac Turville-Petre's *The Alliterative Revival* (1977). Turville-Petre discusses the general question of audience on pp. 40-7 of his book, and more recently Anne Middleton has written on 'The Audience and Public of *Piers Plowman*'.[1] No fresh evidence about the contemporary readership of *Piers* has come to light in wills, inventories, or other such documents since 1957; but much more is now known about the *Piers* manuscripts, thanks especially to the labours of Kane and Donaldson in their Athlone editions of the A and B texts, and also to the work of codicologists and philologists.[2]

Of those manuscripts which may be dated before 1400, and which therefore have the best prima-facie claim to provide evidence of the readership for which Langland himself actually wrote, four require special mention here. The two manuscripts referred to in the preceding essay, Vernon and Simeon, are both now said by Dr Doyle to have been produced

---

[1] In David A. Lawton (ed.), *Middle English Alliterative Poetry and Its Literary Background* (Woodbridge, 1982), pp. 101-23. See also E. Salter, 'The Alliterative Revival', *Modern Philology* 64 (1966-7), 146-50, 233-7.

[2] G. Kane (ed.), *Piers Plowman: The A Version* (London, 1960), describing the A MSS on pp. 1-18; G. Kane and E. T. Donaldson (eds.), *Piers Plowman: The B Version* (London, 1975), describing the B MSS on pp. 1-15. On the Vernon and Simeon MSS, see A. I. Doyle in V. J. Scattergood and J. W. Sherborne (eds.), *English Court Culture in the Later Middle Ages* (London, 1983), pp. 167-8. M. L. Samuels reports the results of a study plotting the scribal language of thirty-six *Piers* MSS on a dialect map: *English Studies* 44 (1963), 94. He concludes that 'the B-texts had a more cosmopolitan circulation' than either A or C.

'about 1390–1400, by scribes of north Worcestershire orthography'. Doyle suggests that Vernon was originally intended for an 'armigerous owner or donor', but in the event 'may have gone to a religious community'; and elsewhere he describes both manuscripts as 'ledgers or couchers for a community or a household, in a church, refectory, hall, chapel, chamber or cell'.[3] A much clearer—indeed, a very striking—instance of clerical ownership of a *Piers Plowman* in or very shortly after Langland's lifetime may be provided by MS Bodley 851, if the copy of *Piers* which this volume contains formed part of the original compilation, and if that compilation belonged, as A. G. Rigg argues, to John Wells, monk of Ramsey, scholar and later *prior studentium* of Gloucester College, Oxford, and noted opponent of Wyclif. For Wells is known to have died in 1388.[4] Whether or not Rigg is right in holding that the first part of the Bodley *Piers* represents a pre-A-text version of the poem, its presence in such a volume, belonging to a learned Oxford Benedictine, would provide notable evidence, to set beside Walter de Bruge's will, of the early interest taken by prosperous and learned churchmen in Langland's poem. The fourth manuscript to be mentioned here, the Ilchester copy of the C text (University of London Library MS [S.L.] V. 88), provides an early example of the London book trade taking a hand in the dissemination of *Piers*. Doyle and Parkes date this manuscript in the 1390s and attribute it to a professional London copyist (their scribe 'D'), whose hand they also trace in six copies of Gower's *Confessio Amantis*, two of the *Canterbury Tales*, and one of Trevisa's *On the Properties of Things*.[5] Thus *Piers* has already

---

[3] *English Court Culture*, p. 167; 'The Shaping of the Vernon and Simeon MSS', in B. Rowland (ed.), *Chaucer and Middle English Studies in Honour of R. H. Robbins* (London, 1974), p. 331.

[4] A. G. Rigg, 'Medieval Latin Poetic Anthologies (II)', *Medieval Studies* 40 (1978), 387–407; and A. G. Rigg and Charlotte Brewer (eds.), *William Langland, Piers Plowman: The Z Version* (Toronto, 1983). The Bodley 851 text of *Piers* is a composite: a text of the Visio regarded by Rigg and Brewer as antedating the A version (the 'Z version'), and a C text of the rest. The latter was added in the fifteenth century; but the former, according to Rigg and Brewer, 'was probably written in Oxford by John Wells of Ramsey Abbey and Gloucester College, some time between 1376 (or earlier) and 1388' (*Z Version*, p. 5). Even the later of these dates would make Bodley 851 the earliest dateable MS of *Piers*.

[5] A. I. Doyle and M. B. Parkes, 'The Production of Copies of the *Canterbury Tales* and the *Confessio Amantis* in the Early Fifteenth Century', in M. B. Parkes

taken its place, as early as the 1390s, in the repertoire of works which were to be copied over and over again in the following century for the growing reading public.

The preceding essay attempted to relate certain stylistic features of Langland's poem to the fact that he either envisaged from the start, or else soon found, an audience of readers more heterogeneous in their literary experience, and in particular less reliably knowledgeable about alliterative verse, than was normal for an alliterative poet of his day. Turville-Petre and Middleton have both objected, justifiably, that my argument overstated the occupational and social differences between Langland's audience and that of other alliterative poets. Turville-Petre characterizes the latter as consisting of 'the gentry . . ., knights, franklins and the clergy, the educated men often with positions of local authority';[6] and such a view of the typical alliterative audience leaves much less room than was allowed by Hulbert's 'baronial' hypothesis for drawing social distinctions between it and Langland's audience, as this is characterized by Middleton: 'Whether laymen or ecclesiastics, their customary activities involve them in counsel, policy, education, administration, pastoral care—those tasks and offices where spiritual and temporal governance meet'.[7]

Yet even if Langland wrote for exactly the same kinds of people as read other alliterative poems, an essential difference remains: 'The difference in the readership of *Piers Plowman* is less one of social class than of geographical distribution, at least in the fourteenth century. Langland's poem was designed to be understood by a far-flung audience, centred particularly on London and the midlands. Most other alliterative poems are composed with a more localised audience in mind, though later manuscripts often show that their readership had expanded far outside the west midlands.'[8] Since there is good reason to believe that formal alliterative verse flourished in certain parts of England (especially the West

and A. G. Watson (eds.), *Medieval Scribes, Manuscripts and Libraries: Essays Presented to N. R. Ker* (London, 1978), 163–210, pp. 195–6.

[6] *The Alliterative Revival* (Cambridge, 1977), p. 46.
[7] 'The Audience and Public of *Piers Plowman*', p. 104.
[8] Turville-Petre, *The Alliterative Revival*, p. 46.

Midlands and the North) and not in others, the ambition for such a 'far-flung audience' would itself be enough to face an alliterative poet with the requisite challenge. The fourteenth-century evidence is enough to show that Langland's poem did indeed achieve, as Middleton says, 'a virtually nationwide distribution within a generation', no doubt through both clerical and commercial networks of distribution: copied both in Worcestershire and in London, read by a canon of York, a hedge priest in the Home Counties, and (probably) a monk in Oxford. The character of the poem's style, not to speak of its message, suggests that such a supra-regional audience did not lie beyond the range of Langland's original ambition.

7. HONOUR AND SHAME IN *SIR GAWAIN* *AND THE GREEN KNIGHT*

Social anthropologists have devoted a good deal of attention to the twin themes of honour and shame. Their work has had an influence on classical studies, but it has generally been ignored by students of medieval English literature, with the notable exception of Derek Brewer.[1] In the case of *Sir Gawain and the Green Knight*, most readers seem to have taken matters of shame and honour for granted, as common-places of knightly romance. Perhaps the dubious reputation of previous 'anthropological interpretations' of this particular poem has deterred them from pursuing the matter.[2]

Two quotations from social anthropologists will recall the theoretical distinction which they make between 'shame cultures' and 'guilt cultures'. The first is from Ruth Benedict's study of Japanese society in the immediate aftermath of the Second World War:

True shame cultures rely on external sanctions for good behaviour, not, as true guilt cultures do, on an internalized conviction of sin. Shame is a reaction to other people's criticism. A man is shamed either by being openly ridiculed and rejected or by fantasying to himself that he has been made ridiculous. In either case it is a potent sanction. But it requires an audience or at least a man's fantasy of an audience. Guilt does not.[3]

[1] D. S. Brewer (ed.), *The Morte Darthur: Parts Seven and Eight* (London, 1968), Introduction, pp. 23–35 ('The Tragedy of the Honourable Society'); and 'Honour in Chaucer', *Essays and Studies, 1973* (London, 1973), pp. 1–19, reprinted in Brewer, *Tradition and Innovation in Chaucer* (London, 1982). See also Mark Lambert, *Malory: Style and Vision in 'Le Morte Darthur'* (New Haven, Conn., 1975), pp. 176–94.

[2] Exceptions are Edward Wilson, *The Gawain-Poet* (Leiden, 1976), pp. 125–31, referring to Brewer's essay on Chaucer, and A. C. Spearing, *The Gawain-Poet* (Cambridge, 1970), pp. 226–7. In his discussion of renown or fame as the main theme of *Sir Gawain*, Larry D. Benson makes many relevant points; but, using only literary evidence, he credits the poet with too critical an attitude towards a way of thinking which Benson regards (wrongly, I think) as obsolescent in the fourteenth century: *Art and Tradition in Sir Gawain and the Green Knight* (New Brunswick, NJ, 1965), pp. 207–48. Yvonne Robreau's lexical study of honour and shame in the French Vulgate prose romances, *L'Honneur et la Honte* (Geneva, 1981), contains many observations directly applicable also to *Sir Gawain*.

[3] *The Chrysanthemum and the Sword: Patterns of Japanese Culture* (London, 1947), p. 223.

The second quotation comes from J. K. Campbell's study of a community of Greek mountain shepherds:

Both guilt and shame are internal states of conscience but whereas shame is concerned with a man's failure to approach some ideal pattern of conduct, the reference of guilt and personal sin is to the transgression of interdicted limits. Shame relates to failure especially in comparisons with the achievements of others. It has an external sanction in the social abandonment which in some degree always accompanies public shame. The sense of guilt, on the other hand, is the consequence of acts which defy the commandments of God, whether they concern the relations between man and God, or social responsibilities that follow from common membership in a group. The external sanction against sin is the punishment inflicted by God and sometimes by a social group. An act may, of course, provoke both a sense of guilt and feelings of shame.[4]

As can be seen from these quotations, anthropologists' accounts of guilt and shame vary considerably in emphasis— partly, no doubt, because they have different societies in mind. It should be noted, too, that the distinction between 'shame cultures' and 'guilt cultures' is far from being an absolute one, as Benedict may be taken to suggest. Most cultures, certainly including that of fourteenth-century England, employ both kinds of sanction, in complex and varying combinations. Yet a reading of Campbell's book, and of the volume of essays entitled *Honour and Shame* to which he also contributed, cannot fail to prompt anyone interested in *Sir Gawain and the Green Knight* to further thought about the workings of honour and shame in its Arthurian world.[5]

I

Two main issues merit attention. First, the relation between the honour of an individual and that of the group to which

---

[4] *Honour, Family and Patronage: A Study of Institutions and Moral Values in a Greek Mountain Community* (Oxford, 1964), pp. 327–8.

[5] J. G. Peristiany (ed.), *Honour and Shame: The Values of Mediterranean Society* (London, 1966). See especially the essay by J. Pitt-Rivers, 'Honour and Social Status'. My own *Reading of Sir Gawain and the Green Knight* (London, 1965) paid too little attention to points of honour and failed to take sufficient account of the distinction between guilt and shame.

he belongs; and second, the relation of honour to virtue. Both these relationships take a problematical form in the latter phase of *Sir Gawain*—from the moment, that is, when Gawain agrees to conceal the lady's girdle from her husband. Up to that point, however, events at Camelot and Hautdesert raise no such problems. Whoever the poet may have been, he here displays an easy and apparently untroubled familiarity with principles of honour. In this first phase of the poem, in fact, the matter will present difficulties only to readers who belong to societies in which the concepts of honour and shame are no longer familiar, and who may therefore need to turn to anthropology for guidance.

The main business of the Green Knight at Camelot, as he later tells the hero, is to

> assay þe surquidré, ȝif hit soth were
> Þat rennes of þe grete renoun of þe Rounde Table.
> (2457-8)[6]

This reference to *surquidré* has been cited as evidence that the Arthurian court suffers from the sin of pride; but whatever the merits of that view, the present passage lends it no support. One does not test or 'assay' a deadly sin to see if it is well grounded. The pride in question here is evidently that of which Pitt-Rivers speaks: 'Honour is the value of a person in his own eyes, but also in the eyes of his society. It is his estimation of his own worth, his *claim* to pride, but it is also the acknowledgement of that claim, his excellence recognized by society, his *right* to pride.'[7] In this case it is the 'claim to pride' of a whole society, the brotherhood of the Round Table, which is being put to the test; and the test is of that severe and definitive sort which only an adversary can administer.[8]

---

[6] All quotations are from the Tolkien and Gordon edition, revised by Norman Davis (Oxford, 1967).

[7] *Honour and Shame*, p. 21.

[8] J. K. Campbell observes that social prestige among his Greek shepherds 'depends overwhelmingly on the opinions of enemies' and especially on 'the inability of enemies effectively to denigrate a family's reputation', *Honour, Family and Patronage*, pp. 264-5. See also *Honour and Shame*, pp. 202-3, on the 'agôn or ritual game' in which adversaries put each others' honour to the test.

The Green Knight's intention of challenging 'þe grete renoun of þe Rounde Table' appears from the very first, when, finding the place of honour on the high table vacant, he looks round to see 'quo walt þer most renoun' (231). In his first long speech (256-74) he refers to the *los* or fame of Arthur himself and the reputation of his knights for prowess and courtesy, with a provocative reservation (*'if* þou be so bold as alle burnez tellen') which is followed up in his speech of challenge by the deliberate insult of 'berdlez chylder' (280). When Arthur and his knights fail to respond immediately to this challenge, the Green Knight takes the first opportunity of declaring that the honour of the Round Table is now overthrown (*overwalt*):

'What, is þis Arthures hous,' quoþ þe haþel þenne,
'þat al þe rous rennes of þur3 ryalmes so mony?
Where is now your sourquydrye and your conquestes,
Your gryndellayk and your greme, and your grete wordes?
Now is þe revel and þe renoun of þe Rounde Table
Overwalt wyth a worde of on wy3es speche,
For al dares for drede withoute dynt schewed!'   (309-15)

Arthur reacts to this dishonouring claim with a hot flush of shame, followed immediately by violent anger:

     þe blod schot for scham into his schyre face
        and lere;
      He wex as wroth as wynde,
      So did alle þat þer were.   (317-20)[9]

Arthur's position, however, is paradoxical. The honour of the Round Table resides most of all in his person; and the Green Knight has singled him out for particular provocation ('if *þou* be so bold'). Yet he is also a crowned king; and a king, like the king in chess, stands to lose more than gain from being hazarded on offensive operations, especially on dubious operations such as that proposed by the Green Knight. Success

---

[9] Wilson, *The Gawain-Poet*, p. 128, notes the parallel between Arthur's shame and Gawain's at lines 2371-2.

could bring only a minimal gain in honour, but failure would be a disaster.[10]

It is in this context that one should understand the speech which Gawain makes when he offers to take the affair upon himself. His extravagant formality serves to affirm that the famed courtesy of the court can survive such incursions: it is a display of self-possession, comparable to the cool joking of Arthur later (470-7). The humility, too, is directed at the Green Knight. So far from requiring a response from the king, Gawain declares, his challenge can be met by the weakest (*sic*) of Arthur's followers—by a pawn, not a king. Humility is no more a Christian virtue here than pride is a deadly sin. If Gawain can claim no other merit than that Arthur's blood runs in his veins (356-7), then the Round Table stands to gain the greatest possible honour if he succeeds, and the least dishonour if he fails—'lest lur of my lyf'.

From this point on, the collective honour of the Round Table is invested in the person of Sir Gawain; and when he plights his troth to fulfil the terms of the Green Knight's contest, his word of honour carries with it more than his own personal reputation for integrity. The 'renoun of the Rounde Table' has been formally staked on his performance in the Adventure of the Green Chapel. Individual honour and the honour of the group are here inseparable, as in the traditional societies described by Peristiany: 'When the individual is encapsulated in a social group an aspersion on his honour is an aspersion on the honour of his group. In this type of situation the behaviour of the individual reflects that of his group to such an extent that, in his relations with other groups, the individual is forcibly cast in the role of his group's protagonist.'[11]

With the emergence of Gawain as protagonist, the poem first approaches the more difficult question of the relation of honour to virtue, but here too it seems for the time being to

[10] 'The possibility of being represented by a champion in the judicial combat was restricted to those who were judged unable to defend their honour personally: women, the aged or infirm, or persons of a social status which prohibited them from responding to a challenge, in particular, churchmen and, of course, royalty.' (Pitt-Rivers, *Honour and Shame*, p. 28.)

[11] *Honour and Shame*, p. 11.

see no problem. Indeed, the passage describing the pentangle, at the beginning of the second fit, clearly implies the inseparability of virtue from honour. Gawain's inner quality of *trawþe* or integrity—his faith in Christ and Mary, and his virtues of *fraunchyse*, *felaȝschyp* and the rest—is there displayed symbolically in the coat of arms which he presents to the world on his shield and coat armour. The significance of a knight's coat of arms in relation to his honour or dishonour ('blame') is expounded in Caxton's *Book of the Ordre of Chyvalry* as follows:

A token or esseygnal of armes is gyven to a knyghte in his shelde and in his cote by cause that he be knowen in the bataylle and that he be allowed [praised] yf he be hardy and yf he do grete and fayr feates of armes; and yf he be coward faulty or recreaunt, the enseygnal is gyven to hym by cause that he be blamed, vytupered and reprevyd. Th'esseygnal is also gyven to a knyght to th'ende that he be knowen yf he be a frende or enemy of chyvalrye, wherfor every knyght ought to honoure his esseygnal, þat he be kepte fro blame, the whiche blame casteth the knyght and putteth hym out of chyvalry.[12]

Since a knight in full armour with his visor down showed nothing of his face or body, heraldic signs were necessary for his identification in battle or tournament. The chief point of such identification, according to the *Book of Chyvalry*, was that the knight should receive his due of either praise or blame, honour or dishonour, for his performance. Hence the sign comes to be seen as itself, like its bearer, capable of being honoured: 'every knyght ought to honoure his esseygnal'. Similarly, to dishonour a coat of arms is to dishonour its bearer, as when a knight provokes an adversary to combat by striking with a spear-butt at the coat of arms displayed on his shield.

In the case of Sir Gawain, the relationship of peculiar intimacy between knight and sign is explained in moral terms. The pentangle, says the poet, 'apendez' to its bearer because, being itself a 'token of trawþe' both by its very nature and also on the authority of Solomon, it provides an ideally appropriate coat of arms for a knight who is himself supremely 'true'—'ay faythful in fyve and sere fyve syþez'.[13]

---

[12] Ed. A. T. P. Byles, EETS o.s. 168 (1926), p. 88.
[13] See *A Reading of Sir Gawain*, pp. 41-51.

Hence the pentangle represents both Gawain's moral being and his honour as a knight, in a fashion which discourages any attempt to disengage one from the other. His virtues are themselves *displayed* ('Gawan watz for gode *knawen*', 'he watz *funden* fautlez in his fyve wyttez'), and the comprehensive term which embraces them all, *trawþe*, itself also expresses the essence of knightly honour. For a medieval knight, as for the modern Greek shepherds studied by Campbell, 'honour is a condition of integrity'.[14]

Gawain's honourable standing does not lack for recognition in the household of Hautdesert. When he first arrives there, 'mony proud mon þer presed þat prynce to honour' (830, cf. 910-14); and subsequent conversations with host and hostess frequently revert to his honour and reputation (*honour, worschyp, prys, los, mensk*), as when the lady says:

> For I wene wel, iwysse, Sir Wowen ȝe are,
> Þat alle þe worlde worschipez quere-so ȝe ride;
> Your honour, your hendelayk is hendely praysed
> With lordez, wyth ladyes, with alle þat lyf bere.
>
> (1226-9)

The lady has her own questionable motives for this particular bit of honouring; but in any case the very *hendelayk* of which she speaks would make it impossible for Gawain simply to accept the bouquet. He responds with self-depreciation ('I am wyȝe unworþy'); and here as in the first fit, though in a different way, his humility serves the purposes of honour—and even, more paradoxically, of pride.[15] One of his favourite defensive moves is to turn his hosts' imputations of honour back upon them by invoking the doctrine that 'honour from the honourer proceeds'. Honour, unlike virtue, is 'always something imputed by others';[16] but only those who themselves possess the quality are capable of bestowing it, so the honour which they bestow may be said to be theirs in the first place. As a medieval French proverb puts it: 'L'honneur

---

[14] *Honour, Family and Patronage*, p. 269.

[15] 'Humilité, si est une virtus par coi l'en puet plus s'onor et son preu essaucier et avancier', French prose *Lancelot* cited by Robreau, *L'Honneur et la Honte*, p. 91.   [16] *Honour, Family and Patronage*, p. 270.

n'est pas en celuy qu'on honnore, mais en celuy qui l'honneur fait.'[17] Hence, when the host thanks him for the *worschip* and *honour* he has bestowed on the house by his presence over the Christmas season (1031-6), Gawain can reply with 'hit is yowrez, / Al þe honour is your awen'; and with the lady later, when more is at stake, he can claim that the honour she so sedulously does him 'is þe worchyp of yourself, þat noȝt bot wel connez' (1267). In the sophistry of honour, in fact, Gawain is more than a match for his hostess, as he shows when he declines her parting request for a glove as a memento:

> Bot to dele yow for drurye þat dawed bot neked,
> Hit is not your honour to haf at þis tyme
> A glove for a garysoun of Gawaynez giftez.   (1805-7)

Faced with the embarrassing necessity of refusing yet another of the lady's requests, Gawain neatly takes refuge in the honorific character of gifts. Ignoring the fact that what she really wants is a love-token, to which the calculus of intrinsic value does not apply, he observes that a trifling gift such as a glove would only dishonour her. Spearing rightly says that 'he also implies that no mere glove would be worthy of *his* honour', adding that 'it seems symptomatic that, like Shakespeare's Julius Caesar, he should now be referring to himself in the third person'.[18] But there is nothing new in this, as Spearing seems to imply: as we have seen, Gawain's acts of self-depreciation, so far from being at odds with his honour, have consistently served to maintain it.

Gawain's concern to maintain his honour in a household only too ready to celebrate it may well seem over-scrupulous; but he should not be regarded as ridiculously self-important, still less as sinfully proud. He sees himself, and is seen by his hosts (901-5), as a representative of Arthur's court. Indeed, the whole collective 'renown of the Round Table' rests, while the adventure lasts, upon his shoulders.

[17] J. W. Hassell (ed.), *Middle French Proverbs, Sentences, and Proverbial Phrases* (Toronto, 1982), H60.
[18] *The Gawain-Poet*, p. 204.

II

Up to this point in the story, towards the end of his last bed-room encounter with the lady, Gawain has succeeded in preserving his integrity and in upholding both his own honour and that of the Round Table; but in what follows, once he has agreed to conceal the girdle from the host, things become more complicated, both because it now becomes necessary to observe the distinction between guilt and shame, and also because individual and collective honour can no longer be simply identified.

The general distinction between guilt and shame is by no means free from obscurities, as can be seen by comparing the two accounts quoted at the beginning of this essay. In particular, it becomes much harder to isolate guilt from shame if one happens to regard God as just another case of what Benedict calls 'a man's fantasy of an audience'. However this may be, it is clear that in practice the 'internalized conviction of sin' fostered by Christianity has rarely if ever been able to dispense with the 'external sanction' of shame. In the later Middle Ages, as T. N. Tentler has shown, shame played an important part in the theory of the confessional.[19] It is a subject on which, as Tentler shows, theologians of the period exhibit mixed feelings. On the one hand, shame is suspect, both because 'confession should not spring from the coercion of human shame' and also because shame may lead to the hiding of sins; on the other hand, it is a powerful 'tool of discipline'. The shame which a sinner feels in the confessional is itself salutary (a good confession should be 'verecunda'), as is the belief that sins which he cannot bring himself to display to his priest will cause him more public shame later on: 'for it was popularly taught and believed that if one did not disclose his sins to a priest in private, they would be disclosed to all—saints, angels, and all creation—at the Last Judgement'.[20] The 'fantasy of an audience' can hardly go further than that.

From a theologian's point of view, Gawain's behaviour after his act of *untrawþe* could only show the dangerous

[19] T. N. Tentler, *Sin and Confession on the Eve of the Reformation* (Princeton, NJ, 1977), pp. 128-30.
[20] Tentler, p. 129.

limitations of the 'coercion of human shame' as a tool of penitential discipline, especially in knights. Shame, like honour, is bestowed upon knights by their peers.[21] Hence, it is only when Sir Bertilak de Hautdesert reveals his knowledge of the hero's dishonourable act (without, be it noticed, adding any aggravating circumstance to what Gawain already knows about it) that the latter appears to 'realize what he has done' and respond with the right degree of intensity:

> Þat oþer stif mon in study stod a gret whyle,
> So agreved for greme he gryed withinne;
> Alle þe blode of his brest blende in his face,
> Þat al he schrank for schome þat þe schalk talked.
>
> (2369–72)

Whatever view one may take of Gawain's confession to the priest at Hautdesert, it is clear that such intense shame and mortification (*greme*) plays no part in it; and the hero's manifestations of unease in the ensuing scene with his host reveal little more than a desire to get the awkward business over with. It would seem, as Spearing observes in his penetrating discussion of the point, that 'for him, as for many chivalric heroes, the criteria of conduct are not fully internalized'.[22] Gawain's act of *untrawþe* (not to speak, as he later does himself, of his cowardice and covetousness) is profoundly dishonourable; but only when he is actually dishonoured by the censure of a fellow knight does he feel its shame. This is in accordance with the principle stated by Pitt-Rivers: 'an action *may* be potentially dishonourable, but it is only when this action is publicly condemned that it dishonours'.[23]

The intensity of Gawain's shame is a dominating fact in the poem from this point on.[24] It is as if, in being delayed, it

---

[21] 'A man is answerable for his honour only to his social equals', Pitt-Rivers, *Honour and Shame*, p. 31.

[22] *The Gawain-Poet*, p. 226.

[23] Pitt-Rivers, *Honour and Shame*, p. 37. Compare Robreau, *L'Honneur et la Honte*, p. 167: 'le sentiment de honte semble ne jamais être ressenti sans qu'il y ait déshonneur public. Il ne se trouve en effet nul exemple, dans le *Lancelot-Graal*, où ce malaise soit ressenti par un personnage solitaire'.

[24] This shame, representing 'dishonour imposed, accepted and finally felt', is to be distinguished from that which Gawain feels when the lady first enters his

has accumulated at compound interest, like that of the sinner whose unconfessed faults are revealed to all creation at the Doomsday. Whereas Arthur's shame at the taunts of the Green Knight finds relief in justified wrath, Gawain, faced with the same adversary's unanswerable censure at the Green Chapel, can find relief only in a dubious outburst against women. And when he returns to Camelot, he must admit his shameful *unleuté* again, most painfully, to his companions of the Round Table:

> He tened quen he schulde telle,
> He groned for gref and grame;
> Þe blod in his face con melle,
> When he hit schulde schewe, for schame.
>
> (2501-4)

Here he can at least claim, as he could not at the Green Chapel, the honour of having voluntarily confessed his fault; but the shame of a knight, unlike that of a penitent, is not purged by confession.[25] A blot on the scutcheon is not so easily wiped off. Hence, Gawain declares that he must wear the green lace as a 'token of untrawþe' and a 'bende of blame' (mark of shame) for the rest of his life. This is evidently that 'shame to the world's end' of which Borns warns Lancelot in Malory's *Morte Darthur*.[26]

Yet there is another principle in the laws of honour which conflicts with the high principle of 'shame to the world's end', and which appears to override it in the poem's closing lines. This principle may be stated by saying that the verb *to honour* is a performative in older usage. If persons who themselves belong to the circle of honour, that is, choose to honour a person, then he is *ipso facto* honoured—and also *a fortiori* honourable, for how could a man be honoured if he

bedroom ('þe burne schamed' 1189): Pitt-Rivers, *Honour and Shame*, pp. 41-4. The latter represents that honourable sensitivity to the possibility of dishonour known in Middle English as 'shamefastness' (e.g. the *Book of the Ordre of Chyvalry*, pp. 77-8). See also Robreau, *L'Honneur et la Honte*, pp. 159-62.

[25] Contrast *Cleanness* 1115: 'þou may schyne þurȝ schryfte, þaȝ þou haf schome served'.

[26] Brewer, *The Morte Darthur*, p. 28. Cf. 'knyghtes ons shamed recoverys hit never', *The Works of Sir Thomas Malory*, ed. E. Vinaver, Ist edn (Oxford, 1947), p. 218. My discussion in *A Reading* misses the point of honour.

were not capable of being honoured?[27] The same curious logic applies to shame. Sir Thomas More cites 'a common proverbe, that shame is as it is taken', which means that a thing is only shameful if it is judged as such by those with the power to do so.[28] The corollary of this is that anyone who insists on seeing shame where competent judges have declared that there is none merely brings shame upon his own head. This is the point of the Garter motto, subjoined by someone, perhaps the poet himself, to the last stanza of *Sir Gawain*: 'Hony soyt qui mal pence', 'Shame be to him that evil thinks'. The famous story of King Edward and the lady's garter provides a striking instance of how a king, the supreme 'fount of honour', could convert an object of shame, or at least embarrassment, into an object of conspicuous honour, simply by declaring it to be so.[29]

This, of course, is just what happens to Gawain's 'bende of blame'. King Arthur and his knights agree to adopt and wear the lace as a mark of high honour:

> For þat watz acorded þe renoun of þe Rounde Table,
> And he honoured þat hit hade evermore after.
>
> (2519-20)

By this act, 'shame to the world's end' would appear to be converted into honour for evermore after.[30] There is an interesting parallel to this triumphal conversion in the writings of the mystic Julian of Norwich (striking evidence of the

---

[27] Cf. Cicero in the *Brutus*: 'Since honour is the reward for excellence given to someone by the judgement and enthusiasm of the citizens, he who has received it by their opinion and choice seems to me both honourable and honoured [*et honestus et honoratus*]'; cited by D. J. Gordon, 'Name and Fame: Shakespeare's *Coriolanus*', in *The Renaissance Imagination* (Berkeley and Los Angeles, 1975), p. 210.

[28] B. J. Whiting, *Proverbs, Sentences, and Proverbial Phrases from English Writings Mainly Before 1500* (Cambridge, Mass., 1968), S195.

[29] The story is first recorded by Polydore Vergil and John Selden, but may well go back to some actual event in 1347: see Richard Barber, *The Knight and Chivalry* (2nd edn., Ipswich, 1974), pp. 304–5. On the motto, see Pitt-Rivers, *Honour and Shame*, p. 37.

[30] In the later version, *The Grene Knight*, the conversion is only partial, for the Knights of the Bath here wear the lace only 'Untill they have wonen their shoen, / Or else a ladye of hye estate / From about his necke shall it take, / For the doughtye deeds that hee hath done' (504–7), ed. J. W. Hales and F. J. Furnivall, *Bishop Percy's Folio MS* (London, 1867–8).

deep penetration of shame-thinking into Christianity). Medi-
tating on her thirteenth revelation, Julian reflects that in
heaven 'synne shalle be no shame, but wurshype to man . . .
for there the tokyn of synne is turnyd to worshyppe'.[31] Just
so Gawain's token of sin is turned to worship at Arthur's
court.

Yet the end of the poem is not simply triumphal. We see
king and court offer Gawain 'comfort' (2513), but we do not
see him take it; and even the public acclamation of the lace
cannot dispel suspicion that it will remain for Gawain himself a 'bende of blame'. If there is indeed, in the poem's final
tableaux, some such unresolved contrast between collective
honour and individual shame, what does it signify? One
interpretation, favoured by many, is that Gawain has learned
from the Adventure of the Green Chapel (or perhaps possessed
from the start) higher standards of honour and ethics than
those of his brother knights, so that success by their standards
is failure by his. 'Shame', as Campbell observed, 'is concerned
with a man's failure to approach some ideal pattern of conduct'; and perhaps only Gawain perceives the ideal pattern
clearly enough to know how far he has failed to achieve it.
The court does not understand the pentangle.

However, in defence of Gawain's comrades, it should
be recalled that their collective honour—the 'renoun of
the Rounde Table'—was staked specifically on their representative's performance in the Green Knight's Christmas
game under the rules laid down with such emphasis and
precision at Camelot (285-98, 382-5, 395-7, 448-53): he is
to strike a single blow, and then present himself at an ap-
pointed time and place to receive, without offering any
resistance, a single return blow. Gawain, on behalf of the
court, has fulfilled all these testing conditions to the letter.
The knights can therefore legitimately claim that, despite
a couple of moments of understandable apprehension, they
have succeeded in vindicating that proud reputation which

---

[31] *A Book of Showings to the Anchoress Julian of Norwich*, ed. E. Colledge
and J. Walsh (Toronto, 1978), Long Text, Chapter 39 (pp. 445, 447). Later in the
same chapter, Julian speaks of the wounds of sin which, though healed through
contrition, 'be sene before god, nott as woundes but as wurshyppes' (p. 452).
Cf. the passage from Mirk's *Festial* quoted in *A Reading of Sir Gawain*, p. 143.

Bertilak set out to 'assay'. The renown of the Round Table is not 'overwalt': on the contrary, yet another marvellous and perilous adventure has been added to the roll of honour. From this point of view, the court's, Gawain's failure at Hautdesert may justifiably be considered as a side-issue; for the exchange of winnings agreement was entered into by the hero on his own account, and did not form part of the conditions of the adventure as registered at Camelot. On the other hand, it is equally easy to see that it would have been adding to his personal dishonour for Gawain to have concealed his failure in *trawþe* from his fellow knights, or indeed to have too readily accepted their comfort in the matter. For him it cannot be a side-issue, for his personal honour was at stake in the exchange of winnings agreement just as much as in the beheading game; and his failure to honour his word in that agreement is a real, and perhaps a lasting, cause of personal shame.[32]

Readers belonging to modern industrialized societies are quick to take a sceptical view of sentiments of honour and shame, and to impute similar views to old authors. The fact, in particular, that these sentiments depend so much upon what other people know and think (as in the case of Criseyde's honour in Chaucer's poem) arouses cynical reflections. So it is by no means unnecessary to be reminded by social anthropologists such as Campbell and Pitt-Rivers that considerations of honour and shame can play a fundamental part in thought-structures of societies other than our own. Such is the case, I have suggested, in the societies of Camelot and Hautdesert, as portrayed in *Sir Gawain*. The poem is not *about* honour and shame. Rather, it seems to take them largely for granted in its Arthurian world, and displays from start to finish an ingrained familiarity with principles which are at best strange to the modern reader, and at worst thoroughly objectionable—honour from the honourer proceeds, for

---

[32] There is no need to insist on the fact that, as Barber observes, it was 'the particular mystique of the word of honour . . . perhaps more than any other single feature, that distinguished the way of thought of the knight', *The Knight and Chivalry*, p. 44. Compare the passage from the French prose *Lancelot* cited by Robreau, *L'Honneur et la Honte*, p. 131: 'puis que nous l'avons juré nous ne poons pas aler encontre. Car dont ferions nous desloialté et puis que hons est de desloialté atains il ne puet estre miex honnis'.

instance, or shame is as it is taken. Certainly the *Gawain*-poet's vision of the world was not bounded by the limitations of a chivalric shame culture. His poem marks those limitations in showing how Gawain's moral self-scrutiny remains dormant until it is woken by the reproaches of a fellow knight. Yet Gawain's fear of shame is not an ignoble thing; and for him, as for Chaucer's pilgrim knight, honour is the inseparable companion of that 'truth' or integrity which the pentangle represents.

8. FANTASY AND LANGUAGE IN
THE CLOUD OF UNKNOWING *

I

The Cloud of Unknowing is a treatise on contemplation, dating probably from the later fourteenth century. In it the anonymous author sets out to instruct a young 'spiritual friend' in the *via negativa*, a way of contemplation associated with the mystical writer known as pseudo-Dionysius the Areopagite. His teaching, baldly summarized, is as follows. God himself is unknowable. There lies between him and the human soul 'a derknes, and as it were a cloude of unknowing, thou wost never what'. This darkness is perpetual, except that God may 'sumtime paraventure seend oute a beme of goostly light, peersing this cloude of unknowing that is bitwix thee and him, and schewe thee sum of his privetè' (p. 62).[1] Such moments provide the supreme rewards of the contemplative life; but the author says that he dare not attempt to describe them, and would not wish to do so even if he dared. His subject is not what God, but what man can do: the 'work' of the contemplative. This work is twofold. The *via negativa* first requires the contemplative to 'foryete alle the creatures that ever God maad and the werkes of hem' (p. 16). The author expresses this idea in the image of a 'cloud of forgetting', a cloud which, unlike the cloud of unknowing, lies underneath the soul of the contemplative, cutting him off from all thoughts of created things. To forget these things is his negative work. His positive work is to strive to pierce the darkness above him 'and smite apon that thicke cloude of unknowing with a scharp darte of longing love' (p. 26). Man cannot know God; but he can love him, with a 'nakid entente directe unto God for himself' (p. 58). So, by the action of will rather than mind, he may hope to pierce the darkness in which God is enclosed, and achieve the mysterious goal of contemplation.

* First published in *Essays in Criticism* 27 (1977), 283–98.

[1] All quotations from *The Cloud of Unknowing and the Book of Privy Counselling*, ed. P. Hodgson, EETS o.s. 218 (1958). Spelling has been slightly modernized.

The author, writing with a certain informal frankness for the benefit of his friend, insists throughout upon the extreme difficulty of this contemplative work, even for those who are ready to devote themselves to it. The difficulties have their root in the very nature of the human mind, which the author expounds in one of the few systematic sections of his book (Chapters 63-67). The soul, he says, has four active powers ('worching mightes'): Reason, by which we may distinguish good from evil; Will, by which we may choose the good and love God; Imagination, by which we 'portray alle images of absent and present thinges'; and Sensuality, by which we 'have bodely knowing and feling of alle bodely creatures'. Since the chief source of the difficulties discussed in *The Cloud* lies in the 'imagination', the chapter devoted to this power (Chapter 65) is of special interest. Before the Fall of Man, we are told, imagination was ruled by reason. 'Bot now it is not so. For bot yif it be refreinid by the light of grace in the reson, elles it wil never sese, sleping or waking, for to portray diverse unordeind images of bodely creatures; or elles sum fantasye, the whiche is nought elles bot a bodely conseite of a goostly thing, or elles a goostly conseite of a bodely thing. And this is evermore feined and fals, and aneste [joined] unto errour.' (p. 117.) This passage, upon which my whole discussion is founded, asserts that the disordered imagination feeds the mind with 'fantasies'—that is, either physical apprehensions ('conseites') of spiritual things, or else spiritual apprehensions of physical things. I shall return later to the mysterious counsel against the 'goostly conseite of a bodely thing', after having first considered the less puzzling kind of fantasy: 'a bodely conseite of a goostly thing'.

II

The 'bodely conseite of a goostly thing' presents any contemplative with a problem which is simple to state but difficult to surmount. The *via negativa*, expounded here in the two cloud images, requires him to 'forget all the creatures that ever God made' and see God blind, as it were, without any attempt to 'conceive' him in creaturely terms. But the nature of the fallen imagination is such that even if we successfully stop thinking *about* created things, we will still go on thinking *with* them. The author allows, admittedly, that this difficulty may be overcome 'by the light of grace in the reason'; but such grace is not to be counted on, and in its absence the contemplative faces an endless struggle to transcend bodily 'fantasies' arising from his disordered imagination. 'Al the whiles that the soule wonith in this deedly body, evermore is the scharpness of oure understonding in beholding of alle goostly thinges, bot most specialy of God, medelid with sum maner of fantasie; for the whiche oure werk schuld be unclene, and bot if more wonder were, it schuld lede us into moche errour.' (p. 33.)

The author is acutely aware of how the readers of his own book may fall into this kind of error through an 'unclean' response to what he has written: 'Be wel ware that thou conseive not bodily that that is seide goostly. For trewly I telle thee that bodely and fleschely conseites of hem that han corious and imaginative wittis ben cause of moche errour.' (p. 94.) 'Curious' here implies a love of abstruse speculation for its own sake—a quality which the author regularly associates with 'imaginativeness' when sketching the kind of reader he does not want. The right kind of reader, by contrast, approaches spiritual mysteries in humility, not looking for exact or literal formulations; but even he will need constant warning and guidance. Thus, the author explains how metaphors drawn from physical experience occur in the discussion of sacred subjects. Christ, for example, cannot literally be said to 'stand' in heaven. 'By stonding is understonden a redyness of helping. And herfore it is seide comounly of oo frende to another, whan he is in bodely bataile: "Bere thee wel, felaw, and fight fast, and yive not up the bataile over lightly; for I schal stonde by thee." He meneth not only bodely stonding, for paraventure this bataile is on hors and not on fote, and paraventure it is going and not stonding.' (p. 109.) Here the author does no more than point out, in his customary downright style, an everyday metaphor which may occur in spiritual discourse. But spiritual discourse differs from its everyday counterpart in being radically metaphorical throughout. Even simple little words like 'up' and 'down', 'in' and 'out', are to be understood by the contemplative in transferred, spiritual senses (p. 114). For the *via negativa* transcends all physical categories—sensory, spatial, motor, and the rest—and leads, in terms of ordinary language, 'nowhere'. The author expresses this uncompromising truth in a memorable passage towards the end of *The Cloud.*

Wher another man wolde bid thee gader thy mightes and thy wittes holiche withinne thyself, and worschip God there—thof al [though] he sey ful wel and ful trewly, ye! and no man trewlier, and he be wel conseivid—yit for feerde of disseite and bodely conceiving of his wordes, me list not bid thee do so. Bot thus wil I bid thee. Loke on no wise that thou be withinne thyself. And schortly withoutin thyself wil I not that thou be, ne yit aboven, ne behinde, ne on o side, ne on other. 'Wher than,' seist thou, 'schal I be? Nowhere, by thy tale!' Now trewly thou seist wel; for there wolde I have thee. (p. 121.)

The masterly timing of this last exchange illustrates how the author's concern to engage with his reader serves to animate his prose.

Those who, despite such warnings, fall victim to the 'bodily conceiving' of spiritual words enter a realm of fantasy. The author dwells upon this with a certain dry humour. It is a dim and ridiculous region lying between, or outside, the two real worlds of the body and the spirit. Its errors or 'deceits' are sometimes quite simple, as when young disciples, hearing that men should lift their hearts up to God, stare up into the sky: 'As fast they stare in the sterres as they wolde be aboven the mone, and herkin when they schul here any aungelles singe oute of heven' (p. 105). It is easy enough to explain, as the author duly does, that God is not there to be seen in the sky; but that is not the end of the matter. A disciple may be weaned away from naïve physical literalism and still fall victim to 'fantasies' of a more insidious kind. Thus, in Chapter 52, the author gives a vigorous account of how conscientious contemplatives may misapply the physical notion of 'inwardness'.

They reden and heren wel sey that they schuld leve utward worching with theire wittes, and worche inwardes; and forthy that they knowe not whiche is inward worching, therfore they worche wronge. For they turne theire bodily wittes inwardes to theire body ayens [against] the cours of kinde; and streinin hem, as they wolde see inwardes with theire bodily iyen, and heren inwardes with theire eren, and so forthe of alle theire wittes, smellen, taasten, and felin inwardes. And thus they reverse hem ayens the cour of kinde, and with this coriousté they travaile theire imaginacion so undiscreetly, that at the laste they turne here braine in here hedes. (p. 96.)

Such well-meaning attempts to internalize 'outward workings' lead to a form of inward activity which, attempting to be both physical and spiritual at once, succeeds in being neither. Men who try to 'see inwards with their bodily eyes' will not see at all, either physically or spiritually. They 'feine a maner of worching, the whiche is neither bodily ne goostly' (p. 23, cf. 96). Such activity is against the course of nature (cf. pp. 23, 124) and results only in an unnatural 'straining' (cf. pp. 85, 89, 91, etc.) both of the spirit and of the body. In tracing these abortive internalizations of sensory and motor experiences, the author shows considerable perception. His discussion of how the words 'in' and 'up' may be misconceived (Chapters 51 to 61), in particular, explores some of the obscure processes by which the mind adopts spatial categories in thinking about non-spatial matters.

However, the discussion of 'bodely conseites of a goostly thing' in *The Cloud* is not entirely negative. A contemplative cannot be always 'nowhere'. Fantasies are inevitable, and not always distracting. Some may even be recommended, if only to beginners, as positively helpful. The author first suggests this in his discussion of two 'goostly sleightes', or spiritual tricks, in Chapter 32. If a contemplative finds difficulty in controlling his thoughts of sin, he should try to 'loke as it were over theire schuldres, seching another thing: the whiche thing is God, enclosid in a cloude of unknowing' (p. 66). The second trick is more subtle: 'When thou felist that thou maist on no wise put hem doun, koure thou doun under hem [the thoughts of sin] as a cheitif and a coward overcomen in bataile, and think that it is bot a foly to thee to strive any lenger with hem; and therfore thou yeeldest thee to God in the handes of thin enmyes.' (pp. 66–7.) Here the author substitutes for the familiar fantasy of spiritual warfare a fantasy of capitulation which, as he goes on to explain, can lead to self-knowledge and humility and so to God. Hence his striking paradox: 'thou yeeldest thee to God in the handes of thin enmyes'. In a later chapter he suggests another device of the same sort. Instead of trying to show God how much he desires him, the contemplative may think of himself as trying to hide his desire, 'right as thou on no wise woldest lat him wite hou faine thou woldest see him and have him or fele him' (p. 87). The author apologizes for suggesting such a childish trick. He wishes, he says, 'by soche a hid schewing bring thee oute of the boistousté [grossness] of bodely feling into the pureté and depness of goostly feling' (p. 88). The fantasies of hiding and capitulation are (or may be) less 'physical' than those of showing or fighting—less likely, that is, to be misconceived in a physical sense. 'For thou and I, and many soche as we ben, we ben so abil to conceive a thing bodily, the whiche is seide goostly, that paraventure, and I had boden thee schewe unto God the stering of thin herte, thou schuldest have maad a bodily schewing unto him . . .' (p. 90).

III

Above everything else the author of *The Cloud of Unknowing* prizes 'pureté and depness of goostly feling'; and he is poign-antly aware, as we have seen, of how 'bodily conceits' always threaten to contaminate this purity of feeling, in himself as much as in his readers: 'we ben so abil to conceive a thing bodily, the whiche is seide goostly'. However, such 'bodily conceits' are not the only sort of fantasy thrown up by the workings of the disordered imagination. The author's formal definition of 'fantasye', quoted earlier, includes two varieties: 'a bodely conseite of a goostly thing, or elles a goostly conseite of a bodely thing'. The first limb of this definition is undoubtedly the more important, so far as concerns the spiritual purpose of *The Cloud*; but the second has significance too—especially, as I shall suggest later, for an understanding of the book's style.

'A goostly conseite of a bodely thing': it may seem strange that this sort of fantasy should be coupled with the other, in a work such as *The Cloud*, as a potent source of deception, falseness, and error. Spiritual apprehension of physical things does not, after all, sound like a danger for contemplatives. One might even expect them to cultivate it. However, the implication of the author's double definition seems to be —must be, indeed—that the physical world has its own necessary and proper integrity as well as the spiritual world, and that to conceive either world in terms of the other imperils the integrity of both. The author nowhere states the matter in quite this form; but his real respect for what I have called the 'integrity' of the physical world appears unmistakably in many places in his work.

One such place is the beginning of Chapter 48. Here the author anticipates, as he often does, a misunderstanding. His warnings against 'bodily showings' of the heart to God do not mean, he says, that a contemplative should never express his devotion in audible words. 'God forbede that I schuld departe that God hath couplid, the body and the spirit; for God wil be servid with body and with soule, bothe togeders, as seemly is, and rewarde man his mede in blis bothe in body and in soule' (p. 90). Body and soule are both the creation of God, and both will participate in the joys of heaven after the general resurrection. Such ideas represent an orthodoxy established very early in Christian tradition. Only heretics, such as the Manichaeans, rejected the body in the interests of the soul. God created 'bothe togeders', and their coupling does not—or should not—impair the integrity of either. The author's sense of this twofold integrity appears even in his repetition (which might otherwise seem merely rhetorical) of small function-words: 'the body and the spirit', 'with body and with soule', 'in body and in soule'.

But what does it mean for God to be served 'with body and with soule, bothe togeders, as seemly is'? Other passages in *The Cloud* make the author's ideal of 'seemliness' quite clear. A discussion of the 'bodily bearing' of contemplatives, in Chapters 53 and 54, is particularly illuminating. The author here describes an amusing variety of eccentric habits: wild gestures, staring eyes, piping voices, gaping mouths, and the like; and he expresses his disapproval of them in no uncertain terms: 'bot yif God schewe his merciful miracle to make hem sone leve of, they schul love God so longe on this maner that they schul go staring wood to the devil' (p. 98).

Such 'unsemely and unordeinde contenaunces' (p. 99) are either simple hypocrisy or else they derive from the fantasies of the disordered imagination. For just as spiritual activities can be disturbed by bodily things, so bodily activity can be disturbed by spiritual things. The attempt to act physically in a 'spiritual' way leads to absurdity, to madness, or even to damnation. The true contemplative, by contrast, will respect the distinction between the bodily and spiritual realms, and observe the differing properties of each: 'Whoso had this werk [sc. of contemplation], it schuld governe him ful semely, as wele in body as in soule' (p. 100). Such a man will avoid ostentatious 'spiritual' eccentricities; but he will not necessarily be soft-spoken or unobtrusive. Like later anti-puritan satirists, indeed, the author of *The Cloud* regards soft or 'piping' utterance with some suspicion, as a possible sign of hypocrisy. 'Semely' behaviour is essentially natural behaviour. So if a man has a naturally loud voice, then he should speak out, not 'poerly and pipingly' but 'in hoelness of voice' (p. 101). The author goes so far as to assert that a true contemplative will always have a certain fulness of physical presence: 'His chere and his wordes schuld be ful of goostly wisdam, ful of fire and of frute, spoken in sad sothfastness, withouten any falsheed, fer fro any feining or piping of ypocrites' (pp. 100–1).

Another ringing affirmation of the integrity of the physical world occurs a little later, in the author's discussion of visions and revelations. He starts by explaining that bodily visions such as those of St. Martin or St. Steven are not to be understood literally. Their true significance is spiritual. 'And therfore late us pike of the rough bark [shell], and fede us of the swete kyrnel' (p. 107). The metaphor of nutshell and kernel is a commonplace in exegetical tradition; the nutshell is the literal sense, the kernel the inner spiritual sense. But the author fears that he may be misunderstood. Nutshells, after all, have no value at all; they are simply broken and thrown away. To treat the physical world like that would be heresy. Heretics 'ben wel licned to wode men having this custume, that ever whan they have dronken of a faire cup, kast it to the walle and breke it. Thus schul not we do, yif we wil wel do. For we schul not so fede us of the frute that we schul dispise the tree; ne so drinke that we schul breke the cuppe when we have dronken.' The similitudes of tree and cup certainly suggest, what the author later states, that 'alle bodely thing is sogette unto goostly thing' (p. 113); but they also affirm the indispensability of the physical world, and even its beauty. The cup is a *'faire* cup', and it is madness to smash it against the wall.

From passages such as these we can see that the author's double definition of 'fantasye' is not just a neat formal anti- thesis. It corresponds to a kind of doubleness, or dialectic, in his thinking about 'goostly thinges' and 'bodely thinges'. The dialectic starts from a presumed position of naïve literalism, which understands even statements of spiritual truths in a physical sense. The first and main movement is then to correct such erroneous physical fantasies: 'conseive not bodily that that is seide goostly'. The movement from physical to spiritual, however, will itself lead into erroneous fantasies of a different kind—the 'spiritual' fantasies of heretic or hypocrite—if it is carried too far. So it is checked by a second, opposite movement from spiritual to physical. This phase in the dialectic is marked by warnings against 'goostly conseites of bodely thinges' and by affirmations of the in- tegrity of the physical world.

IV

This zig-zag, to-and-fro dialectic between physical and spiritual may be observed in many places throughout *The Cloud*. It is one of the most characteristic movements of the author's thinking. Naturally, in a mystical treatise, the first movement of the dialectic (physical to spiritual) gets more stress than the second (spiritual to physical); but the latter, I want now to suggest, has a special interest for literary students in *The Cloud*. For the author's affirmations of the integrity of the physical world help to make sense of certain features of his language and style which might otherwise seem incongruous.

Since the *via negativa* requires a contemplative to 'foryete alle the creatures that ever God maad and the werkes of hem', we may expect any exposition of it to display some uneasiness with the language in which it is of necessity expressed; for language is itself the chief instrument and repository of all those creaturely ways of thinking and seeing which the contemplative must attempt to transcend. The author of *The Cloud* expresses this dilemma most clearly in the following passage: 'Beware that thou conceive not bodely that that is mente goostly, thof al it be spokin in bodely wordes, as ben thees: UP or DOUN, IN or OUTE, BEHINDE or BEFORE, ON O SIDE or ON OTHER. For thof al that a thing be never so goostly in itself, nevertheless yit yif it schal be spoken of, sithen it so is that speche is a bodely werk wrought with the tonge, the whiche is an instrument of the body, it behoveth alweis be spoken in bodely wordes.' (p. 114.) The phrase 'bodely wordes' has a double meaning here. It refers to the fact that language is a physical activity (a 'werk wrought with the tonge'), and also to the fact that language expresses ideas in physical terms ('up', 'down', etc.). The implication seems to be that the one fact follows from the other: i.e. that it is *because* language is a physical activity that it can only express ideas in physical terms. Perhaps the author did not mean anything quite so specific. In any case, the passage clearly expresses his awareness of an intrinsic unsuitability in human language for the expression of spiritual things.

A spiritual writer may respond to this difficulty by attempting in one way or another to change language. He may, that is, try to create special forms of expression more suited to his purposes than the customary 'bodily words'. From time to time the author of *The Cloud* seems to be doing this, when he employs unusual negative formations: 'unfele' (p. 45), 'unbe' (p. 84), and 'unknowing' itself. It should be noticed, however, that such negative formations appear to have enjoyed something of a vogue during the fourteenth century: Chaucer's Troilus speaks of 'unloving' Criseyde. 'Unfele' and 'unbe' may therefore not have seemed as strange to the original readers of *The Cloud* as they do to us. In any case, the author only rarely attempts such innovations. He is rather more inclined to another stratagem, which might be described as a minimizing of language. Thus in Chapter 7, he recommends for purposes of meditation such short, preferably monosyllabic, words as 'God' or 'love': 'for ever the schorter it is, the betir it acordeth with the werk of the spirite' (p. 28). He returns to the same theme in Chapters 36–40, where the two words 'God' and 'sinne' are recommended as suitably brief for meditations and also for prayer. In prayer, he says, the fewer words the better.

Such passages suggest the possibility of a special 'language of the spirit', distinguished from ordinary discourse by an extreme and challenging brevity and by abnormal formations such as 'unbe'. But this is not the language of *The Cloud of Unknowing*. So far from negating or minimizing ordinary language, indeed, *The Cloud* accepts and exploits it so fully that a modern reader may well be struck by the positively *un*spiritual manner of the book. The author often addresses his young friend in a highly idiomatic and colloquial fashion: 'They schul love God so longe on this maner that they schul go staring wood to the devil'. Nor does he show any inclination to avoid the 'bodily words' of ordinary language. On the contrary, sensory and physical images play an important part in his work. This is most obvious in the first part of the book, which is dominated by the two cloud images, each with its associated imagery. There is the 'cloud of unknowing' itself, upon which the contemplative is to 'smite' or 'beat' with his 'dart' of love; and there is the other cloud of forgetting, under which the contemplative is to 'cover' the creaturely thoughts which he has 'cast' or 'trodden' down. These two powerful image-clusters admittedly almost disappear in the later part of the book (after Chapters 31 and 32); but the author continues to use, as he has from the start, a rich variety of more casual, unfixed imagery. Metaphors abound throughout, some of them commonplace, like the 'fire' of God's love, but many of them strikingly vivid and physical. Thus we read about a 'lyame' (leash) of longing (p. 14), and a 'scharpe double-eggid dreedful swerde of discrecion' (p. 68). Sin is a 'rust' (p. 43), a 'foule stinking fen and donghille' (p. 46), and a 'lumpe' (p. 73). The soul may spring up to God 'as sparcle fro the cole' (p. 22), or fix its gaze on God 'as the iye of a schoter is apon the prik that he schoteth to' (p. 24), or take God's word as its 'mirour' (p. 72), or snatch at God's grace 'as it were a gredy grehounde' (p. 87), or 'wrechidly and wantounly weltre, as a swine in the mire' (p. 119).

I should like to make a brief digression here. Imagery such as I have just illustrated—we may call it 'homely', or 'physical', or 'concrete'—occurs in practically all Middle English writings. So widespread is such imagery, indeed, that one may well wonder whether an English author of this period could possibly have avoided using it, even if he had wanted to. It seems to have been a characteristic of Medieval English itself, of the language at large. If this is indeed so, then it cannot be enough simply to demonstrate, as criticism often does, that this or that writer exhibits the inevitable down-to-earth characteristics in his style. Such qualities may simply represent the English of the day, in which case they are better left unmarked by any special comment. Otherwise, the whole critical problem is to determine how, in a particular work, the idiomatic language functions or is accommodated. The concreteness is significant, in fact, only when it is made significant, as part of an author's whole effort to realize a story or explore an idea; and the nature of its significance can be understood only in this whole context. In Middle English styles, concreteness has no single, because no intrinsic significance.

It might appear at first sight that the 'bodily words' of Middle English, however appropriate they might be for the purposes of popular preaching, could only impede and subvert an exposition of the *via negativa*. In *The Cloud* the contradiction seems blatant: on the one hand, the author insists upon the need to 'forget all the creatures that ever God made' in the work of contemplation; on the other, his own exposition of this work teems with unpurged and creaturely imagery of a very solid and physical kind. However, this very solidity and physicality, which seems to exasperate the contradiction, in fact points towards its resolution. The author of *The Cloud*, as we have seen, believed that all human language expresses ideas in physical terms. There is therefore no question, for him, of escaping into a purely spiritual language. The task is rather to express spiritual things in such a way that the 'bodily words' do not become confused with their spiritual referents. To avoid such confusion, it is best that the inevitable physical imagery should be clearly recognized for what it is: physical. Thus the author's deep concern to uphold the spiritual character of 'goostly thinges' serves also to guarantee the physical character of the 'bodely thinges'. There is in his style no 'interfusing' of the spiritual and the physical, to use Wordsworth's term—still less, the kind of 'spiritualization' of the physical world associated with the poets of the later nineteenth century. The Cloud of Unknowing has nothing in common with the Celtic Twilight.

The style of *The Cloud* is thus characterized by a sharp definition of physical imagery which, so far from merely reflecting the English of the day, reflects the author's earnest and sustained thought about the relationship between physical and spiritual realities. The physical world is 'sogette unto goostly thing'; but it has its own integrity. Indeed, the author's sense of this integrity sometimes leads him into explanations which may strike a modern reader as almost comically literal-minded. We have already seen an example of this, in the passage explaining how a promise to 'stand by' a companion in battle is to be understood metaphorically: 'He meneth not only bodely stonding, for paraventure this bataile is on hors and not on fote, and paraventure it is going and not stonding'. The two pairs of alternatives, 'on hors' and 'on fote', 'going' and 'stonding', cover all the possibilities with the easy authority of a man who knows what real battles are like. Another passage shows how even the two prime spiritual symbols of cloud and darkness retain, on the literal level, their full physical reality: 'Wene not, for I clepe it a derkness or a cloude, that it be any cloude congelid of the humours that fleen in the aire, ne yit any derkness soche as is in thin house on nightes, when thy candel is oute' (p. 23). What he means, he says, by darkness is a 'lacking of knowing', and by the cloud a 'cloude of unknowing, that is bitwix thee and thy God'. These characteristic explanations present the reader with a strongly marked contrast between tenor and vehicle: on the one side, a fully physical cloud 'congealed of the humours that flee in the air' and an equally physical darkness 'such as is in thine house on nights, when thy candle is out'; and on the other side, fully spiritual states of 'unknowing'. The author's uncompromising insistence that he means the one and *not* the other may strike a modern reader as rather primitive: for we are accustomed, especially in post-romantic poetry, to symbols which seem to carry something of their physical reality over into the realm of the spirit. But this is precisely what the author of *The Cloud* does not want. Such symbols, to his thinking, would encourage readers to 'feine a maner of worching, the whiche is neither bodily ne goostly'. The two realms of the 'bodily' and the 'ghostly' have been joined by God; but that is no reason for confusing (or interfusing) them one with the other. Physical images are unavoidable in all human language; but we must constantly struggle to keep them distinct from the spiritual realities about which they enable us to speak. And that, paradoxically, means keeping them physical. It is dangerous to attempt to 'spiritualize' them. 'Ghostly conceits of bodily things', we recall, are among the fantastic products of the disordered imagination of fallen man.

V

All readers of *The Cloud* will see the difficulty of summing up the author's attitudes towards the relationship of physical to spiritual things. It would be easy to credit him with nothing more than a rather conventional 'wisdom'—a relaxed awareness that both physical and spiritual have their due place in the scheme of things. Such orthodox truisms do little justice to the living quality of the author's thought, the energetic tautness of his mind. Yet he does not go in much for formal, intellectually articulated exposition. It is as if, having submitted himself to the prolonged discipline of meditation, he feels no call to submit to the lower scholastic discipline of consecutive argument. He seems to trust his own developed sense of what is true and 'seemly' to save him from any errors into which his disjointed exposition might otherwise lead him.

Instead of a summary, then, let me conclude by looking briefly at a section of *The Cloud* which illustrates the main points I have been trying to make in this essay. I refer to the treatment of the story of Mary and Martha, in Chapters 17-21. The author adopts the traditional interpretation of this story (Luke 10: 38-42), according to which Mary and Martha are types—or, as he says, 'ensaumples'—of the contemplative and active lives respectively. Following Christ's words, which he translates as 'Marye hath chosen the best partye', the author stresses the superiority of the contemplative life, and warns 'actives' against judging what they cannot understand: 'Ye wote not what hem eileth. Lat hem sit in here rest and in here pley' (p. 55). Yet he is scrupulously fair to Martha and her complaint to Jesus:

> For me thinketh that sche schuld be ful wel had excusid of hir pleinte, taking reward to the time and the maner that sche seide it in. For that that sche seide, hir unknowing was the cause. And no wonder thof sche knewe not that time how Marye was ocupied; for I trowe that before sche had litil herde of soche perfeccion. And also, that sche seide it was bot curtesly and in fewe wordes. And therfore sche schuld alweys be had excusid. (p. 50.)

This passage illustrates how far the author's devotion to spiritual things is from an unbalanced fanaticism. Mary's total absorption represents the 'perfection' of the contemplative life; but Martha is not merely *im*perfect. 'Lord, dost thou not care that my sister hath left me to serve alone? bid her therefore that she help me'. Martha complains because she has 'little heard of' the perfection of Christian contemplation; and she cannot be blamed for that, at a time when Christ himself is still on earth. Also, her complaint is expressed 'courteously and in few words'. Both these excuses illustrate the author's typical fair-mindedness towards non-contemplatives. They also illustrate his concern for the literal or historical sense of the biblical narrative. The events carry spiritual significance without losing their integrity as physical events. Indeed, their 'time and maner' are fully present to the author's imagination. We can see this again in his interpretation of Christ's reply to Martha's complaint: 'Martha, Martha, thou art careful and troubled about many things . . .'. The author suggests that Christ realized that Mary was too 'fervently occupied' to answer on her own behalf, and therefore 'courteously' answered for her. Martha appealed to him as a judge, but he answers as an advocate; and he begins by naming Martha twice, 'for he wolde that sche herd him and toke hede to his wordes' (p. 52). In this way, the author develops the brief biblical account into a little drama, amplifying the part played by each of the persons involved. The whole section shows medieval exegesis at its rare best, exploring at the same time general spiritual truths and a particular dramatic situation. In such an interpretation, 'spirit' and 'letter' both flourish, each in its own way. Here, as throughout his work, the author of *The Cloud* is true to his ideal of man serving God 'with body and with soule, bothe togeders, as seemly is'.

9. HENRYSON: *THE PREACHING OF THE SWALLOW**

The Preaching of the Swallow belongs to the collection of animal fables which Robert Henryson left uncompleted, apparently, at the time of his death in about 1500. Its story, taken from Aesopic tradition, is very simple. A swallow warns other birds that the flax, which they see planted and growing, will eventually be made into nets to trap them. They ignore the warnings and are duly netted. Out of this unpretentious material, Henryson made one of the best of his fables. The *Preaching*, indeed, deserves to be counted as one of the minor masterpieces of medieval English poetry; but despite an excellent essay by Denton Fox, the poem has failed to get due recognition, outside Scotland.[1]

I

Unlike some of Henryson's better-known fables (*The Town-Mouse and the Country-Mouse* is an obvious example), *The Preaching of the Swallow* does not adopt the point of view of its small creatures or attempt to engross the reader in their world. Its point of view is, indeed, distinctively human, for it is the only one of the fables to introduce a human observer into the story. At the beginning of his narrative, this observer is a mere *ficelle*, walking out to the greenwood to see the spring flowers grow, in the conventional fashion of narrators in *chansons d'aventure* and dream poems. But in the course of his walk he stops by a hedge to watch men at work in the fields, and at this point he comes alive:

> Movand thusgait, grit mirth I tuik in mind
> Of lauborers to see the besiness,
> Som makand dike, and som the pleuch can wind,
> Som sawand sedis fast fra place to place,
> The harrows hoppand in the sawers trace.

* First published in *Essays in Criticism* 25 (1975), 25–37.

[1] D. Fox, 'Henryson's *Fables*', *ELH* 29 (1962), 337–56, to which I am indebted. See also J. MacQueen, *Robert Henryson: A Study of the Major Narrative Poems* (Oxford, 1967), pp. 153–65.

It was grit joy to him that lufit corn
To see thame labour sa at evin and morn.
                                                    (99–105)[2]

The man's joy in the field, and in the labours of his fellow-
men who work it, colours the rest of his story. It is present in
the little glowing idyll of the field in June, when

sedis that war sawin of beforn
War growin heich, that haris micht thame hide
And als the quailye crakand in the corn.   (156–8)

Even the fowler, whose activities are so ominous from the
point of view of the birds, delights the narrator. The stanza
describing how, in autumn, he and his wife make thread and
so bird-nets out of the ripe flax celebrates human skills:

It steipit in the burn and dryit syne,
And with a bitill knockit it and bet,
Syne scutchit it weill and heclit it in the flet.
His wife it span and twane it into threid . . . (206–9)

And when winter comes, bringing hardships which Henryson
does full justice to, the season derives a certain Brueghelesque
charm from the diligent activities of the fowler, engrossed in
laying his nets, shovelling a patch of ground clear of snow,
and scattering chaff to attract the birds.

    This human point of view prevails, inevitably, at the ex-
pense of the autonomy of the animal world in the poem. The
inividual birds are not very interesting, by comparison with
the town and country mice, or the fox, or the wolf. The role
of Cassandra, assigned by tradition to the Swallow for no
very evident reason (Fox cites a patristic source), might
better have gone to an owl. Henryson's Swallow is no more
than a Wise Bird. The best the *Preaching* has to offer in
the way of animal humours is the moment when the Lark,
acting as spokesman for the other birds, responds to the
Swallow's first warning with a speech of exuberantly larky

[2] All quotations are from the normalized text in *English Verse 1300–1500*, ed.
J. A. Burrow (London, 1977).

irresponsibility. However, the birds do have a kind of reality in the poem—not as individuals, or as species, but as a flock. This is in keeping with the human point of view; for it is as a flock that the man sees the birds.

Henryson's treatment of this crowd of small birds, as observed by the narrator, is one of the successes of the poem. The sudden, darting movements of the flock suggest exhilaration, hysteria, and finally panic. At the same time, these movements serve to establish the unified space within which the action of the fable occurs. The birds first appear, in a big flock, after the man has stopped by the hedge, in the shade of a hawthorn tree, to watch the labourers:

> Of small birdis thair com a ferly flicht
> And doun belive can on the levis licht
> On every side about me whair I stude,
> Richt mervelous, a mekle multitude.   (109–12)

After rejecting the Swallow's advice, the birds fly off, some away across the open field ('bent'), some into the greenwood:

> The fowlis fersly tuke their flicht anon;
> Som with a bir they braidit owr the bent,
> And som agane are to the grenewod gone.
> (149–51)

'Fersly' ('fiercely', furiously) and 'bir' (rush), both words strengthened by alliteration, convey not only the shock of a sudden mass take-off, but also the violence with which the birds reject the Swallow's advice. Later, when the man revisits the same spot in June, the same flock of birds alights in the same hawthorn tree ('I think because it was their customary place of resort, being safer or else more solitary', Henryson says). They hear the Swallow again, and again fly off regardless:

> The counsal of the swallow set at nocht,
> Bot tuik their flicht and on togidder fure,
> Som to the wod, som markit to the mure.
> (199–201)

'Mure' looks past the hedged field, which together with the greenwood has formed for the man a pleasant area for walks, to the treeless, uncultivated land beyond. Later, when winter comes, the birds lose their exuberant freedom of movement. They take refuge in houses, in barns and haystacks, until at last they all (except the Swallow) cluster over the chaff in the one patch of snowless ground. The fable ends with the Swallow flying away alone:

> Sho tuik hir flicht, bot hir I saw no moir. (266)

II

Through the eyes of Henryson's human observer, we can see the activities of men and birds across one piece of country-side in vivid, sometimes luminous, detail. The country world itself is lightly but firmly sketched: wood, field, moor, barn. The actions and movements of the farm-labourers, the fowler and his wife, and the flock of small birds are all 'great joy to see'. The fable, then, has its own convincing reality. But the fable is by no means all of the *Preaching of the Swallow*. Indeed, the first third of the poem has no narrative content at all, being devoted to cosmological and calendrical matters. The connection between this introduction and the ensuing fable is not obvious. The poem as a whole, in fact, may well seem loose and rambling—more ambitious, perhaps, but less satisfying than other fables in the collection. Certainly, for a modern reader at least, the structure of the piece requires justification. Let us consider first its surface structure.

The fable itself, to begin with, consists of four scenes. There is one scene for each of the four seasons. The story opens, at line 92, in spring. On a 'soft morning', in accordance with poetic tradition, the poet sets off into the country, where he has a marvellous experience. He hears the birds' dispute, after which he picks up his stick and returns home, 'So ferliand as I had sene a fary'—'as much amazed as if I had seen magic' (154). Time passes. Then, in June, the poet visits the same spot again, but at a later time of day, 'between midday and morn', matching the later time of the year. Again, he hears the birds' dispute, after which

> I tuke my staff, when this was said and done,
> And walkit hame, whill it drew neirhand none.
>
> (202–3)

Up to this point in the story there is a very clear parallel between scenes, and also between time of year and time of day (the end of June being the noon of the year). Perhaps Henryson felt it would have been laborious to add an afternoon walk in autumn and an evening walk in winter. At any rate, he drops the narrator at this stage. Autumn is represented by the stanza describing how the flax ripens and is made into nets. Then comes winter:

> The winter cam, the wickit wind can blaw,
> The woddis grene war wallowit with the weit,
> Baith firth and fell with frostis war maid faw,
> Slonkis and slack maid sliddery with the sleit.
>
> (211–14)

To appreciate the structural significance of these seasonal divisions in the story, it is necessary to look back before line 92. What immediately precedes the beginning of the fable at that point is, in fact, a formal poetic description—in part, an allegorical pageant—of the four seasons (57–91). The series starts with summer and ends with spring. This unusual order provides Henryson with the smoothest of transitions into the spring opening of his story:

> Syne comis Ver [Spring], when winter is away,
> The secretar of Somer with his seill,
> When columbie up keikis throw the clay
> Whilk fleit was before with frostis feill.
> The mavis and the merle begins to meill;
> The lark on loft, with uthir birdis smale,
> Than drawis furth fra derne, on doun and dale.
>
> That samin seasoun, into a soft morning,
> Richt blith tha bitter blastis were ago,
> Unto the wod, to see the flouris spring
> And heir the mavis sing and birdis mo,
> I passit furth . . .
>
> (85–96)

The small birds of the vivid *descriptio* of spring take their place in the spring opening of the story, to become later its chief actors. The same spring which is the last of one series of seasons becomes the first of another. In this fashion, story is fastened to introduction with a long, strong hinge.[3]

The *descriptio* is itself connected just as securely with what precedes it in the introduction. This introduction is of an encyclopaedic character. It has a cosmic range which contrasts, in a bold but satisfying way, with the narrow world of the fable. Its subject is God and his Creation, no less. The first four stanzas speak of God himself and of the inability of man's mind to comprehend him. Nevertheless (line 29), God's goodness and wisdom can be understood from his works. The rest of the introduction (29-91) develops this second point at length. After an opening reference to the beauty and variety of flowers, Henryson, in his best school manner, sets out to expound the order of the created universe, starting from the top. First there is the firmament; then the planets; then the four elements, named in descending order— fire, air, water, earth; then the creatures who inhabit the elements—fish, animals, birds (unlike Langland, Henryson overlooks the cricket); and finally, Man. All creatures serve the needs of man, as do all the seasons of the year:

> The differens of time and ilk seasoun
> Concordand to oure oportunitie
> As daily by experiens we may see.　　(54-6)

This serves to introduce the *descriptio* of seasons. The *descriptio* supplies the conclusive demonstration, from common 'experiens', of the benevolent order governing the changeful variety of nature—and at the same time introduces the fable. Thus the main constituent parts of the poem prove to be constructed and articulated in a notably formal and orderly fashion. The schoolmaster of Dunfermline knew how to lay his materials out.

[3] See MacQueen, pp. 160-1.

III

So much for the joinery. But it is not enough to show how deftly Henryson joints the parts of his piece together. We must ask why he wanted to put them together in the first place. What, in particular, is the deeper structural relationship between the encyclopaedic introduction and the animal fable, the macrocosm and the microcosm of the poem?

The key to the problem lies in identifying, and correctly understanding, Henryson's main moral theme. The key term is present, together with clues to its understanding, in the opening stanza of the poem:

> The hie prudence and wirking mervellous,
> The profound wit of God omnipotent,
> Is so perfite and so ingenious,
> Excelland fer all mannis argument,
> Forwhy till him all thing is ay present
> Richt as it is or ony time sall be,
> Befoir the sicht of his devinité.   (1-7)

The key term is 'prudence'; and the clues occur in the last three lines. By invoking the doctrine that all time is eternally present to God (recalling Boethius, *De Consolatione*, V, pr. 6) as proof of the supreme and perfect prudence of the Divine Mind, Henryson is implying a specific relationship between the virtue of prudence and time. A God who sees all things as eternally present cannot fail to be perfectly prudent, because prudence, according to an ancient and widely received tradition, consists precisely in the ability to hold in mind not merely the present time, but also the past and the future. Here is one formulation, current in the Middle Ages: 'Prudence consists in the recollection of things past, the ordering of things present, and the contemplation of things to come' ('In praeteritorum recordatione, in praesentium ordinatione, in futurorum meditatione'). Iconographically, this idea was expressed in the three faces, or three eyes, of Prudence, looking to past, present, and future. This is the emblem to which Chaucer's Criseyde alludes when she laments that she always lacked one of Prudence's 'eyen thre': she could not see future time (*Troilus*, V. 744–9). There is a beautiful picture of three-faced Prudentia by Titian, now in the National Gallery, which occasioned a masterly study of the tradition by Panofsky.[4]

Henryson does not use any emblems; but the conception of Prudentia is clearly in his mind throughout the poem, most clearly in the first scene of the fable. Here the Swallow gives a formal definition of prudence, derived, probably, from some scholastic source:

> 'For clerkis says it is nocht sufficient
> To consider that is befoir thine ee;
> Bot prudence is ane inward argument
> That gars a man provide befoir and see
> What guid, what evil is likly forto be
> Of every thingis at the final end,
> And so fro perrell ether him defend.'   (134–40)

Prudence makes a man anticipate the future by recalling—it is a necessary implication, though unstated by Henryson—the past. To consider only the present time is 'not sufficient'. Later, in the final scene, the Swallow has a stanza of moralizing on the imminent death of the other birds, which culminates in the following lines:

> 'Grit fule is he that na thing hes in thocht
> Bot thing present, and eftir what may fall
> Nor of the end hes na memorial.'   (243–5)

The key term is not used here; but, after the death of the birds, the Swallow sums up:

> 'Lo!' quod sho, 'thus it happins oftin syis
> Of thame that will nocht tak counsal nor reid
> Of prudent men or clerkis that are wis.'
>
>   (261–3)

---

[4] E. Panofsky, 'Titian's *Allegory of Prudence*: A Postscript', *Meaning in the Visual Arts* (Harmondsworth, 1970), pp. 181–205. The medieval formulation cited in the text is from Berchorius, cit. Panofsky, p. 185.

Here the theme of prudence is combined with the secondary, but closely related, theme of 'taking counsel' (compare 199, 241–2, 248).

The theme of prudence provides the unifying principle in the *Preaching*. All the major parts of the poem bear upon this theme, more or less obviously. Henryson displays not only the practical and moral significance of the cardinal virtue, but also something of its philosophical and spiritual implications. The philosophical point is a double one. The nature of prudence is bound up with 'differens of time'. One may call God perfectly prudent; but it hardly makes ordinary sense to attribute this particular virtue to a being who by his nature perceives all time as present. His creation, however, is ruled by time. The firmament, 'fra eist to west rolland in circil round' once every twenty-four hours, divides the days. The planets, each 'in his propir sphere', divide the seasons. It is because man is subject to such differences of time that prudence is necessary to him. At the same time, the virtue is possible only in so far as the changes in life and nature exhibit some order and regularity. In a random universe, recollection of the past and observation of the present would tell one nothing about the future. Hence Henryson, both in introduction and fable, stresses not only the changefulness of the sublunary world but also the 'dew proportioun' (53) to be observed in its changes. The chief function of the introduction is to set up, for the purposes of the poem, a universe which exhibits both change and order, and in which, therefore, prudence is both necessary and possible. It is because the passing seasons so well represent both aspects of this universe that they are so prominent in the poem.

In such a universe, a wise man will obviously attempt to come to terms with the changes to which he is subject, by recalling the past, observing the present, and anticipating, so far as he can, the future. Simple, practical examples of such prudence are provided in the poem by the farm-workers, sowing corn in springtime in anticipation of a harvest in autumn, and by the fowler, sowing hemp and flax in anticipation of his future need for nets. But the poem is most concerned with the practical and moral necessity of anticipating future changes for the worse. The small birds provide bad

examples in this respect. In the first scene of the fable, the
Lark counters the Swallow's warnings with a string of blatantly
anti-prudential proverbs:

> The lark lauchand the swallow thus coud scorn,
> And said sho fishit lang befoir the net:
> 'The barn is eith to busk that is unborn;
> All growis nocht that in the ground is set;
> The neck to stoup when it the strake sall get
> Is sone eneuch; dede on the feyest fall.'   (141–6)

The dramatic ironies are evident: as the story progresses,
planted seeds do grow, a net is made, and necks are cut
through. In the second scene, the unwise birds employ a different argument: not that the future should be left to look
after itself, but that it will turn out alright:

> They cryit all and baid the swallow ceis
> And said, 'Yon lint heireftir will do guid,
> For linget is to litil birdis fuid.'   (180–2)

Such optimism is a form of self-delusion, what Henryson
earlier calls 'fantasy' (20), because the future generally brings
changes for the worse. The joy and prosperity of spring and
summer are followed by the misery and deprivation of
winter. While there is still time, the prudent man will 'be
ware' (168, 193, 238) and 'provide before' (118, 137). In this
way he may avert, or at least reduce, the dangers facing him
in the future.

This idea is summed up by the Swallow in a Latin maxim,
which stands at the mathematical centre of the poem—at line
133 in a poem of 266 lines (excluding the Moralitas):

> 'Out of the erd scraip we yon sede anon
> And ete it up; for gif it grows, we sall
> Have caus to weip hereftir ane and all.
> See we remede thairfore furthwith instante,
> *Nam levius laedit quicquid providimus ante.*'
>
> (129–33)

Commentators have not noticed, I believe, that this Latin line comes from the Distichs of Cato, an elementary Latin text much used in grammar schools. Like the Latin Aesop, which was also used in schools, this text must have been especially familiar to Henryson. Distich II. 24, from which Henryson quotes the second line, runs as follows: 'Anticipate events which are to come, and consider that they will have to be borne; for whatever we see in advance does us less harm.'[5] This same Distich is imitated by Gualterus Anglicus, author of the Latin Aesop used by Henryson, in his version of the fable of the Swallow, which also alludes to the traditional idea of prudence.[6] Perhaps it was Henryson's custom, when expounding this passage of Gualterus in the school at Dunfermline, to use the parallel with Cato as a way of introducing discussion of the fable's moral significance. In any case, the line he quotes points straight to the main moral implicit in his own version of the story.

We must now, however, briefly notice the 'Moralitas' which Henryson appends to this fable, as to all the others in his collection. In this moralization, Henryson goes beyond the antique, or pseudo-antique, Stoic ethics of his textbooks, and gives the story a specifically modern, Christian application. The fowler, according to this 'spiritual' interpretation, is the Devil; the seeds are wicked thoughts, sown in men's souls and growing into sins, by means of which the Devil traps his victims; the small birds pecking at the chaff are 'wretches' deceived by the false pleasures of the world; and the Swallow is the 'holy preacher' warning men to beware. Modern historical criticism has had no difficulty in showing that such allegorical moralizations belong to a venerable tradition. Nevertheless, most present-day readers of Henryson's fables find his Moralitates at best unpleasing and at worst desperately confusing; and I think they are often justified, despite the

---

[5] 'Prospice qui veniant casus: hos esse ferendos; / Nam levius laedit quidquid praevidimus ante', *Disticha Catonis*, ed. M. Boas (Amsterdam, 1952), II. 24.

[6] Ed. J. Bastin, *Recueil Général des Isopets*, vol. ii (Paris, 1930), p. 26, 'De Hirundine et Avibus', line 10: 'Nam praemissa (v. 1. praevisa) minus laedere tela solent' ['For weapons sent (or seen) in advance do less damage']. Gualterus, who was Henryson's main source for the *Preaching*, refers in his Moralitas to past, present, and future (15–17), but in connection with 'consilium', not 'prudentia': see Panofsky, p. 185 and n. 11.

best efforts of Professor Fox and Professor MacQueen to prove the contrary. Fortunately, however, the Moralitas to the *Preaching of the Swallow* is no worse than unpleasing. It may be said to continue and complete the thematic development of the poem. Although the term 'prudence' itself is not used in these stanzas (a fact which, admittedly, requires some explanation), what they expound is evidently just prudence applied to spiritual matters. Christians must look forward to the future, and anticipate the inevitable changes of Fortune and the equally inevitable consequences of sin. The message is the same, 'be ware' (318); but it is delivered not merely by the wise counsellor, but by the preacher of God's word. This is the final development anticipated in the poem's title.

IV

In his book *Chaucer and the English Tradition* (1972), Ian Robinson speaks of Henryson's fables as 'those very lively and charming poems which one yet sometimes feels like calling *only* charming and lively' (p. 244). He goes on to refer to the author as a 'comfortable old schoolmaster'. There is a good deal of the schoolmaster in the *Preaching of the Swallow*, as we have seen; but this fable, at least, should never be called '*only* charming and lively'. It is hardly charming at all, and its lively sketches of nature and country life serve a larger purpose. I have tried to show how the encyclopaedic, didactic and narrative parts of the poem all contribute to the treatment of a single, named, moral topic. The poem displays various aspects of Prudence, as that virtue was understood in Henryson's day, by means of formal exposition and narrative example. Thus Prudence plays the same part in this poem as Patience does in the *Gawain*-poet's *Patience*, or Justice in the Fifth Book of Spenser's *Faerie Queene*. Generally speaking, whatever the other attractions of the poems concerned, this type of ethical construct has found little favour with modern readers. They think it wrong that a poet should be content merely to expound and illustrate a familiar moral idea such as prudence, justice, or patience. It seems too servile or too scholastic an exercise. The obvious answer to this objection is that much can be done, by a skilled and imaginative poet, with a familiar moral topic, as the *Preaching* itself shows. But the case of Henryson's poem prompts a more fundamental reflection.

Many traditional moral ideas still regarded as familiar, even commonplace, survive in modern times only in drastically simplified and weakened versions. 'Prudence' is an extreme case of this simplification and weakening, since the term in modern English (where it is rarely used) denotes little more than the not-always-lovable quality which saves people from overspending or going out without a raincoat. The connection between such common caution and the noble capacity to hold in view past and future, as well as present, has been broken off, with the result that we would not want to call God (or Blake's Bard) 'prudent'. Prudence is, in fact, a shadow of its former self, like at least two of the other three cardinal virtues—justice, temperance, and fortitude. In her last book, Rosamond Tuve showed how the theory of the cardinal virtues, originating in classical antiquity, was integrated into Christian thought, producing the rich and complex ethical tradition drawn upon by Spenser.[7] Henryson belongs to the same line. *The Preaching of the Swallow*, like the Second and Fifth Books of the *Faerie Queene*, provides an opportunity to rediscover, as Tuve did, what a cardinal virtue was like in its heyday. Much that must have been familiar teaching to an audience around 1500 is there in the poem for us to learn, brought to life—as it must have been also for a contemporary—by the power of Henryson's imagination.

[7] R. Tuve, *Allegorical Imagery* (Princeton, NJ, 1966).

10. THE POET AS PETITIONER*

Since medieval literature generally appears more impersonal than that of modern times, it is something of a paradox that medieval writers should refer to themselves by name more often than their modern successors. Whereas in recent times the author's name tends to be confined to cover and title-page, a medieval work will not infrequently find a place for it within the text itself. Quite often, too, the name will be accompanied there by further particulars about the author: occupation, age, place of residence, and so on. Where other evidence is available to check them, these particulars usually turn out to be factual ('Mandeville' is a rare exception); and it seems reasonable to suppose that other similar passages which cannot be checked against external evidence are also more likely to be fact than fiction. E. T. Donaldson adopts this position in the course of his penetrating analysis of the long 'autobiographical' passage in *Piers Plowman*, C VI: 'it seems best to assume that Langland was telling the truth about himself and not whimsically devising an elaborate fiction'.[1]

In such cases it is, I think, either false historicism or undue scepticism to deny that the author is most likely 'telling the truth about himself'. Where this is agreed, however, a further question immediately arises. What *occasions* these autobiographical passages? In literature, as in life, there are many different reasons for speaking about oneself; and one's purpose on any particular occasion will at least partly determine the kind of truth one tells. The question of purpose is by no means a simple one—it may, for instance, be necessary to distinguish between the ostensible and the real purpose—but it cannot be avoided, if we are to understand why the author speaks of himself in the way he does. The favourite term 'autobiographical' has tended to obscure this question, because it suggests answers which are not appropriate to most

* First published in *Studies in the Age of Chaucer* 3 (1981), 61-75.

[1] E. T. Donaldson, *Piers Plowman: The C-Text and Its Poet*, 2nd edn. (London, 1966), p. 220.

of the medieval instances. Autobiography proper, after all, is a highly specialized, literary way of speaking about oneself; and, although there are no doubt many possible reasons for writing one's autobiography, the term itself suggests aims which are at any rate not basely practical. It is not *autobiography* when I give my name and address to a policeman. But in many medieval texts the reasons which lead an author to speak of himself are, precisely, practical—or at least purport to be so. What the medieval author is doing is not (in most cases) 'writing his autobiography'. Rather he is doing some practical thing such as claiming credit for his book, greeting his friends, complaining about his lot, or (as in *Piers* C VI) making a public confession. Most commonly of all, I think, the occasion is the presentation of a petition on the author's behalf. I shall argue here that it is this petitionary intention which lends to many 'autobiographical' passages in medieval English literature their distinctive tone and emphasis—even where, as in Chaucer and Gower, the petition is no longer meant quite seriously.

Personal petitions for the favour of the great play relatively little part in the public life of modern Western democracies; but medieval men were dependent upon the good will of those set above them; and one way for them to win that good will was to plead for it, either directly or else through an intercessor. God was the supreme source of favour and grace. Men could solicit his good will by direct prayer; or they could solicit it indirectly, either by praying the Virgin or the saints to plead their cause with God, or else by praying or paying other human beings to act as petitioners on their behalf. On earth the same pattern is repeated, both in secular and ecclesiastical courts. Men asked favours (benefices, offices, pensions) from lords and from bishops, both directly and through the intercession of courtiers or chaplains who had the ear of the great.

When seeking the favour of God or some earthly patron, an obvious prime requirement is that one should be identified—otherwise the favour might go to the wrong person. Hence the writer of any petitionary document has a strong practical incentive to register his name. There is also a natural tendency to add a few further particulars in order to support the identification. Such particulars may also perform another function, for the petitioner often introduces some account of himself and his circumstances in order to strengthen his plea. He will claim to need the favour, or to have deserved it, or both. Need is a common theme in petitions of all sorts: the petitioner needs God's grace because he is a miserable sinner, or he needs a lord's favour because he is broke. No merits can establish a claim on God's grace; but the petitioner may claim to have deserved, by his labours, the prayers of his readers for that grace; and he can certainly claim to have done enough to deserve a benefice or a pension. At the same time, he will attempt to preserve the humble tone appropriate to a man at least metaphorically on his knees.

The main purpose of this essay is to consider some passages of petitionary self-reference in the poetry of Chaucer and Gower; but before turning to these passages, which are rather complex, I shall more briefly discuss some selected examples from other medieval English writers. The most common form of petition in the literature of this period is the author's request for the reader's prayers. In the course of such requests, the author often gives his name. When this happens, a modern reader may be inclined to regard the request for prayers as itself little more than a formality—a conventional occasion for declaring authorship. In the absence of copyright laws, however, medieval writers had little direct practical interest in declaring authorship; whereas it was, for them, an eminently practical thing to be prayed for by name. Men, after all, left large sums of money in their wills in order to shorten their time in the pains of Purgatory through the prayers of beadsmen. Admittedly, not all requests for readers' prayers in medieval literature can be taken at their simple face value; but the avowed religious motive is enough to account for many of them. The very first English poet to declare his name does so in the course of just such a devout request. Four Anglo-Saxon poems are 'signed' with the name Cynewulf, spelled out in runic letters. In his essay, 'Cynewulf and his Poetry', Kenneth Sisam pointed out that all four signatures occur in passages which refer to the Day of Judgement, and that two of the passages (in *The Fates of the Apostles* and *Juliana*) expressly ask the reader to pray for the soul of the author—which, like all souls, faces the terror of God's judgement on that great Day.[2] Sisam quotes from *Juliana*: 'I beg every man who repeats this poem to remember me *by name* in my need'. On the subject of his 'need' the poet enlarges a little, speaking of his own sinfulness and also, in *Elene*, of his sorrowful old age. Even in this last passage, however, Cynewulf is content to speak of himself in general terms derived from the elegiac traditions of Old English verse. He evidently regards a perfectly conventional 'autobiography' as sufficient to amplify his need and move the reader to a pious response in prayer. But to ensure the efficacy of that prayer, something more particular is needed—a name. Like the number of a bank account, the name has to be right.

Recent historians have spoken of a 'discovery of the individual' in the eleventh and twelfth centuries; and certainly, by about the year 1200, we find English poets speaking of themselves, on occasion, with more individual detail than any Anglo-Saxon provided. One might compare Cynewulf's epilogues with Laȝamon's prologue to his *Brut*. Laȝamon begins his prologue by naming himself, his father, and his place of residence; and he ends it by bidding the reader say prayers for himself, his father, and his (unnamed) mother.[3] In the intervening lines he describes how he conceived the work and gathered materials for its composition. The petitionary function of these lines is presumably to establish the author's claim upon the reader's good will. Whereas Cynewulf's emphasis falls upon his sad and sinful condition (need), Laȝamon stresses his diligent efforts on the reader's behalf (desert). When Laȝamon can claim to have done so much, runs the concealed argument, the reader cannot in conscience refuse him a prayer. Yet Laȝamon's claim surely also betrays some simple pride of authorship. His prologue, in fact, seems to over-shoot the strict requirements of a prayer-petition in the interests of displaying writer to reader—which is not to say, however, that the petition is a mere pretext.

---

[2] K. Sisam, 'Cynewulf and his Poetry', in *Studies in the History of Old English Literature* (Oxford, 1953), pp. 23-5. The four passages are: *The Fates of the Apostles*, 88 ff., *Juliana*, 695 ff., *Elene*, 1236 ff., and *Christ*, 779 ff.

[3] Laȝamon's *Brut*, ed. G. L. Brook and R. F. Leslie, vol. i, EETS o.s. 250 (1963), Cotton Caligula text, ll. 1-5 and 29-35.

A poem perhaps nearly contemporary with the *Brut*, *The Owl and the Nightingale*, presents a more complex case, which anticipates, in some respects, the subtleties of the Ricardian poets. Early on in the debate between the two birds, the Nightingale proposes 'Master Nichol of Guildford' as a suitably wise and discriminating judge between them. The Owl agrees: Nicholas was too fond of nightingales in his wild youth; but he has since cooled off and become mature ('ripe').[4] At the end of the long debate which follows, the Wren tells the two birds where Nicholas is to be found, at Portesham in Dorset, and adds her own word in praise of his wisdom. It is a shame, she says, that bishops give livings to unworthy recipients while allowing a man of Nicholas's calibre to live in the obscurity of a remote country parish.[5] If, as most recent scholars agree, it was Nicholas himself who wrote the poem, then he has produced a subtle and telling plea on his own behalf—a petition for preferment, in this case, addressed to some ecclesiastical patron.[6] The poet's need for such patronage is stated, without any nagging complaint, in the Wren's rapid description of the humble circumstances of his life in a Dorset village. He deserves the favours of a patron, too, by virtue of the moral qualities of wisdom and maturity which the birds affirm and the poem, by its own 'ripeness', displays. Nicholas is equally acceptable to the solemn Owl and the joyous Nightingale because his maturity places him, as it were, at the apex of an equilateral triangle, equidistant from both. When the Owl suggests that Nicholas has simply followed a natural order of moral development from wild youth to sober age, that is no more than the Owl's version. The fact that Nicholas proves equally acceptable to the Nightingale suggests a more subtle kind of maturity. The poet is evidently not, as Montaigne says of himself in old age, 'but too much settled, too heavy and too ripe'. His maturity somehow incorporates, rather than supersedes, the energies of youth. Hence both birds can join with the Wren

---

[4] *The Owl and the Nightingale*, ed. E. G. Stanley (London, 1960), ll. 189-214.
[5] Ed. Stanley, ll. 1750-91.
[6] E. G. Stanley doubts Nicholas's authorship, pp. 20-1; but see E. J. Dobson, *N & Q* n.s. 8 (1961), p. 373, and Kathryn Hume, *The Owl and the Nightingale: The Poem and Its Critics* (Toronto, 1975).

to act as intercessors on his behalf. The poet neither himself addresses the patron nor invites the reader to speak for him. His plea is conducted more insidiously, within the fiction of the poem. But it is not itself a fiction.

A full survey of passages of petitionary autobiography in Middle English literature would, I believe, reveal a rich variety of instances. Prayers and requests for intercession lead authors to register their names, either simply or (like Cynewulf) cryptically;[7] and they may add, as Malory does in *Morte Darthur*, some further particulars about themselves, the circumstances in which the work was composed, and so on.[8] In the later Middle English period, too, we find petitions of a different kind—pleas addressed to kings, lords, and other secular patrons. Hoccleve in England and in Scotland Dunbar depended upon favours from courts which, by the fifteenth century, regularly spoke and wrote English; and the petitionary poems which they addressed to their benefactors represent

[7] Cryptic signatures occur in connection with prayers or requests for prayer in Thomas Usk's *Testament of Love*: see *Chaucerian and Other Pieces*, ed. W. W. Skeat (Oxford, 1897), pp. xix–xx; and in Osbern Bokenham's *Mappula Angliae*: see his *Legendys of Hooly Wummen*, ed. M. S. Serjeantson, EETS o.s. 206 (1938), pp. xvi–xvii. Professor E. J. Dobson has argued convincingly that the author of *Ancrene Wisse* indicates his name, Brian of Lingen, by etymological allusion and anagram in the course of asking for his readers' prayers: *The Origins of Ancrene Wisse* (Oxford, 1976), pp. 327–68. Dobson makes the following general observation: 'most commonly, in religious works and sometimes also in secular, [the author's name] is embodied in or comes in the immediate neighbourhood of a request for the readers' prayers, or else is mentioned in a direct prayer by the author himself to God for his mercy' (p. 329). For examples of the same pattern in Middle High German poetry, see Julius Schwietering, *Die Demutsformel mittelhochdeutscher Dichter* (Berlin, 1921) and 'The Origins of the Medieval Humility Formula', *PMLA* 69 (1954), 1279–91; both reprinted in Schwietering, *Philologische Schriften*, ed. F. Ohly and M. Wehrli (Munich, 1969).

[8] *The Works of Sir Thomas Malory*, ed. E. Vinaver (Oxford, 1954), pp. 133, 623, 741, 816, and esp. 883: 'I praye you all jentylmen and jentylwymmen that redeth this book of Arthur and his knyghtes from the begynnyng to the endynge, praye for me whyle I am on lyve that God sende me good delyveraunce. And whan I am deed, I praye you all praye for my soule. For this book was ended the ninth yere of the reygne of King Edward the Fourth, by Syr Thomas Maleoré, Knyght, as Jesu helpe hym for Hys grete myght, as he is the servaunt of Jesu bothe day and nyght.' Compare John Audelay, who refers to himself sixteen times in his poems, nine times in a context of religious petition: *Poems of John Audelay*, ed. E. K. Whiting, EETS o.s. 184 (1931), 2. 1008, 3. 102, 12. 66, 13. 122, 15. 208, 18. 6, 18. 507, 23. 202, 55. 48. The author of *Mandeville's Travels* ends his book with a similar passage, audaciously presenting the fictional autobiography of his John Mandeville, Knight, in a petitionary context from which the reader would have expected fact: ed. M. C. Seymour (Oxford, 1967), p. 229.

one of the high-water marks of autobiographical writing in medieval England. The detail is so rich that a modern reader may sometimes lose sight of the petitionary intention altogether. Yet when Hoccleve in his *Male Regle* asks the Lord Treasurer to pay his annuity, or when Dunbar in *To the King* ('Schir, yit remembir as of befoir') asks James IV for a benefice, these are not mere excuses for the poet to talk about himself. The self-portrait is elaborate, but it still has a practical purpose; and that purpose largely dictates its dark tones and gloomy pose.[9]

In the rest of this essay, however, I want to consider certain passages from the poetry of Chaucer and Gower which are of a somewhat different character. In the passages I have chosen, the practical petitionary intention is either almost refined away or else entirely fictionalized, as it is not in Hoccleve or Dunbar. Petitionary forms, in these Ricardian poets, become detached from their original function, while retaining their power to control the way the poet portrays himself in his work. The role of petitioner is here a part which the poet plays largely for his own purposes, with a freedom from practical intention which makes possible some incongruous and, in Chaucer, comical developments.

Although not strictly speaking a dream poem, John Gower's *Confessio Amantis* follows many of the conventions of dream poetry, among them the convention stated by Professor Kane: 'authors of dream-vision poems signed these by naming the dreamers after themselves'.[10] Gower times and

[9] Dunbar's *To the King* is one of fifteen poems classified as Petitions in W. M. Mackenzie's edition, *The Poems of William Dunbar* (London, 1932). Other examples are *Remonstrance to the King, The Petition of the Gray Horse, Auld Dunbar*, and *To the Lordis of the Kingis Chalker*. Among the shorter petitionary poems of Hoccleve are his balades *To My Lord the Chancellor, To Mr. Henry Somer, Subtreasurer, To King Henry V*, and *To My Maister Carpenter*: Nos. xii, xiii, xv, and xvi in *Minor Poems*, ed. F. J. Furnivall, EETS e.s. 61 (1892). The melancholy description of the poet's life in the first part of Hoccleve's *Regement of Princes* leads up to the old man's suggestion that he should complain to Prince Henry and petition the Prince for his annuity to be paid more regularly: *The Regement of Princes*, ed. F. J. Furnivall, EETS e.s. 72 (1897), ll. 1832–1904 (cf. 4383–9). Hoccleve introduces his own name twice into this petitionary passage (1864, 1865) and nowhere else in the poem. Cf. the discussion of Gower's *Confessio Amantis* below. A collection of Anglo-Norman petitions from the time of Hoccleve is edited by M. D. Legge, *Anglo-Norman Letters and Petitions from All Souls MS. 182*, Anglo-Norman Text Society III (Oxford, 1941).

[10] George Kane, *Piers Plowman: The Evidence for Authorship* (London,

manages this signature to perfection. Towards the end of
Confessio Amantis, after completing his confession to Genius,
Amans (who corresponds to the dreamer in dream poems)
writes a letter of petition and complaint to Venus and Cupid,
asking to be relieved of his sufferings in love. Genius presents
the letter on his behalf, and he receives a visit from the
goddess:

> To grounde I fell upon mi kne,
> And preide hire forto do me grace:
> Sche caste hire chiere upon mi face,
> And as it were halvinge a game
> Sche axeth me what is mi name.
> 'Ma dame', I seide, 'John Gower'.
> 'Now John', quod sche . . .[11]

This is the first time Gower has named himself in the poem;
and he does so in the time-honoured petitionary context. A
great lady has received, by the hand of her confessor, a 'sup-
licacioun'; and before she replies to her kneeling petitioner,
she must ascertain his identity. It is a familiar pattern.

Gower's petition, however, differs from those of Cynewulf,
La3amon, Nicholas of Guildford, Hoccleve, Malory, and
Dunbar, in that it is purely fictional. Doubly so, indeed. An
appeal to the goddess Venus, itself necessarily fictional in a
Christian poem, might mask a real appeal to a real lady; but
there is no sign of such a lady in this affair. One of Gower's
Latin sidenotes, opposite Book I line 60, speaks of the
author 'quasi in persona aliorum, quos amor alligat, fingens
se . . . esse Amantem' ['feigning himself to be a lover, as if in

---

1965), p. 65. The chapter 'Signatures' gives many French examples of poets
naming themselves in dream poems.

[11] *Confessio Amantis*, VIII. 2316–22, in *The English Works of John Gower*,
ed. G. C. Macaulay, EETS e.s. 81–2 (1900–1). Charles d'Orléans names himself
in a very similar context in his *Songe en Complainte*. Like Gower, Charles represents himself as submitting a letter of petition to Cupid and Venus, asking to be
relieved of his sufferings in love: 'Supplie presentement, / Humblement, / Charles,
le duc d'Orlians, / Qui a esté longuement, / Ligement, / L'un de voz obeissans
. . .', *Songe en Complainte*, ll. 179–84 (cf. 251–3), ed. P. Champion, *Poésies*,
CFMA, vol. i (Paris, 1971). The equivalent English passage is ll. 2718–23 in
The English Poems of Charles of Orleans, ed. R. Steele and M. Day, EETS o.s. 215
and 220 (1941 and 1946, repr. 1970).

the role of those others whom love constrains']; and the figure of Amans indeed bears all the marks of poetic fiction. He is one kind of conventional Lover—faithful, long-serving, unrewarded. It is not the real Gower who introduces the petition in Book VIII. Rather, one might say, it is the petition which introduces the real Gower. When Venus, replying to the petition, says 'Mi medicine is noght to sieke / For thee and for suche olde sieke' (VIII. 2367-8), she alludes for the first time to a fact about the narrator which is to play a significant part in the poem's closing scenes. He is *old*. The Amans who submitted his supplication had served his mistress long and unsuccessfully; but there had been no reason, even at that late stage, to suppose that he faced any but the usual lover's obstacles.[12] Once Venus has drawn attention to his age, however, 'Gower' realizes that his passion is worse than hopeless:

> 'Ma dame', I seide, 'be your leve,
> Ye witen wel, and so wot I,
> That I am unbehovely
> Your Court fro this day forth to serve'
>
> (VIII. 2882-5)

Gower was himself old at the time of writing (see VIII. 3120-31), and he portrays the renunciation of love with real feeling; yet there can be no question of reading these closing scenes in any strict autobiographical sense. The autobiographical details of name and age which the petition introduces do not point outwards into real life; rather they point forwards to the end of the poem—towards the 'beau retret' of which Venus speaks (VIII. 2416). The incongruity of a love petition from such an 'unbehovely' servant of Venus helps to prepare Gower's poem for its powerful moral conclusion. In Chaucer, as we shall see, a similar incongruity is turned to different, comic effect.

---

[12] *Pace* Donald Schueler, 'The Age of the Lover in Gower's *Confessio Amantis*', *Medium Aevum* 36 (1967), 152-8. The passages Schueler cites are indeed consistent with the idea of an elderly Amans; but they could only establish that idea in the mind of a reader already (as Schueler implausibly suggests) thinking of the real Gower.

Chaucer made surprisingly little use of his art for practical
purposes of petition. He must have depended more than
Gower on the favour of the great. We may see it as a testimony to his sense of the dignity of his art that he did not
more often write like Hoccleve; or perhaps his salary was
paid more regularly. Only three of his poems directly betray
any impurity of intention: *Fortune*, *The Complaint of
Chaucer to his Purse*, and *Lenvoy to Scogan*. In *Fortune*, a
stilted philosophical dialogue between Le Pleintif and Fortune
leads abruptly to an envoy in which Fortune prays the King's
three uncles or Richard himself to relieve the poet's distress.
In the *Complaint*, a rather silly pseudo-amorous complaint
to his purse is followed, in the envoy, by a solemn address
and 'supplication' (Chaucer uses the same word as Gower) to
the new king, Henry IV. The uncertain and uneven character
of both these poems suggests that Chaucer was not quite
happy—as a poet, at least—in the role of humble petitioner to
the great. At any rate, *Scogan* is a much better poem.

Lenvoy to Scogan presents its petition in the last of its
seven stanzas:

> Scogan, that knelest at the stremes hed
> Of grace, of alle honour and worthynesse,
> In th'ende of which strem I am dul as ded,
> Forgete in solytarie wildernesse, —
> Yet, Scogan, thenke on Tullius kyndenesse;
> Mynne thy frend, there it may fructyfye!
> Far-wel, and loke thow never eft Love dyffye   (43-9)

Nobility, honour, and favour flow down from a high source—
in this case the king, the very 'fount of honour', and his
court. All three manuscripts write 'Windsor' against line 43
and 'Greenwich' against line 45. The stream is not only a
'stream of honour'[13] but also the River Thames- a touch of
transfigured geography which anticipates Spenser and Milton.
Both literally and metaphorically, Chaucer is downstream of
his friend. Scogan, a member of Richard II's household, may

---

[13] The phrase is Dr Johnson's, speaking of Cardinal Wolsey: 'Turned by his
nod the stream of honour flows, / His smile alone security bestows' (*Vanity of
Human Wishes*, 102-3, pointed out to me by my colleage David Hopkins).

not himself be a source of favour; but the gracefully posed
image of the courtier 'kneeling at the stream's head' serves
to remind him that he is well placed to put in a word for his
friend: 'Mynne thy frend, there it may fructyfye'. The
petition is unspecific, but presumably Scogan was expected
to understand what he could do. And the words of the poem
are addressed, steadily and unmistakably, to *him*. His name
occurs no less than seven times in the poem's forty-nine lines,
twice in the petitionary last stanza quoted above. Invoking
Cicero's *De Amicitia*, Chaucer bases his claim to Scogan's
good offices on the fact of their friendship; and he takes
every opportunity to evoke his own unhappy circumstances.
The weather is frighteningly bad (1–14); he is grey-haired and
overweight (27, 31), too old for love (26–8), and no longer
ambitious for his poetry (37–40); and he is living alone, dull
and forgotten, in a part of the world which, as he describes
it (45–6), is scarcely better than Nicholas of Guildford's
obscure parish in Dorset.

Yet anyone who had not read *Scogan* would get a quite
incomplete idea of it from my description so far. *Scogan*
presents a real petition, and it does not neglect the perennial
topics of the petitioner: his claim upon favours and his need
for them. Yet here, much more than in the *Brut* or the *Owl*,
the autobiographical writing tends to leave its petitionary
occasion behind. Chaucer is writing a letter to a friend, and
he addresses Scogan in a tone of ease and familiarity. Scogan
may be on his knees, we feel, but Chaucer is not—certainly
not to Scogan. Although the poem does not neglect the
realities of human lordship and dependence, it in fact gives
greater prominence to the fictive lordship of Venus and
Cupid; and in relation to that court, Chaucer and Scogan are
both at an equal disadvantage. Like Gower in *Confessio
Amantis*, they are both too old to expect any favours from
the God of Love. If anything, it is Chaucer who is better
placed than Scogan here; for he at least has not committed
the blasphemy of giving up his mistress, like a rented house,
on a quarter-day. Hence the poet can claim a certain superiority over his friend and benefactor. One must do full justice
to Chaucer's diplomatic touch in this matter. His claim to be
somewhat less out of favour with Cupid and Venus than the

rebellious Scogan could not offend the latter, because it is obviously just a friendly joke: 'Lo, olde Grisel lyst to ryme and playe'. Indeed, one might say that the playful fantasy actually strengthens Chaucer's petition, for it helps him to avoid that nagging tone of humble complaint which can so easily irritate potential benefactors. However, when 'petition-ary autobiography' becomes as subtle as this, it begins to seem irrelevant to insist upon the practical intention. The display of personality in *Scogan*, indeed, is so absorbing that many readers hardly notice the petition when it is finally presented.

In Chaucer's longer works there are (leaving aside the Retraction) three main passages in which he refers to himself (twice by name) and to his circumstances and writings: *The House of Fame*, 605 ff., the Prologue to *The Legend of Good Women*, G, 234 ff., and the Introduction to *The Man of Law's Tale*, 45 ff. Although the last does not belong to the present subject, we may note in passing that it does involve some-thing not unlike a petition. Its formal model seems to be the bill of complaint; and this, like the bill of petition, is a public, non-literary form. Chaucer employs it in a playful and extravagant fashion. One of his creations, the Man of Law, makes a public complaint against his own creator, alleging that he has irresponsibly used up all the good stories. Auto-biographical details are therefore given a most peculiar twist. The same thing happens, we shall see, in *The House of Fame* and *The Legend of Good Women*, both of which distort the pattern of petition in a fashion just as fictive and outrageous.

Chaucer's vision of Cupid in the Prologue to *The Legend of Good Women* presents the God of Love as a king, accom-panied by Queen Alceste and followed by a train of ladies forming part of his 'court' (G, 328). Chaucer portrays the lordship of Cupid quite realistically: like Theseus in the *Knight's Tale*, he bears the heavy responsibility of deciding difficult cases.[14] As Queen Alceste reminds him:

> he that kyng or lord is naturel,
> Hym oughte nat be tyraunt and crewel,

---

[14] Cupid is a god as well as a lord, Chaucer a penitent as well as a petitioner; but as we have already seen, a god (heavenly lord) and a lord (earthly god) would stand in much the same relation to their dependants.

As is a fermour, to don the harm he can.
He moste thynke it is his lige man,
And that hym oweth, of verray duetee,
Shewen his peple pleyn benygnete,
And wel to heren here excusacyouns,
And here compleyntes and petyciouns,
In duewe tyme, whan they shal it profre.

(G, 356-64)

Alceste's terms 'compleynt', 'petycioun', and 'excusacyoun'
precisely indicate what is going on in the central scene
between Cupid, Chaucer, and Alceste. After the poet has
identified himself (though not by name, G, 240), Cupid in-
dignantly and scornfully rehearses the complaints and accusa-
tions which have been made against Chaucer in his court (see
G, 326-39). Like Scogan, Chaucer has uttered heresy (G,
256) against the God of Love—in this case, by translating
the *Roman de la Rose* and telling the story of Criseyde's
infidelity. Cupid threatens vengeance on his renegade liege-
man, to which Alceste responds with what is in effect a
petition for clemency, suggesting 'excusacyouns' for the two
offending works. When the decision is delegated to the
Queen, Chaucer drops to his knees (G, 445) and addresses to
her his own plea of excuse. After responding at first rather
sharply—'Love ne wol nat counterpletyd be'—Alceste releases
the poet with a light penalty.

This summary will have shown how Chaucer's references
to himself and his writings occur, in the Prologue to *The
Legend*, as part of a quite elaborately developed court scene
of complaint and petition. The scene is, of course, entirely
fictive in itself, and the fiction does not, as in *The Owl and
the Nightingale*, serve a serious petitionary purpose. At most
Chaucer is asking the ladies in his audience to forgive him for
his portrait of Criseyde—and that half-jokingly, 'halvinge a
game'. Yet the petitionary context, fictive and humorous
though it is, largely determines what Chaucer says about himself. The role of petitioner is itself inimical to any heroics.
Like Gower in *Confessio Amantis*, Chaucer is discovered on
his knees to a higher power; and it would be hard for any
poet, from that humble posture, to make lofty claims for

himself or his art. Furthermore, Chaucer represents himself as
cutting an incongruous figure in the court of Love. Like
Gower, again, he is an 'old fole' (G, 262, 315). His days of
love are over (G, 400-1).[15] When the God of Love passes him
on to Alceste, we may be reminded of his own words to
Scogan:

> He wol nat with his arwes been ywroken
> On the, ne me, ne noon of oure figure.   (26-7)

Cupid does not so much forgive Chaucer as dismiss him from
consideration, treating him, as Alceste advises him to, as a
lion treats a troublesome fly: 'Hym deyneth nat to wreke
hym on a flye' (G, 381).

Chaucer's account of his own work as a poet takes on,
in this extravagant petitionary context, a very peculiar
character. Cupid's hostile description seems unfair; but the
'excusacyouns' offered by Alceste and later by the poet himself only make things worse. Like the Man of Law, Alceste
implies that Chaucer writes more than is good for him. He
translates to order and 'taketh non hed of what matere he
take', not caring—perhaps not even noticing—what he writes.
When Alceste speaks of his 'innocence', consequently, she
is sacrificing a good deal of the petitioner's dignity in order
to win him a reprieve—as friends at court no doubt often did.
Chaucer's own plea to Alceste does little to restore his standing. His excuses are admittedly not ridiculous, as is his
apology to the ladies at the end of *Troilus* (V. 1772-85); but
they do not carry conviction:

> a trewe man, withoute drede,
> Hath nat to parte with a theves dede.   (G, 454-5)

And so on. Alceste's brisk rejoinder, 'Lat be thyn arguynge',
saves her protégé from further abasement.

There is a passage in *Troilus* which describes a type of
humour very characteristic of Chaucer's work. Pandarus is
doing his best to amuse Criseyde:

[15] All three allusions to the dreamer's age are absent from the F version of the
Prologue, where he sometimes speaks like a conventional lover: F, 50-9, 84-96,
249-77.

> And he gan at hymself to jape faste,
> And seyde, 'Nece, I have so gret a pyne
> For love, that everich other day I faste—'
> And gan his beste japes forth to caste,
> And made hire so to laughe at his folye,
> That she for laughter wende for to dye.
>
> (II. 1164-9)

Like Pandarus, Chaucer takes special pleasure in 'japing at himself'; and the role of humble petitioner offered a variety of opportunities for comedy of this self-depreciating sort. In the Prologue to *The Legend*, as in *Confessio Amantis*, the poet represents himself pleading for a favour which he is unlikely to receive from an unsympathetic patron; in *The House of Fame* he is shown reluctantly enjoying a favour which he did not want from a patron who is only too sympathetic.

The best-known of all Chaucer's autobiographical passages, the description of his life as a customs official, forms part of a comically distorted pattern of petition in the second book of *The House of Fame*. The first requirement for such a pattern is the presence of an exalted source of patronage, capable of dispensing grace and favour. In *The House of Fame*, this role is played by Jupiter. 'Thorgh hys grace' (661), Jupiter decides to grant Geoffrey the reward or 'guerdon' which the poet has for so long failed to receive from Cupid and Venus:

> And thus this god, thorgh his merite,
> Wol with som maner thing the quyte.   (669-70)

In contrast to the god, the poet—addressed 'by his name' at line 558 and identified as 'Geoffrey' at line 729—cuts a comically undignified figure. In *The Legend of Good Women* he was compared to a fly and a worm (G, 244, 381); here, rigid with fear in the claws of the giant eagle, he is compared to a lark (546; cf. *Troilus* III. 1191-2). When the eagle explains his mission, he portrays the poet as a humble but deserving case for favourable treatment. He deserves a guerdon because he has laboured long and selflessly as a writer in praise of love; and he needs it because he leads such an obscure and dully bookish life. The eagle's double portrait of the poet as a comically indefatigable writer (614–40) and reader (641-60) combines the fantasy of Chaucer as a servant of the servants of Love with the realities of Chaucer as a servant of the servants of the King—ill-rewarded, by implication, in both capacities. It is the perfect portrait of a petitioner.

But, unlike the dreamer in the *Legend*, the dreamer here is *not* a petitioner. He is apparently quite happy among his books (there is even a hint of discreet self-indulgence in line 660); and he receives Jupiter's unsolicited favours with a distinct lack of enthusiasm. 'Can you believe this?' 'No'; 'Can you see any towns?' 'No'; 'Do you want to learn about the stars?' 'Certainly not.' He is too old to learn astronomy; his eyes are not good enough to look at the stars; and so on. It is, by common consent, one of Chaucer's 'best japes'–to portray himself as not only an unlikely, but also an unwilling recipient of the favours of the great. The theme of petition is, as it were, inverted in this most extravagant variation.

Confessio Amantis, *Scogan*, *The Legend of Good Women*, and *The House of Fame* thus all display a certain playfulness on the part of the Ricardian poet in his role of petitioner. Forms of autobiographical utterance which originally had, and could still have, serious and practical functions tend in their work to shed those functions, either completely or in part. When these poets represent themselves as dependent upon the favours of the great, they most often write 'halvinge a game'—half (at least) in jest. Yet their work presents an image of the writer which is still recognizably shaped and coloured by those circumstances of petitionary dependence in which their medieval predecessors and successors so often appeared before their readers.

11. 'YOUNG SAINT, OLD DEVIL':
REFLECTIONS ON A MEDIEVAL PROVERB*

Dunbar's poem 'The Merle and the Nychtingaill' describes a
debate between two birds. The nightingale asserts that 'all
lufe is lost bot upone God allone'; the blackbird defends 'a
lusty life in luves service'. One stanza from the blackbird's
defence runs as follows:

> 'Seis', quod the merle, 'thy preching, nychtingale,
> Sall folk thair yewth spend in to holines?
> Of yung sanctis growis auld feyndis but faill;
> Fy, ypocreit in yeiris tendirness,
> Agane the law of kynd thow gois expres,
> That crukit aige makis on with yewth serene,
> Quhome natur of conditionis maid dyvers;
> A lusty life in luves service bene.'[1]

This attack on 'holiness' in youth takes the form of an appeal
to the Law of Kind. Nature has made youth different from
age, and to disturb this natural order is morally dangerous.
Those who cultivate in youth the holiness reserved for age,
the 'yung sanctis', will infallibly grow into wicked old men
and women. The blackbird suggests that the nightingale herself, in the tenderness of her years, has no business to be
preaching sanctity. She must be a hypocrite.

The line 'Of yung sanctis growis auld feyndis but faill' is
based on a pithy English saying: 'Young saint, old devil'. This
proverb appears in two fifteenth-century proverb collections,
in British Library MSS Additional 37075 and Harley 3362.[2]
Both these manuscripts are gatherings of texts intended for

---

* First published in *Review of English Studies*, n.s. 30 (1979), 385-96.

[1] 'The Merle and the Nychtingaill', ll. 33-40, from *The Poems of William
Dunbar*, ed. W. M. Mackenzie (London, 1932), omitting the editor's comma after
ypocreit.

[2] BL Add. MS 37075 fo. 70b; Harley MS 3362 fo. 2a. For these and other
references see B. J. Whiting, *Proverbs, Sentences, and Proverbial Phrases from
English Writings Mainly Before 1500* (Cambridge, Mass., 1968), S19: 'Young
Saint old devil'.

educational purposes; and in each case the English proverb is accompanied by a Latin hexameter which expresses the same idea: 'Angelicus iuvenis senibus satanizat in annis' ('An angelic young man becomes a devil in old age').[3] No doubt the Latin was meant for schoolboys to construe and scan. One wonders what they made of the sentiment.

Dunbar shows what he thinks of the proverb by assigning it to the frivolous blackbird, in a context which serves to neutralize dangerous implications. The pious nightingale replies that man should look to the love of God whatever his age, 'both in yewth and eild, and every hour' (42); and the debate ends with the ignominious capitulation of the blackbird:

> Than said the merle, 'Myne errour I confes;
> This frustir luve all is bot vanite;
> Blind ignorance me gaif sic hardines,
> To argone so againe the varite'.   (97–100)

Dunbar thus makes it clear that he regards the proverb as mistaken and perhaps dangerous. In this he was not alone. Indeed, 'young saint, old devil' seems to have acquired a certain notoriety in the medieval and Renaissance periods. Quite frequently pious writers cite the proverb as expressing a dangerous, even diabolical error. These passages have considerable interest, both for their own sake and for the light they shed on certain ways of thinking which have been, on the whole, censored from the official record.

The two earliest passages known to me come from thirteenth-century France. One appears in a Latin treatise dated in the late 1240s, the *De Eruditione Filiorum Nobilium* of Vincent of Beauvais. In his chapter 'De morali puerorum

---

[3] The same hexameter appears, without English equivalent, in three other fifteenth-century proverb collections written in England: Bodleian Library MS Douce 52 fo. 20b; Trinity College Oxford MS 7 fo. 109b; John Rylands Library Latin MS 394 fo. 10a. For the last see *Bulletin of the John Rylands Library* 14 (1930), 99. The hexameter is Item 1042 in H. Walther, *Proverbia Sententiaeque Latinitatis Medii Aevi* (Göttingen, 1963–7), where other occurrences are listed. There are a number of related Latin sayings in Walther: Items 1043, 1045, 1046, 1047, 1049, 2322, 9603, 18092, 20394, 24375 ('Qui nimium sanus puer est, vivet male canus; Qui puer est letus, fit bonus ille vetus'), 27273.

instruccione', after stressing the importance of moral discipline in boyhood, Vincent observes: 'Illud ergo prouerbium est detestabile, quod uulgariter solet dici, sc. de iuuene sancto dyabolum senem fieri'.[4] This proverb, Vincent continues, is factually incorrect, as well as wicked. Boys, admittedly, do sometimes pretend to be good 'uel ob parentum fauorem uel ob flagelli timorem' ('either to win their parents' favour or because they fear the whip'), and that kind of simulated virtue will not last. But a true virtuous disposition, confirmed by good discipline, will not easily go wrong in later life.

The vulgar (i.e. French) proverb referred to here by Vincent appears in a remarkable vernacular treatise by Philippe de Navarre, written a few years after the *De Eruditione*. In this work, *Les Quatre Ages de l'Homme*, Philippe treats in turn each of the four ages of man. In the section on the second age, Youth, he remarks on the need for men to remember God when they are young: 'Il i a aucunes foles genz qui dient une grant folie ou mençonje en leu de proverbe, mais ce est contraire a proverbe et a raison, quant il dient: *De jone saint, viel diable*. Ainsis n'est il pas.'[5] Virtue cultivated in youth, Philippe, says, becomes 'seconde nature' and lasts into later life. 'Mais il puet bien estre que li faus proverbes fu diz por les ypocrites.' But even hypocrisy, Philippe reflects subtly, is better than outright wildness; for a young hypocrite may set a good example for others—and

---

[4] Ed. A. Steiner (Cambridge, Mass., 1938), ch. xxxiii, ll. 116-18: 'Therefore that commonly cited proverb is detestable, that is, that a young saint becomes an old devil'.

[5] *Les Quatre Ages de l'Homme*, ed. M. de Fréville, Société des Anciens Textes Français (Paris, 1888), p. 34. 'De joene saintel veil dyable' is No. 509 in J. Morawski, *Proverbes français antérieurs au XVe siècle* (Paris, 1925), citing from *Li Proverbe au Vilain*. One MS of *Les Quatre Ages* substitutes *paperlarz* (hypocrite) for *saint* — a much less interesting version of the proverb, cited by Morawski from two French collections (see his note to No. 509). Another French variant, also recorded by Morawski, substitutes *angelot* for *saint*. Huizinga cites this version: 'As early as the fifteenth century people liked to show themselves *esprits forts* and to deride piety in others. The word "papelard", meaning a hypocrite, was in frequent use with lay writers of the time. "De jeune angelot vieux diable" (a young saint makes an old devil), said the proverb, or, in solemn Latin metre, *Angelicus juvenis senibus sathanizat in annis*. "It is by such sayings", Gerson exclaims, "that youth is perverted. A brazen face, scurrilous language and curses, immodest looks and gestures, are praised in children. Well, what is to be expected in old age of a *sathanizing* youth?"' (J. Huizinga, *The Waning of the Middle Ages*, Harmondsworth, 1955, p. 165.)

he may, after all, himself become truly virtuous, if he goes on pretending long enough: *lons usages torne presque a nature*.

The first known English discussion of the proverb occurs about a hundred years later, in a treatise on the Psalm *Qui Habitat* often ascribed to the fourteenth-century mystic Walter Hilton. A young man newly turned to God, says the author, may expect unfriendly comment: 'As whon worldly louers sen a mon or a wommon stured bi grace forte dispise hemself & þe likyng of þe world and fulliche and mekeliche ȝiuen hem to þe seruyse of god, anon þei are vuel payed with hit And callen hem ypocrites or ȝong seyntes, olde deueles. Þei halde hem fooles and seyn þat þei schal neuere bringe to ende þat þei beginne.'[6] Although this is the first recorded English occurrence of the 'detestable proverb', the author's manner of introducing it suggests that it was already familiar —and already associated, in English minds, with the idea of hypocrisy.

Three passages attest the currency of the proverb in fifteenth-century England. In a sermon from early in the century, one preacher observes that many young men foolishly declare that they will delay repentance until they are old: 'Itt is a comond prouerbe bothe of clerkes and of laye men, "ȝounge seynt, old dewell". And so þei arn disceyveyd. For often tymes sonere þou seyst a ȝounge man die þan an old man. And þerfore beware of þise wordes, ȝounge men.'[7] We may get some idea of how 'laye men' used the proverb from a nearly contemporary work, *Dives and Pauper* (1405-?1410). This treatise takes the form of a dialogue between a preaching Friar (Pauper) and a rich, worldly layman (Dives). Pauper speaks of the natural perversity of man, which may be made worse by lack of discipline and good example in youth. He cites one of the proverbs of Solomon: 'A young man according to his way. Even when he is old he will not depart from it' (Prov. 22: 6). Dives objects: 'And þow it is a comoun prouerbe: ȝong seynt, eld deuyl'. To this Pauper retorts

---

[6] *An Exposition of Qui Habitat and Bonum Est in English*, ed. B. Wallner, Lund Studies in English xxiii (Lund, 1954), pp. 8-9. The editor introduces a conjectural *and* between ȝ*ong seyntes* and *olde deueles*; but this is unnecessary, given the asyndetic form of the proverb.

[7] *Middle English Sermons Edited from British Museum MS Royal 18 B. xxiii*, ed. W. O. Ross, EETS o.s. 209 (1940), pp. 159-60.

sharply: 'It is a synful prouerbe, to drawyn meen to synne
from vertue, from God to þe fend.' He goes on to cite authorities and examples in favour of God-fearing youth: 'in holy
wryȝt Seynt Ion Baptist, Tobye, Ieremie, Sampson, Samuel
and manye othere been preysid for here holynesse in here
ȝougthe'.[8]

Like Dunbar's 'The Merle and the Nychtingaill', *Dives and
Pauper* is a simple dialogue. In another fifteenth-century
English text we can see the proverb in a more fully dramatic
context—being used by a devil, in fact, to 'draw a man to sin
from virtue', just as Pauper says. The text in question is
headed 'Of þe seuen Ages' in the only surviving manuscript.
Although it extends to only fifty-seven short verses, it has
justly been described as an 'embryonic morality play'. It consists of speeches by Man and by his Good and Bad Angels.
The Bad Angel draws Man to sin in six of his seven ages, only
to lose him when he turns to God in the last. The following
lines cover the second, third, and fourth ages (Boyhood,
Youth, and Maturity):

þe childe	I will go play with my felowe
þe angel	To goode vertews loke þou drawe
þe fende	Ȝonge saynt alde devell is ane alde sawe
	Begyn not þat Iape to kepe gode lawe
	Ȝouthe spekes to his selfe & says
	With women me lyst both play & rage
Angel	To þi saule it is gret dammage
þe fende	If þou be holy in þi ȝong age
	Þi sorrow sal incres & þi myght swage
	Man spekes to hym selfe & says
	Now I am in strenthe who dar to me say nay
Angel	Man hafe mynde of þine endyng day
þe fende	Whils þou art ȝonge be Ioly & lyght
	With al ryall & ryche aray
	When þou art olde & fayles myght
	þan is tyme to do foly away.[9]

---

[8] *Dives and Pauper*, ed. P. H. Barnum, vol. i, Part I, EETS o.s. 275 (1976),
p. 128. All the biblical figures mentioned here, except Sampson, were ancient
types of the *puer senex* or wise youth: see C. Gnilka, *Aetas Spiritalis* (Bonn,
1972), Index.

[9] BL Add. MS 37049 fo. 28b. The whole text is edited by E. C. York, *MLN*

Here it is the fiend himself who, within the context of the
natural order of the ages, invokes the sinful proverb. 'Normal'
boys, as we would call them, want to play with their friends.
To be 'virtuous' is, at that age, itself no more than a 'jape'.
Youth also has its own kinds of play; and holiness in youth is
merely depressing and weakening. Maturity is a time of
strength, pleasure, and prosperity—no time to think of death
or 'do folly away'. These diabolical arguments are answered,
as in Dunbar's poem, by injunctions to 'remember thy
creator in the days of thy youth'.

Let me conclude this anthology of examples with two
from famous writers of the generation after Dunbar. A fellow
Scotsman, Sir David Lindsay, uses the proverb in a context
very like that in 'Of the seuen Ages'. In Lindsay's *Ane Satyre
of the Thrie Estaitis*, the morality-play hero, young Rex
Humanitas, is approached by Placebo the flatterer, Solace,
and Wantonness. When they tempt him with talk of women,
he responds with pious horror; so Placebo attempts to encourage him:

> Beleiue ȝe that we will begyll ȝow,
> Or from ȝour vertew we will wyle ȝow,
> Or with euill counsall overseyll ȝow,
>   Both into gude and euill?
> To tak ȝour graces part wee grant
> In all ȝour deidis participant,
> Sa that ȝe be nocht ane ȝoung sanct,
>   And syne ane auld deuill.[10]

Lindsay here follows the medieval tradition of using the proverb in dramatic or semi-dramatic contexts. The other,
homiletic, tradition is equally clearly represented in the
following passage from a sermon by Lindsay's great English
contemporary, Bishop Hugh Latimer: 'If [a man] be young
and lusty, the devil will put in his heart, and say to him:
"What! thou art in thy flowers, man; take thy pleasure; make

[10] 1554 version, ed. D. Hamer, *Works of Sir David Lindsay*, vol. ii, STS Third
Series, No. 2 (1931), ll. 227–34. There is a similar use of the proverb by Riot in
the Interlude *Youth*, ll. 605–8.

merry with thy companions; remember the old proverb, 'Young saints, old devils'". Which proverb in very deed is naught and deceitful, and the devil's own invention; which would have parents negligent in bringing up their children in goodness.'[11]

The sinful proverb continued to interest people long after Dunbar, Lindsay, and Latimer. M. P. Tilley, in his *Dictionary of the Proverbs in England in the Sixteenth and Seventeenth Centuries*, cites twenty-three occurrences in that period, ending with a quotation from 1721 which is very much in the manner of our earlier examples: 'A young Saint may prove an old Devil. It were a thousand pities he should; this is a devilish Proverb, and often as devilishly apply'd.'[12] I cannot attempt here, however, to follow the history of the proverb in modern times. No doubt the religious controversies of the sixteenth and seventeenth centuries brought new significances to the phrase 'young saint'. Perhaps, too, the attitudes expressed by the proverb gained strength in the age of the French Revolution. 'Young saint, old devil' would not have been out of place among William Blake's Proverbs of Hell, alongside a saying such as 'The road of excess leads to the palace of wisdom'.

II

All the writers I have cited disapprove of the proverb 'Young saint, old devil'. It is variously described as 'detestabile', 'une

---

[11] The Seventh Sermon upon the Lord's Prayer, in *Sermons by Hugh Latimer*, ed. G. E. Corrie, Parker Society (Cambridge, 1844), p. 431. Erasmus ascribes a similar Latin proverb to the Devil's invention in his *Pietas Puerilis*, a dialogue between two boys: 'Erasmius: Religiosior tu quidem es quam pro aetate. Gaspar: Imo nullam aetatem non decet religio ... Erasmius: Aiunt vulgo pueros angelicos in satanam verti, ubi consenuerint. Gaspar: Sed ego proverbium istuc ab autore satana natum arbitror', *Colloquia* (1522), ed. L. E. Halkin, F. Bierlaire, R. Hoven, in *Opera Omnia*, I. iii (Amsterdam, 1972), p. 172: 'Erasmius: You are more pious than befits your age. Gaspar: On the contrary, there is no age to which piety is not appropriate ... Erasmius: They say commonly that angelic boys turn to Satan when they grow old. Gaspar: But I consider that proverb to be the work of Satan himself.' The English translation by Nathaniel Bailey (1725) uses the traditional English equivalent for the Latin proverb: 'a young saint and an old devil'.

[12] M. P. Tilley, *A Dictionary of the Proverbs in England in the Sixteenth and Seventeenth Centuries* (Ann Arbor, Michigan, 1950), S33, citing James Kelly's *Complete Collection of Scotish Proverbs* (1721). See also Tilley D311 and W324 for related sayings.

grant folie ou mençonje', 'faus', 'synful', 'naught and deceitful', and 'ab autore satana natum'. When Latimer called it
'the devil's own invention', he spoke for all.[13] The saying
was (though not in Blake's sense) a Proverb of Hell. Such
widespread and unanimous hostility suggests that the proverb
expressed ideas which were themselves widespread and also,
in the opinion of pious men, dangerous. I want now to place
these ideas within a general context of medieval ethical thinking about the ages of man. I shall suggest that the proverb
may be taken to represent the less orthodox of two diamet-
rically opposed radical approaches to this subject.

All societies, no doubt, have some notion of a normal
order, sanctioned by nature or by some other authority, in
the development of an individual from infancy to old age. In
the Middle Ages, as in classical antiquity and in the Renaissance, educated people thought of this order in a more
schematic way than we do now. They recognized three, or
four, or six, or seven ages of man.[14] Such schemes were commonly supported by analogies in nature or history. The four
ages correspond with the four seasons, the six ages with the
six ages of the world, the seven ages with the seven planets.
Thus the ages form part of a larger order and obey what
Dunbar called the 'law of kynd', the Law of Nature.

The natural laws of human development not only govern
the growth and decay of the body; they also affect character
and behaviour. Each age has its own passions and preoccupations, and hence its own characteristic virtues and vices. For

[13] I have found only one early passage which cites the proverb with approba-
tion. It is in Lord Berners's *Golden Book of Marcus Aurelius* (1535, translated
from an original Spanish work by Guevara): 'He [Marcus Aurelius] was wont to
saye, whan any in his presence that were yonge and not welle taught in their
language, gested at the debilytie of age, or olde men at the foly of youth: Leaue
them sith they leue you. Many tymes of wyse yonge men cometh olde foles: And
of yonge fooles customably cometh wyse olde men. Naturalitie at the last maketh
al thynge in kynde', ed. J. M. Gálvez, *Guevara in England*, Palaestra cix (Berlin,
1916), pp. 157–8. The whole passage is of interest, as a quite radical expression of
what I call the 'nature ideal'.
[14] On age-schemes in antiquity see F. Boll, 'Die Lebensalter: Ein Beitrag zur
antiken Ethologie und zur Geschichte der Zahlen', *Neue Jahrbücher für das
klassische Altertum* 31 (1913), 89–145; and E. Eyben, 'Die Einteilung des mensch-
lichen Lebens im römischen Altertum', *Rheinisches Museum für Philologie*,
116 (1973), 150–90. There is no comprehensive study of age-schemes in the
Middle Ages. For Renaissance England see S. C. Chew, *The Pilgrimage of Life*
(New Haven, Conn., 1962), ch. 6.

this reason moralists as well as doctors have to take account of the ages of man. This is a complex subject, and it has been little studied. It seems clear, however, that there are two basically different ways in which moralists can think about the natural order of human development. They can regard it *either* as a low norm to be transcended *or* as a high norm to be achieved.

In practice, these two very different approaches come into conflict most often where the earlier ages are concerned. The reason for this is that the 'natural' characteristics of the later ages tend to look more like virtues than vices to those pious writers who otherwise favour the ideal of transcendence—which they are therefore inclined, in such cases, not to invoke. Such writers could hardly, after all, reject the wisdom of old age merely because it was natural (for so tradition held). In the earlier ages, on the other hand, and especially in boyhood and youth, the natural passions and preoccupations look much more dubious: the playfulness of boys or the wildness of young men are hardly likely to commend themselves to conventional piety. Hence it is in their boyhood and youth, not in their old age, that saints are said by hagiographers to transcend the natural characteristics of their age. The young saint, according to these authors, achieves by grace a peculiar wisdom and sobriety, 'aetatem moribus transiens'.[15]

There is thus a certain asymmetry about the 'transcendence ideal'. By contrast, the 'nature ideal' is, or may be, consistently applied to all the ages. The proverb 'Young saint, old devil', by its very form, asserts this ideal at its most symmetrical and consistent, and so claims for it a kind of strength. The phrase 'young saint' boldly courts comparison with the hagiographic ideal of transcendence in youth; but the proverb converts it into a dubious oxymoron by setting

---

[15] 'Surpassing his age in his conduct'. The Latin phrase was apparently coined by Gregory the Great, speaking of St. Benedict in his *Dialogues*: 'cor gerens senile, aetatem quippe moribus transiens' (*Patrologia Latina*, vol. 66, col. 126): 'having the heart of an old man and indeed surpassing his age in his conduct'. Bede picked it up and applied it to Benedict Biscop in *Historia Abbatum* and to Wilfred in *Historia Ecclesiastica: Opera Historica*, ed. C. Plummer (Oxford, 1896), i. 322, 364. There is an excellent study of what he calls the *Transzendenzideal* in early Christian writers by Gnilka: see n. 8 above.

it alongside 'old devil'. The latter phrase is solidly uncontroversial, since it calls up various images of sin in old age (the *senex amans*, for instance) which no one could fail to find repellent, whether or not he favours the nature ideal. It therefore provides support for the controversial implications of the first phrase. The buried arguments may be stated like this: 'Everyone agrees that vice in old age is unnatural and repulsive; but is not virtue in youth equally unnatural?'

It all depends, clearly, on what you mean by 'virtue'. The proverb was commonly taken to imply that 'virtue' in youth can be false or assumed. As Philippe de Navarre observed: 'il puet bien estre que li faus proverbes fu diz por les ypocrites'. Christ himself said 'Nolite tristes fieri, sicut ypocrite', 'Be not, as the hypocrites, of a sad countenance' (Matthew 6: 16); and the 'sadness' of *young* saints is particularly open to this suspicion of hypocrisy. Most people evidently preferred frank naughtiness in children or wildness in youths to the kind of goodness which seemed to be assumed 'uel ob parentum fauorem uel ob flagelli timorem'.

But even if the elders and (more rarely) the contemporaries of such a young saint allow his goodness to be real, they may still feel uneasy about it. As Erasmius (the normal boy) says to Gaspar (the pious boy) in Erasmus' *Colloquia*: 'Religiosior tu quidem es quam pro aetate'.[16] This uneasiness may have many sources—old wives' fears ('So wise, so young, they say, do never live long'), as well as plain jealousy and dislike. The moral doctrines involved are not entirely clear. People commonly suspect that the virtue of young saints, however real it may be at the time, will not last. Why? Perhaps there is a tacit biological analogy here: such virtue is a premature birth, or a plant that comes up too early in the year.

A slightly different version of this idea is implicit in a dictum uttered by Duke Theseus in Chaucer's *Knight's Tale*. Theseus has come upon the two young lovers fighting in a grove outside Athens. He makes a powerful speech on the folly of love ('The god of love, a, *benedicite*!'). The scorn of this speech, however, modulates into sympathy with the following words:

---

[16] For the passage see n. 11 above.

> But all moot ben assayed, hoot and coold;
> A man moot ben a fool, or yong or oold, —
> I woot it by myself ful yore agon,
> For in my tyme a servant was I oon.   (I. 1811-14)

If a period of folly is indeed inevitable in every man's life,
then it follows that he had better get it over with in youth.
Youthful folly, natural enough in itself, carries a promise of
later wisdom; but a wise youth condemns himself to a foolish
old age. And, to cite another pungent proverb, there is no
fool like an old fool.[17]

III

Students of literature have paid too little attention to the
ages of man and to the traditions of moral thinking associated
with them. Good writers, of course, cannot usually be identified as simple adherents of a 'nature ideal' or of a 'transcendence ideal'; but ideas such as those expressed by the proverb
'Young saint, old devil' do play a part in their more searching
representations of human nature. In the hope of drawing
critics' attention to this largely unexplored subject, I should
like finally to glance at three versions of the young saint
from different periods of English literature: the young hero
of Chaucer's *Prioress's Tale*, Prince John in Shakespeare's
Henry IV Part II, and Blifil in Fielding's *Tom Jones*.

Chaucer's *Prioress's Tale* seems at first sight to fall squarely
within the hagiographical tradition, adopting completely the
appropriate *Transzendenzideal*. The seven-year-old schoolboy
who is its hero appears to be a straightforward example of
the *puer senex* of the saints' lives, 'aetatem moribus transiens'.
He cannot strictly be called a saint; but the Prioress compares
him to St. Nicholas and St. Hugh of Lincoln. His devotion to
the Virgin certainly lifts him well out of the common run of
schoolboys. But on closer scrutiny it turns out that Chaucer
has subtly adapted and, as it were, naturalized the familiar
figure of the *puer senex*.

What Chaucer does is to trace, delicately, but unmistakably, the natural origins of the child's devotion to Mary. The

---

[17] Whiting F452.

boy learns it first from his mother, and it sticks in his mind, as such things do:

> Thus hath this wydwe hir litel sone ytaught
> Oure blisful Lady, Cristes mooder deere,
> Tor worshipe ay, and he forgat it naught,
> For sely child wol alday soone leere.

(VII. 509-12)

Then, in his first term at school, he hears older boys singing a Latin anthem in praise of Mary, *Alma Redemptoris Mater*. He cannot understand it, but asks a friend in a higher form to tell him what the Latin means. Once he finds out, he determines to learn it by heart before the end of term. The naturalism of such touches is remarkable, not least in a Miracle of the Virgin. The boy is almost a saint; but he is also almost a normal boy. He has a child's capacity to learn words he does not understand; and his fatal fascination with the anthem has its beginnings in little more than the curiosity schoolboys feel about the mysterious work done in higher forms (ll. 516-20). He does not learn the anthem 'ob parentum fauorem uel ob flagelli timorem': on the contrary, he risks being beaten for neglecting his other studies (541-3). There is real boyish exuberance, too, as well as Marian devotion, in his bold and merry singing on the way to school. If he were a few years older (as he is in the analogues), perhaps these boyish qualities would not coexist so easily with his piety; but at the age of seven he is only just out of the age of innocence, *infantia*, and still on the threshold of boyhood, *pueritia*.

The proverb 'Young saint, old devil' does not appear anywhere in Chaucer's works; but the nature ideal of which it is an extreme expression evidently commanded from him some degree of assent. One may think, for instance, of the contrast between the Knight and the Squire, and of the contrast between their tales. In the *Prioress's Tale*, he tacitly acknowledges this ideal by portraying a young saint who is so pointedly *not*, in the proverb's sense, a 'young saint'.

Shakespeare's works, like Chaucer's, are exceptionally rich in reflections on natural and unnatural behaviour in youth and old age. This is particularly true of the two *Henry IV* plays, which present a number of variations on this theme. One thinks first, of course, of Falstaff, who exhibits all the incongruities of an 'old devil' ('How ill white hairs become a fool and jester!'). More relevant to our present subject, however, is the contrast between Prince Hal and his younger brother, Prince John, in Part II.

In Act IV of this play, Prince John, at the head of the king's forces, confronts the rebel Archbishop of York and his forces in Gaultree Forest. The play seems about to culminate in a battle, as Part I did at Shrewsbury; but the young prince captures the rebel leaders by a trick, and their forces disperse. This anticlimactic episode concludes with an encounter between Prince John and Falstaff, at the end of which Falstaff expresses his dislike of John in the famous sherry soliloquy: 'Good faith, this same young sober-blooded boy doth not love me, nor a man cannot make him laugh—but that's no marvel, he drinks no wine. There's never none of these demure boys come to any proof, for thin drink doth so over-cool their blood, and making many fish-meals, that they fall into a kind of male green-sickness, and then when they marry they get wenches.'[18] Later in the same speech Falstaff contrasts John, to his discredit, with his brother Hal. Both have inherited the 'cold blood' from their father; but Hal, unlike John, has enriched his by drinking sherry and so has become 'very hot and valiant'.

Shakespeare's contrasting portraits of the two brothers may appear to present a simple antithesis, in the spirit of the proverb, between a young saint (bad) and a young devil (good). Unlike Hal, John is a good son and gives his father no trouble; but the Gaultree episode proves him to be cold, calculating, and unscrupulous—capable, when it suits him, of the most shameless lying and deceit. He is also, according to Falstaff, a coward. By contrast, Hal may appear the most attractive sort of 'young devil'—a high-spirited and courageous young man. He sows his wild oats at just the right time of year; and, when the responsibilities of royalty fall upon him, he shows himself capable of assuming them with mature gravity. But the reality is more complex. Hal's inherited cold blood shows itself in a capacity to calculate almost equal to

[18] Ed. J. Dover Wilson (Cambridge, 1946), IV. iii. 85–92.

John's. There is always something equivocal, a touch of cool-ness, about his wildness. The audience cannot accept him as a natural 'young devil', any more than they can accept Falstaff's outrageous claim, made to annoy the Lord Chief Justice, that he himself is a *puer senex*: 'To approve my youth further, I will not: the truth is, I am only old in judge-ment and understanding' (I. ii. 186-8). In the devious human world of *Henry IV* Part II neither the nature ideal nor the transcendence ideal finds authentic representatives. Hence the figure of the hypocritical 'young saint' appears less ab-normal, though hardly less unlovable, than he might seem in a more stable context.

A more straightforward antithesis than that between John and Hal may be found in Fielding's *Tom Jones*. Here Blifil is the young saint and Tom the young devil. The moral advan-tage lies much more clearly here with Tom than it does with Hal in Shakespeare. As a boy, Tom robs orchards and poaches game; and as a youth, he goes to bed with women of easy virtue. But the book makes it abundantly—even excessively—clear that these are 'faults of wildness and of youth' (Book XVII, Chapter ii) and 'vices of a warm disposition' (XII. xiii). Tom is one of those 'young men of open, generous disposi-tions' who are 'naturally inclined to gallantry' (IV. v). He is imprudent and rash; but he possesses that 'natural goodness of heart' which Fielding values as the guarantee of good faith and true benevolence. Tom's brother Blifil is his exact opposite. 'He was, indeed, a lad of a remarkable disposition: sober, discreet, and pious, beyond his age' (III. ii). It sounds like the admiring description of a *puer senex* in a saint's life; but the reader soon discovers that the piety and discretion of Blifil mask a complete indifference to any but his own interests. He is, in short, a hypocrite and a scoundrel.[19] Sophia (her name means wisdom) sees this from the first: 'To say the truth, Sophia, when very young, discerned that Tom, though an idle, thoughtless, rattling rascal, was nobody's enemy but

[19] My colleague Pat Rogers points out to me another amusing passage where Fielding implies suspicion of young saints. In *Joseph Andrews* (III. vii) the quack doctor says: 'It must greatly raise our expectations of the future conduct in life of boys, whom in their tender years we perceive instead of taw or balls, or other childish play-things, at their leisure hours, to chuse, to exercise their genius in contentions of wit, learning, and such-like.'

his own; and that Master Blifil, though a prudent, discreet, sober young gentleman, was at the same time attached to the interest only of one single person; and who that single person was, the reader will be able to divine without any assistance of ours' (IV. v). At the end of the book, we see Blifil 'lately turned Methodist, in hopes of marrying a very rich widow of that sect' (XVIII. xiii). Thus the old medieval theme of religious hypocrisy, or *papelardie*, takes a distinctly eighteenth-century turn.

Fielding claimed that he was 'not writing a system, but a history'; but the contrast he draws between Tom and Blifil implies a system of ideas very like that implicit in the medieval proverb which I have discussed in this essay. Youthful wildness, in a good nature such as Tom's, carries with it the promise of an equally seasonable gravity in later life. Such is the calm and settled maturity of Allworthy. For Allworthy was himself like Tom, not like Blifil, in his younger days: 'Allworthy was naturally a man of spirit, and his present gravity arose from true wisdom and philosophy, not from any original phlegm in his disposition; for he had possessed much fire in his youth, and had married a beautiful woman for love' (VI. iv). For Blifil the prospects are quite different. His youthful sobriety already betrays a suppressed and perverted sexuality (Book VII, Chapter vi illustrates this); and the figure of the elderly 'philosopher' Square discovered in Molly Seagrim's bedroom may be taken to represent a possible future for Blifil as a grotesque *senex amans*. For, as Falstaff observes, 'there's never none of these demure boys come to any proof'.

12. ALLEGORY: THE LITERAL LEVEL

I

I think that it is true to say that all allegories are fictions. At least they can be considered, from the literary point of view, as fictions. And that is what I should like to do here. I want in particular to consider certain questions about the laws governing allegorical fictions. There are questions of fact and questions of principle. Do allegories obey any laws at all at the fictional, or literal, level? If so, what are they? These questions have been debated for centuries, and it seems clear that there are available three kinds of answer to them. The greater part of this essay will be devoted to a survey of these three approaches; but first I have to clear up two points of terminology. These concern the word 'literal' and the word 'allegory'.

It seems that the use of the word 'literal' in the sense which concerns us here originated with St. Paul. In the Epistles to the Romans and the Corinthians we find the famous opposition between 'spirit' and 'letter' ('pneuma' and 'gramma', in Paul's Greek).[1] Exactly what Paul himself meant by this opposition need not concern us here. The point is that early interpreters of the Bible took the terms up and adapted them to the purposes of their allegorical exposition of the Old and New Testaments. Here, very roughly, the 'letter' is what the Bible actually says, by way of narrative, prophecy, commandment or whatever; and this stands to the 'spirit' as nutshell to kernel. Later on, in the Middle Ages, the term 'literal' was taken up by another learned discipline. The grammarians and rhetoricians borrowed it from the exegetes, and at the same time extended its range of application. The grammarians and rhetoricians of classical antiquity had been accustomed to treat allegory as one of the 'tropes'—a trope being any figure of speech in which words are used in abnormal, or as they would have said 'improper', senses.[2] So it

---

[1] Romans 2: 29, 7: 6; 2 Corinthians 3: 6.

[2] Thus Quintilian discusses *allegoria* in his chapter on *tropi*, defining the latter as 'verbi vel sermonis a propria significatione in aliam cum virtute mutatio' ('the

was natural for their medieval successors to apply the new Christian term 'literal' to the other tropes, as well as allegory, whenever the apparent or surface sense was in question. Hence 'literal' comes in Modern English to be used not only of allegory, but also of such other tropes as metaphor, hyperbole, and irony. So in English (though not in French) 'literal' has taken over the functions of the old term 'proper', so far as tropes are concerned. This use is now very common both in technical and in colloquial English. The word is used in this way, for instance, by John Searle in his illuminating discussion of metaphor in his book of essays, *Expression and Meaning*. Searle distinguishes between what he calls 'word or sentence meaning' and 'speaker's utterance meaning'. 'In literal utterance', he says, 'the speaker means what he says; that is, literal sentence meaning and speaker's utterance meaning are the same.'[3]

A knowledge of the history of the word may help to distinguish the two overlapping senses of 'literal' in modern critical terminology. In many contexts the 'literal meaning' is simply the 'word or sentence meaning' or (in the old sense) the proper meaning of any expression or passage in which some kind of trope is being used. But when allegory is in question, the word 'literal' usually reverts to its remoter exegetical ancestry. For when we speak of the 'literal level' of an allegory, we mean that which the allegory as a whole presents to us as said and done, not the proper meaning of a particular passage. The 'letter' is here, as in medieval exegesis, the 'historia'—or, as we would say, the fiction. Imagine an ordinary, sensible, literal-minded artist sitting down to produce illustrations for an edition of, say, the *Pilgrim's Progress*. Everything which such an artist might include in his pictures is on the literal level. This is, as it were, the fictional body of the allegory.

Allegory, as we understand it, is the only one of the tropes to assert its literal sense in the way that fictions are asserted, and it is because of this unique fictive character that its literal

artistic alteration of a word or phrase from its proper meaning to another'): *Institutio Oratoria*, ed. and trans. H. E. Butler (London and New York, 1920-2), VIII. vi. 1.

[3] J. R. Searle, *Expression and Meaning: Studies in the Theory of Speech Acts* (Cambridge, 1979), pp. 77, 81.

level is capable of sustaining the erection of further tropes upon it. This can cause confusion. In his essay on Dante, for example, T. S. Eliot praised Dante for using few metaphors; 'allegory and metaphor', he said, 'do not get on well together'. But the fact is that most allegories (including, I should have thought, the *Divine Comedy*) have at least a normal amount of incidental metaphor in them. Eliot says that 'as the whole poem of Dante is, if you like, one vast metaphor, there is hardly any place for metaphor in the detail of it'.[4] But it is misleading, in this context at least, to call the whole poem 'one vast metaphor'. Its literal level is *there*, as the literal sense of a metaphor can never be. It is, indeed, a fiction solid enough to sustain any number of other tropes. The truth is that this superfoetation of tropes, to which Eliot objects, is a perfectly normal and acceptable occurrence in allegory. But the double ancestry of the word 'literal' does give rise to difficulties in such cases. For it will be the figurative and not the literal (or proper) sense of the incidental metaphor which will belong to the literal level of the allegory. Aquinas, as often, is very clear on this point.[5]

Eliot's reference to Dante's allegory as 'one vast metaphor' will serve to introduce my second point of terminology, which concerns the word 'allegory' itself. This word has its origins outside Christianity, in the work of the Greek and Roman grammarians. I have already said that these writers regarded allegory as one of the tropes. But if you look at, for example, Quintilian's discussion of the matter (in the Eighth Book of his *Institutio Oratoria*), you will see that 'allegory' did not mean quite the same to him as it normally does to us. One of his examples will make the difference clear. He quotes the passage with which Virgil brings to an end the Second Book of his *Georgics*:

> But now
> A mighty length of plain we have travelled o'er;
> 'Tis time to loose our horses' steaming necks.[6]

---

[4] 'Dante', in *Selected Essays* (3rd edn., London, 1951), pp. 243–4.

[5] *Summa Theologiae*, I. q. 1, a. 10, ad 3: 'sensus parabolicus sub litterali continetur: nam per voces significatur aliquid proprie, et aliquid figurative, nec est litteralis sensus ipsa figura, sed id quod est figuratum'.

[6] *Institutio Oratoria*, VIII. vi. 44–5.

This conforms to the standard rhetorical definition of allegory, the definition which is stated by Quintilian and echoed by Eliot: allegory is a 'continued metaphor'. But would we nowadays call it allegory? I think not. We do not usually call it allegory when Spenser, imitating Virgil, ends a book of the *Faerie Queene* in a similar fashion:

> But now my teme begins to faint and fayle,
> All woxen weary of their iournall toyle:
> Therefore I will their sweatie yokes assoyle
> At this same furrowes end, till a new day.
>
> (*Faerie Queene*, III. xii. 47)

Spencer would certainly have called this an allegory; but we would simply call it a metaphor. The word 'allegory' seems, in fact, quite recently to have narrowed in meaning—perhaps as recently as the nineteenth century, when the old rhetorical tradition collapsed. We are no longer inclined (in ordinary critical usage, at least) to apply the word to straightforward continued metaphors, such as Spenser's ploughing metaphor, where the literal sense is merely metaphorical. The plough is, in a quite simple and unpregnant sense, just not there at the end of the Third Book of the *Faerie Queene*; and this seems to disqualify it as allegory, according to present usage. Allegory, for us, is a special kind of trope, marked by some degree of fictional solidity on the level of the literal sense.

What I have called, for lack of a better phrase, 'fictional solidity' has to be reckoned with as a variable in any discussion of allegorical fiction. The variation occurs, one might say, along a scale running from simple continued metaphor at the zero end up to the opposite extreme where, as in much biblical exegesis, the literal level is taken to represent historical fact. We might visualize Quintilian standing at one end, and St. Paul at the other. Both extremes lie beyond our range, however, since for modern literary criticism the literal level of allegory is always both more than metaphor and less than history. It is fiction. Yet even if we cut off the two extreme ends of the scale, we shall still have to discriminate between the various degrees or kinds of allegorical fiction. Some allegories represent themselves as histories, others as dreams or visions; some are inset or framed in another, larger fiction, others (like the *Faerie Queene*) are not; some serve the purposes of prophecy or preaching, others of satire or of entertainment. So we should not expect every allegory to exhibit the same degree of fictional solidity, or to obey the same laws of fictional coherence. We must be prepared to recognize the special by-laws which govern allegorical prophecies, allegorical dreams, and the rest.

II

I come now to the main questions which I want to consider in this essay: Do allegories, at the literal level, obey laws? And if so, what are they? There are, as I have said, three different kinds of answer to such questions. I shall consider these in turn. It will be convenient to attach labels to them. I shall call the first 'Neo-Medieval' and illustrate it from D. W. Robertson's *Preface to Chaucer* (1963). The second is the 'Neo-Classical' approach, which I shall illustrate from the work of two eighteenth-century critics, Joseph Spence and Hugh Blair. The third and last is the 'Neo-Romantic' approach; and I shall illustrate that from Angus Fletcher's book, *Allegory: The Theory of a Symbolic Mode* (1964).

Let me introduce the Neo-Medieval view first in caricature. This will establish one of the two extreme positions which are possible on the present subject. An extremist Neo-Medieval view, then, might run somewhat as follows: allegorical fictions are (in Aristotelian language) ordered strictly towards an end which lies outside and beyond them; hence they have no autonomy and no laws of their own. It does not matter how their parts stand to each other on the literal level, for their whole function is to contribute to the higher significance. One should look in the fictional world of an allegory neither for sense nor for interesting nonsense. Its ladies may look and behave oddly; its castles may be grotesque and unrecognizable; but the right kind of reader will look straight through these things 'and then the heaven espy'.

Robertson, in his *Preface to Chaucer*, puts forward a somewhat less extreme version of this view. Let me quote from his second chapter, which is entitled 'Some Principles of Medieval

Aesthetics'. At the beginning of this chapter, he discusses a passage from Augustine *On Christian Doctrine* in which Augustine interprets a verse from the Canticles allegorically: I shall return to this later. He then draws the following general conclusions:

The incoherence of the surface materials is almost essential to the formation of the abstract pattern, for if the surface materials—the concrete elements in the figures—were consistent or spontaneously satisfying in an emotional way, there would be no stimulus to seek something beyond them. It follows from these considerations that if the figures were decorative, as they are in much eighteenth-century writing, or if they were spontaneously satisfying to the emotions, as they are in much romantic writing, no such effects as those described by St Augustine would be possible. It follows also that the concrete materials of the figures do not need to be 'realistically' conceived to obtain the effect desired . . . This means that when we consider this kind of figurative expression, either in literary art or in the visual arts, neither surface consistency nor 'realism' is necessary to its effectiveness.[7]

I distinguish two points here: first, that some 'incoherence of the surface materials' is 'almost essential' in allegory; second, that 'surface consistency', though presumably it may be found, is not in any way 'necessary'. Let us consider these points in turn.

One might compare the composition of allegory to the composition of a crossword, in which (in my experience, at least) due attention to the downs inevitably produces some nonsensical acrosses, and vice versa. But Robertson is saying rather that allegories *ought* to have at least some nonsensical acrosses, or we will never bother to look at the downs. Now this is not true, strictly speaking: it is not necessary for the recognition of an allegory as such that it should display some incoherence on its literal level. A small framed or inset allegory, for example, may establish its allegorical character not by any internal incoherence, but by the oddity of its relation to the larger context in which it is enclosed—as when the Fool in *Lear* starts to talk about what cuckoos do to hedge-sparrows. But this is something of a quibble. Many allegories —especially the larger, unframed varieties—do rely heavily on

[7] *A Preface to Chaucer* (Princeton, NJ, 1963), pp. 56–7.

surface incoherences of various kinds in order to alert the reader to their allegorical character in the first instance; and most allegories from time to time employ such devices to keep him on his toes. In the Middle Ages, Bible interpreters were accustomed to regard an oddity as a sign that allegorical meaning was to be looked for: 'recurramus ad allegoriam', 'let us have recourse to the allegory'. They were very quick to detect these signs. One writer, for example, remarked that, when Christ came to Bethany to resurrect Lazarus, we would have expected Mary as well as Martha to go out to welcome him, since she loved him so much. But the Bible says that she remained indoors. This is an incoherence, an unmotivated event, unintelligible on the literal level; but it can be understood figuratively if we will see Mary as representing the life of contemplation, as against Martha who represents the active life. It is common for an allegorical personage to act strangely like this. Why, in Langland's *Piers Plowman*, does Piers tear up the pardon which his master Truth has sent him? Why does Walter, in Chaucer's *Clerk's Tale*, behave as he does towards poor Griselda? The author may attempt to devise some motivation on the literal level, as Chaucer does so unsuccessfully in the case of Walter; but we still feel forced to look elsewhere for the true explanation: 'recurramus ad allegoriam'. And the same is true of all the other kinds of oddness which we meet in allegories: the people who walk forwards with one foot and backwards with the other, the people without teeth or tongue, the strange beasts, the floating islands. The author may cover himself by adopting the form of a romance or a fantastic dream, where marvels are to be expected. But we are not deceived; we have recourse to the allegory.

So 'incoherence of the surface materials' is highly characteristic, whether we like it or not, of allegories; and it does play an important part, as Robertson argues, in directing our attention through to the significations which lie beyond the allegorical fiction. Yet it does not follow from this, of course, that 'surface consistency' is simply not necessary at all in allegory; and I want to argue now that Robertson in fact goes too far when he asserts this.

Robertson's key example, as you will remember, is taken

from the *Christian Doctrine*. Augustine quotes the following
verse from Canticles: 'Thy teeth are as flocks of sheep, that
are shorn, which come up from the washing, all with twins,
and there is none barren among them' (Cant. 4: 2). The
beautiful woman who is being addressed here is traditionally
an allegory of the Church; and Augustine accordingly interprets her teeth as holy men 'cutting off men from their errors
and transferring them to her body after their hardness has
been softened as if by being bitten and chewed'. These men
are like shorn sheep because they have 'put aside the burdens
of the world'; they are like sheep which come up from the
washing because they have been baptized; and so on. Robertson comments: 'Teeth do not in themselves suggest holy
men. In the same way, shorn and washed ewes with twin
lambs are neither empirically nor emotionally connected with
human perfection. There is, moreover, no surface consistency
between teeth and sheep.'[8] All this is true; but we must now
notice that Robertson is talking about 'figurative expression'
in general, and that he makes no distinction between allegory
and the other tropes. This is in keeping with the old rhetorical
tradition, as we have seen, but it confuses the question of
consistency. The point here is that the teeth belong to the
allegorical fiction: they belong to the lady and are consequently 'there'. But the sheep are introduced in simile, and
are consequently not there. This is an example of what I
called the 'superfoetation' of tropes. The question of surface
consistency simply does not arise, since the teeth and the
sheep are not on the same surface.

So this example does not prove Robertson's point; and we
are still free to argue that, so far at least as allegorical fictions are concerned, surface consistency may matter after all.
To show how this is, let me introduce into the discussion the
idea of 'expectation'. This idea is closely related to the idea
of consistency, because one thing is consistent with another
when it does not conflict with the expectations set up by it.
Now any kind of allegorical fiction, whether it is a story or
simply some kind of static, emblematic description, will set
up expectations from the very first in the mind of any
suitably equipped reader. When we read the line 'A gentle

[8] *Preface to Chaucer*, p. 56.

knight was pricking on the plain', we say 'Ah, it is going to be that kind of story'. And of course, despite all the odd things it contains, the *Faerie Queene is* that kind of story. The point is an obvious but important one. Allegorical fictions betray our expectations in many quite startling ways; but these betrayals, or inconsistencies, occur within a larger pattern of fulfilled expectations. And I would argue that we have here a kind of overall surface consistency which is necessary to allegories. To put it another way, they should have structure or form. Let me quote the definition of form given by Kenneth Burke in *Counter-Statement*: 'Form in literature is an arousing and fulfilment of desires. A work has form in so far as one part of it leads a reader to anticipate another part, to be gratified by the sequence.'[9]

This matter of the expectations or 'desires' aroused by allegorical fictions is much affected, I suspect, by the variable which I spoke about earlier: the variation in fictional solidity. But I cannot enter into these complications now. Let me instead conclude my brief discussion of the Neo-Medieval case with an example—a smallish, unframed allegory called *Regeneration*, from Henry Vaughan's *Silex Scintillans*. The poem begins as follows:

> A Ward, and still in bonds, one day
> 　　I stole abroad,
> It was high-spring, and all the way
> 　　Primros'd, and hung with shade;
> 　　Yet, was it frost within,
> 　　　And surly winds
> Blasted my infant buds, and sinne
> 　　Like clouds ecclips'd my mind.
>
> Storm'd thus; I straight perceiv'd my spring
> 　　Meere stage, and show,
> My walke a monstrous, mountain'd thing
> 　　Rough-cast with rocks, and snow;
> 　　And as a pilgrim's eye
> 　　　Far from reliefe,
> Measures the melancholy skye
> 　　Then drops, and rains for griefe,

⁹ *Counter-Statement* (Berkeley and Los Angeles, 1968), p. 124.

So sigh'd I upwards still, at last
　　'Twixt steps, and falls
I reach'd the pinacle, where plac'd
　　I found a paire of scales,
　　I tooke them up and layd
　　　In th'one late paines,
The other smoake, and pleasures weigh'd
　　But prov'd the heavier graines;

With that, some cryed *Away*; straight I
　　Obey'd, and led
Full East, a faire, fresh field could spy
　　Some call'd it, *Jacobs Bed*;
　　A Virgin-soile, which no
　　　Rude feet ere trod,
Where (since he stept there,) only go
　　Prophets, and friends of God.[10]

One does not have to look far here to find incoherences in
the surface materials. The spring landscape of the first stanza
becomes wintry and mountainous in the second, without, it
would seem, time passing or the narrator stirring a foot. And
what is a pair of scales doing on top of a mountain? And
whose are the mysterious voices which cry 'away'? Yet the
effect of the whole poem is not incoherent, because these
things are contained within a larger pattern of expectations
fulfilled. The somewhat enigmatic reference to the narrator
as 'a ward and still in bonds' stealing abroad establishes an
idea of escape and truancy; and the pilgrim simile in the next
stanza adds the idea of a search for some distant goal—a
pilgrimage or a quest. And it is the latter idea which, as in so
many allegories, informs the fiction. Our long-term expectation, as we read the poem, is simply that the quest will reach
its goal; and this expectation is fulfilled at the end:

　　　. . . I heard
　　A rushing wind
Which still increas'd, but whence it stirr'd
　　No where I could not find;

[10] *Poetry and Selected Prose*, ed. L. C. Martin (Oxford, 1963).

> I turn'd me round, and to each shade
>   Dispatch'd an eye,
> To see if any leafe had made
>   Least motion, or reply,
>   But while I listning sought
>   My mind to ease
> By knowing, where 'twas, or where not,
>   It whisper'd; *Where I please.*
>
> *Lord*, then said I, *On me one breath,*
> *And let me dye before my death*!

The encounter with the holy spirit and the nunc-dimittis-like response of the poet make a somewhat enigmatic and unresolved conclusion, like that of Herbert's *Pilgrimage*, which Vaughan is presumably imitating. It is not exactly what we expected, perhaps; yet surely our desires are satisfied. Or if they are not, the poem fails. For here is a kind of consistency or coherence which we must, as readers and as literary men, feel free to demand of an allegorical fiction. It must have form.

III

If we turn now to the Neo-Classical view of allegorical fictions, we will be able to come at the same problems from a different direction; for this view stands in direct opposition to the Neo-Medieval view. In its extreme form, the Neo-Classical case is as follows. Allegorical fictions should, as far as possible, be capable of standing on their own feet as consistent, coherent, and even realistic, creations in their own right. The crossword should make sense across as well as down. Any incoherence in the surface materials represents a fault in the 'machinery' of the allegory, and a failure on the part of the author.

The history of this view might be summed up in a phrase: Quintilian reinforced by Aristotle. Because Quintilian regarded allegory as continued metaphor, it was natural for him to apply the rule against mixed metaphors to any unexpected shift on the literal level; and he is in fact emphatic in condemning such shifts: 'There are many who, after beginning

with a tempest, will end with a fire or a falling house, with
the result that they produce a hideously incongruous effect'.[11]
The view was reinforced, so far as it applied to full allegorical
fictions, by the influence of Aristotle's *Poetics*, which first
makes itself strongly felt in Italy in the course of the sixteenth century. Aristotle inspired many critics to demand
mimetic 'probability', not only of tragedies, but also of
allegorical fables. R. L. Montgomery, in his article entitled
'Allegory and the Incredible Fable: The Italian View from
Dante to Tasso', says that by the end of the sixteenth century
most Italian critics were agreed in demanding 'surface credi-
bility and logic' in the construction of allegories—a view to
which Boccaccio, for instance, would have objected strongly.
Thus Sassetti makes a distinction between 'enigma' and 'true
allegory', the former corresponding to mixed metaphor in
that things are joined together in improbable combinations,
the latter corresponding to the metaphor logically continued. Only the latter meets Aristotle's requirements; and
only the latter is acceptable.[12]

Let me now illustrate this view with a couple of quotations
from eighteenth-century English critics. The first is Joseph
Spence, the friend of Pope, whose essay on mythology was
published in 1747 under the title *Polymetis*. Spence's principles might be described as a very commonsensical pseudo-
Aristotelianism. This is what he says, in the course of a
discussion of Spenser, about allegory:

You will easily, I believe, allow me here the three following postulata.
That in introducing allegories, one should consider whether the thing
is fit to be represented as a person, or not. Secondly, that if you chuse
to represent it as a human personage, it should not be represented with
any thing inconsistent with the human form or nature. And thirdly,
that when it is represented as a man, you should not make it perform
any action which no man in his senses would do.[13]

Since Spence means all this quite literally, you can imagine
that he finds a good deal to object to in the *Faerie Queene*.

---

[11] *Institutio Oratoria*, VIII. vi. 50.
[12] 'Allegory and the Incredible Fable', *PMLA* 81 (1966), 45-55.
[13] *Polymetis* (1747, facsimile New York and London, 1976), p. 305. For an
illuminating discussion of Spence, see D. J. Gordon, *The Renaissance Imagination*
(Berkeley and Los Angeles, 1975), pp. 55-73.

My second quotation, which is more in the manner of Quintilian, comes from Hugh Blair's *Lectures on Rhetoric and
Belles Lettres* (1783)—one of the books with which the
pedantic Mr Tilney attempted to 'overpower' the ladies in
Northanger Abbey. Blair, after defining allegory as 'continued metaphor', gives an example from the 80th Psalm,
'where the people of Israel are represented under the image
of a vine, and the figure is supported throughout with great
correctness and beauty':

Thou hast brought a vine out of Egypt, thou hast cast out the heathen
and planted it. Thou preparedst room before it, and didst cause it to
take deep root, and it filled the land. The hills were covered with the
shadow of it; and the boughs thereof were like the goodly cedars. She
sent out her boughs into the sea, and her branches into the river. Why
hast thou broken down her hedges, so that all they which pass by the
way do pluck her? The boar out of the wood doth waste it; and the
wild beast of the field doth devour it . . .

Blair's comment runs as follows:

Here there is no circumstance (except, perhaps, one phrase at the beginning, 'thou hast cast out the heathen') that does not strictly agree to a
vine, whilst at the same time, the whole quadrates happily with the
Jewish state represented by this figure. This is the first and principal
requisite in the conduct of an allegory, that the figurative and the literal
meaning be not mixed inconsistently together.[14]

There are some rather obvious objections to views such as
these, which I will not labour here. We are not likely,
nowadays, to demand that an allegorical personage behave, as
Spence puts it, like 'a man in his senses'. Let me rather con-
centrate on an idea which I think valid and useful: Blair's
notion of 'quadration'.

When Blair says that the Psalmist's allegory of the vine
'quadrates happily' with the circumstances of the Jewish
state, he is using what appears to have been a critical term of
his day. *The Oxford English Dictionary* cites Erasmus Darwin
as saying that 'the similes of Homer do not quadrate, or go
upon all fours'. The term might be revived, since it expresses
precisely enough one of the ways in which allegorical fictions

---

[14] *Lectures on Rhetoric and Belles Lettres*, Lecture XV *ad fin.*

fit with the things they signify: A stands to B on the literal
level as X stands to Y in the signification. The contriving of
such quadrations is one branch of the art of allegory, and the
recognition of them is one of the pleasures which allegory
affords. This is not the only legitimate kind of allegory, and
the Neo-Classical critics were wrong to suggest that it was.
Yet it is certainly *a* legitimate kind; and one should not
neglect the guidance of those critics who best understood it.

The fundamental condition of quadrating allegory is, as
the Neo-Classical critics insisted, that the 'circumstances' of
the literal level should agree naturally together. The author
must avoid any suggestion that he is rigging or forcing his
parallel. He should attempt to preserve the independence and
integrity of both levels. The relationship between A and B
should be recognizably true and probable in its own right,
while at the same time matching the relationship of X to Y
in the signification. A good quadrating allegory is therefore
rather like a good pun. We feel that the author has simply hit
upon a likeness which has only to be stated and developed to
be thoroughly convincing. A good punster should not have to
mispronounce his ostensible word in order to suggest his
hidden one; and in the same way, a good quadrating allegorist
will not distort his literal fiction in order to suggest his intended significance. 'Incoherence of the surface materials'
will for him be no less than a confession of failure.

I do not think one need feel forced to choose between this
and the Neo-Medieval view (though one may choose to do
so). Some allegories are of the quadrating kind, and others
are not. It is not wise to set up general laws for allegory on
the basis of either kind. Both can give pleasure, though of a
different sort. Thus, when we read the opening stanzas of
Vaughan's *Regeneration* and come to the pair of scales on the
pinnacle, our pleasure clearly cannot derive from recognizing
a quadration or natural fit between the experience of stock-
taking after moral effort and the experience of coming upon
a pair of scales at the top of a mountain. Yet I would not
myself want to say that Vaughan has here forced or rigged his
allegorical fiction. We feel, I suggest, not that he has failed to
produce a correct quadration, but that he has produced
something else. In Dryden's *Absalom and Achitophel*, on the

other hand, it is important that David's relations with Absalom should be presented in accordance with the biblical narrative. In so far as Dryden distorts the Bible in order to force the fit with the contemporary dealings between Charles and Monmouth, the allegory fails to quadrate and we acknowledge the justice of Dr Johnson's criticism: 'The original structure of the poem was defective; allegories drawn to great length will always break; Charles could not run continually parallel with David.'[15]

It would seem that quadrating allegory, of the kind admired by Neo-Classical critics, occurs most commonly where the writer's purpose is either satire or plain exposition. In satire, the fiction may be kept intact in order to shield the writer, while at the same time providing the base for witty and outrageous sallies against his opponents—as in *Absalom and Achitophel* or Orwell's *Animal Farm*. In exposition, the fiction is kept intact in order to suggest that the writer is grounding his argument on the very 'nature of things'. This is commonly the case with parables and exempla, such as Menenius' tale of the body and its members in *Coriolanus*. Such small framed allegories are more likely to work consistently by quadration than are, say, dream-allegories; and they are therefore more to the Neo-Classical taste.

IV

Allegory fell into disrepute during the Romantic period. This was largely due, it seems, to the unflattering distinction between allegory and symbolism, first drawn apparently by Goethe, and adopted by Coleridge in England. Coleridge has many brilliant things to say about allegory; but his view of the proper conduct of allegorical fictions is not very different from that of Blair and even Spence. There is a passage in the *Pilgrim's Progress* which runs as follows: 'Then I saw that one came to Passion, and brought him a bag of treasure, and poured it down at his feet; the which he took up, and rejoiced therein, and withal laughed Patience to scorn; but I beheld but awhile, and he had lavished all away, and had nothing left him but rags.' And this is Coleridge's comment:

[15] Life of Dryden, *Lives of the English Poets* (Oxford, 1906), i. 308.

One of the not many instances of faulty allegory in *The Pilgrim's Progress*; that is, it is no allegory. The beholding 'but awhile', and the change into 'nothing but rags' is not legitimately imaginable. A longer time and more interlinks are requisite. It is a hybrid compost of usual images and generalised words, like the Nile-born nondescript, with a head or tail of organised flesh, and a lump of semi-mud for the body.[16]

The imagery is unmistakably Coleridge's; but the argument is, in my terminology, purely Neo-Classical, because it rests on an appeal to what is 'legitimately imaginable'—in other words, to the canon of probability.

It is only in more recent times that there has emerged a thorough-going romantic view of allegory. One of the fullest statements of this in English is Fletcher's book; and I shall therefore adopt this as my starting-point. A different version of the same view, laying emphasis on the roots of allegorical fictions in word-play, may be found in Maureen Quilligan's book: *The Language of Allegory* (1979).

The Neo-Romantic view, as stated by Fletcher, is clearly distinguishable from both the older views. Indeed, it might be said to form with them a triangle—even an equilateral one. Fletcher argues that the classical canons of probability and daylight common sense cannot be applied to allegorical fictions, for they are not mimetic works in the Aristotelian sense. So far he agrees with Robertson. Yet he does not agree with the Neo-Medievalists in holding that the literal level need exhibit no form or coherence of its own at all. Appealing to psychology, anthropology, and like disciplines, he argues that allegorical fictions are similar to surrealist paintings: they do make sense, but it is night-time sense. The typical allegorical protagonist is a man obsessed, or possessed by a demon—not 'a man in his senses', at all, but a fixated and neurotic man. The actions in which he engages, furthermore, are more ritual than rational. They fall into very simple patterns, especially those of battle and of quest; and they proceed according to the laws of magical rather than normal causation. On this last point, let me quote Fletcher himself:

In allegorical actions generally events do not even have to be plausibly connected. Reversals and discoveries arbitrarily imposed on the action,

---

[16] Roberta F. Brinkley (ed.), *Coleridge on the Seventeenth Century* (Durham, NC, 1955), p. 478.

the *deus ex machina* introduced to rid the action of an impasse—these do not imitate Nature, though they may imitate ideas and theories. Even so, however, allegorical actions do hold together on their own principles of unity. We shall find that these principles require a suspension of disbelief in magic and magical causation . . . The dramatis personae in allegorical fictions will not have to interact plausibly, or according to probability, as long as they interact with a certain logical necessity. This necessity in turn appears, as a result of the rhythms of allegory, to take on a magical force. The agents of allegory can help, hurt, change, and otherwise affect each other 'as if by magic'.[17]

This general argument deserves serious consideration. The characteristics of dream, of obsession, of ritual, and of magic do appear with special frequency in allegory, notwithstanding the fact that Langland, Bunyan, and the rest had not read Frazer or Freud. Langland's *Piers Plowman* is certainly a dream poem in more than a merely formal way. It is rich in episodes which Spence and Blair would no doubt have dismissed as ridiculous Gothick inventions, but which in fact make good night-time sense. In Passus VI of the B text, for instance, Piers sets the pilgrims to work on his half-acre. Some of them defy him and refuse to work; so Piers 'whoops after Hunger'; and Hunger comes and buffets the wasters back to work:

> Faitours for fere herof flowen into bernes
> And flapten on with flailes fro morwe til even.
> (VI. 183–4)

This episode illustrates some of Fletcher's observations about allegorical actions. Hunger is a *deus ex machina*; and the way Piers summons him suggests a magician or holy man calling down famine upon his adversaries. He is able to act upon the wasters, as Fletcher says, 'as if by magic'. His action makes sense, therefore, on the literal level in terms of what Fletcher calls 'magical causation', quite apart from any deeper significance it may have. The Palm Sunday episode much later in the poem, at the beginning of Passus XVIII, provides another example. Here, the knight who rides into Jerusalem to joust

[17] Angus Fletcher, *Allegory: The Theory of a Symbolic Mode* (Ithaca, NY, 1964), p. 182.

with the fiend is a composite of Christ, the Good Samaritan,
and Piers the Plowman:

> Oon semblable to the Samaritan, and somdeel to
>   Piers the Plowman.
>
> (XVIII. 10)

'Someone like the Samaritan and rather like Piers'. Now we
should be able to explain why, in its context, this is so
powerful. It is not enough just to say that Langland allows
himself a certain incoherence on the literal level in order to
make his point about the human nature and charity of Christ.
We must recognize that the fusing of these three figures is,
in its own way, probable—probable, that is, in dream. I do
not mean that dreams obey no laws, and that anything goes,
therefore, in a dream-poem. This would be both uncritical
and contrary to fact. The point is rather that what Freud
calls 'collective' figures are specifically characteristic of
dreams. Freud talks about this, with examples, in his discussion of 'dream condensation' in *The Interpretation of Dreams*.
Langland's invention therefore makes positive night-time
sense, and this is one of the sources of its power. Elsewhere
in the poem he seems to play the same trick, though more
unobtrusively. Towards the end of the dinner party in Passus
XIII, for example, the Dreamer disappears without explanation, and at the same time Conscience begins to exhibit
suspiciously Dreamerish characteristics. Perhaps he too is, for
the time being, a 'collective figure'.

I do not think that observations such as these can safely be
dismissed on principle as unhistorical. The unconscious mind
is not changed very much by history. They may in fact be
cranky or ill-substantiated; but that is another matter. Yet
Fletcher's approach is a dangerous one; and this becomes
obvious when he brings surrealism into the argument. Surrealism, unlike dreaming, magic, or neurosis, is a phenomenon of
the conscious mind, and a modern one at that. It has something in common with traditional allegory because it draws,
in part, from the same sources; but it is basically different
none the less. The pair of scales on the pinnacle in Vaughan's
Regeneration can easily be conceived as a surrealistic image: we

can readily respond to them as if they appeared in a picture by Dali. But it would be a bad habit if we became accustomed to relish allegorical imagery for its own surreal sake.

If one looks more generally at the romantic view of the literal level in its relation to the signification, one sees that it differs sharply from older views. The Neo-Medieval and the Neo-Classical approaches, as we may now notice, were both based on the same assumption: that the ideas to be expressed through an allegory are already there when the poet starts work, and that they could have been expressed adequately, if not as forcefully, in literal or 'proper' terms. This assumption is clearly stated by Dante in his *Vita Nuova*: 'It would be a great disgrace to a man if he were to express himself under the covering of figurative or rhetorical speech, and then, when he was asked, was unable to strip off that covering and show what he really meant.'[18] But what the modern Neo-Romantic critic looks for, and sometimes finds, in allegory is precisely the meaning which the author could *not* have expressed in proper terms. He is most interested in that kind of allegory where the literal fiction participates in its own signification and is indispensable to it. The contrast with the Neo-Classical view is complete. Instead of a mechanical 'quadration' between a story which can be told as a story in its own right and ideas which can be stated as ideas in their own right, we have, as in dreams, an indissoluble participation between story and idea. The result, so far as concerns the literal level, will be incoherences which themselves contribute to and participate in the meaning. There is a fundamental difference between this kind of meaningful incoherence and the simpler disjunctions recognized alike by Neo-Classical and Neo-Medieval critics. Let me try to illustrate this difference from the first part of *Piers Plowman*, the Visio.

The Visio consists of two visions. The first, which occupies the five five passus, is chiefly concerned with the story of the marriage of Lady Mede. The second (Passus V to VII) concerns the pilgrimage to Truth. So far as form is concerned,

---

[18] *Vita Nuova*, ch. 25 *ad fin*: 'grande vergogna sarebbe a colui che rimasse cose sotto vesta di figura o di colore rettorico, e poscia, domandato, non sapesse denudare le sue parole da cotale vesta, in guisa che avessero verace intendimento', *Le Opere di Dante*, ed. M. Barbi, E. G. Parodi, *et al.* (2nd edn., Florence, 1960), p. 33.

these two dreams have a good deal in common. They both set up expectations which they then disappoint. But whereas the first vision is simply disjointed, the second disappoints the reader's expectations in a subtle and meaningful fashion.

The question raised at the beginning of the story of Lady Mede is who shall she marry? She is about to be given to False; but Theology objects to this; and False agrees to take her up to London to obtain the judgement of the King's Court. All this gives promise of a good solid story; and our expectations are at first not disappointed. The King forbids Mede to marry False, and offers her Conscience instead. Mede agrees, but Conscience refuses. From this point on, however, the marriage recedes into the background, and our interest is transferred to the contest for the King's favour between Mede (who is now unambiguously evil) and Conscience. Conscience is joined by Reason. Peace brings a plea against Wrong into the King's Court. The King refuses Mede's offers on behalf of Wrong, and judges the case according to Conscience and Reason. Mede is discomforted. What happens, then, is that Langland just drops the marriage story in order to get at Mede more directly. The satirical impulse breaks in on the fiction, and the result is a simple case of 'incoherence of the surface materials'. It would be sufficient either to defend it on Neo-Medieval grounds or to attack it on Neo-Classical ones. I should myself want to attack it, since it destroys the basic formal structure of the dream. But either way it is no more than a straightforward disjunction.

The case of the second vision, though superficially similar, is really different.[19] Reason preaches to the people; and they repent and confess and set out on the pilgrimage to St. Truth which Reason has prescribed for them as a penance. By this point in the action, a medieval audience at least would have been entertaining strong expectations about the outcome; for a pilgrimage ends at the shrine of the saint with the receiving of a pardon. But what in fact happens? The pilgrimage is interrupted by Piers Plowman, who sets the people to work on his half-acre; and it is not resumed. Truth sends a pardon; but Piers tears it up. Despite appearances, these unexpected

---

[19] For a fuller discussion, see 'The Action of Langland's Second Vision', Essay 5, above.

developments are not like the shelving of Mede's marriage in the first dream. For they participate, in a subtle way, in Langland's meaning. Sermon, confession, pilgrimage, and pardon form a chain of events chosen, in the first place, to represent the reformation of society. But that reformation is itself really an internal, spiritual thing, and it is not to be identified with any external observance—particularly not with pilgrimages or pardons, both of which Langland is known to have regarded with considerable suspicion. So when Piers interrupts the pilgrimage and when he tears the pardon, his actions express Langland's sense of the demands of the truly spiritual life; and this is so again when, at the end of the dream, Piers resolves to give up even the very life of ploughing and sowing, the 'pilgrimage at the plough', to which he had invited the pilgrims earlier. These quite un-expected twists in the allegorical fiction suggest imaginatively, it seems to me, the continuous corkscrewing movement of the spirit, adopting and then rejecting successive images, definitions, and external observances as it works towards inwardness and truth. Perhaps Langland would have suc-ceeded no better than I have done in expressing 'what he really meant'; for this is not a case where 'the covering of figurative or rhetorical speech' is easily stripped off. The story and the meaning seem to interpenetrate, in a way that Neo-Romantic criticism is specially well fitted to describe.

I have tried to stress, in this very partial survey, the com-plexity and multifariousness of the subject. Allegorical fictions are not all of the same degree of solidity; nor do they all stand in the same relation to their significations. They may interpenetrate, or they may quadrate, or they may well do neither. The only absolutely general law, it seems to me, is that they should satisfy, in however surprising a fashion, the expectations they arouse. They must have form.

INDEX